PRAISE FOR *I Dream with Open Eyes*

"George Prochnik is our great biographer of émigré writers, chronicling lost-and-found souls such as Heinrich Heine, Gershom Scholem, and Stefan Zweig as they flee from (and sometimes toward) disaster. In *I Dream with Open Eyes*, Prochnik turns his exilic gaze on his own departure from New York City in the wake of the Trump election, an ambivalent leave-taking that has inspired this extraordinary reflection on 'home.' What is it exactly? A brownstone filled with mementoes of a family whose members range from early Puritans and friends of Emerson to Southern Confederates and associates of Freud to émigrés, like Freud, from a Vienna on the cusp of catastrophe? A Brooklyn neighborhood whose rich mix of people is threatened by a mercilessly unequal economy? A country that seems thrilled to death by nihilistic behavior of all sorts? A language that is everyday more corrupted by a bullshit artist turned President and a social media complex fueled by inflammatory takes? In the midst of this conflagration, heightened by a raging virus and a suffering environment, Prochnik seizes on almost utopian moments in which alternative ways of living and loving suddenly appear. This book offers hopeful respite in that unexpected home too." —Hal Foster, author of *What Comes After Farce? Art and Criticism at a Time of Debacle*

"In this thrillingly candid book, Prochnik examines his decision to leave his home—the United States—and addresses questions that are becoming all too familiar and all too pressing for more and more of us: How do we proceed, how do we think, how do we understand ourselves and even our existence on Earth when social and political convulsions shatter our sense of belonging to something—to a nation or culture? Prochnik delights us with his transportive eloquence, kindness, and erudition, the originality of his thought, and astonishing reflections on his family and background. The book shines, and in the darkness where we live now, it leaves us with an orienting and invigorated sense of possibilities."

—Deborah Eisenberg, author of *Your Duck Is My Duck*

ALSO BY GEORGE PROCHNIK

*Putnam Camp: Sigmund Freud, James Jackson
Putnam and the Purpose of American Psychology*

*In Pursuit of Silence: Listening for
Meaning in a World of Noise*

*The Impossible Exile: Stefan Zweig
at the End of the World*

*Stranger in a Strange Land: Searching for
Gershom Scholem and Jerusalem*

Heinrich Heine: Writing the Revolution

I Dream
with
Open Eyes

A MEMOIR ABOUT

REIMAGINING HOME

George Prochnik

Counterpoint
Berkeley, California

To protect the privacy of individuals, some names have been changed.

I Dream with Open Eyes

Library of Congress Cataloging-in-Publication Data
Names: Prochnik, George, author.
Title: I dream with open eyes : a memoir about reimagining home / George Prochnik.
Description: First hardcover edition. | Berkeley : Counterpoint Press, 2022.
Identifiers: LCCN 2021055058 | ISBN 9781640095472 (hardcover) | ISBN 9781640095489 (ebook)
Subjects: LCSH: Prochnik, George. | Prochnik, George—Homes and haunts. | United States—Social conditions—21st century. | Americans—Biography. | Place (Philosophy) | Place attachment. | Essayists—Biography. | Literary historians—Biography. | Immigrants—Biography.
Classification: LCC CT275.P84946 A3 2022 | DDC 973.93092 [B]—dc23/eng/20220128
LC record available at https://lccn.loc.gov/2021055058

Jacket design by Lexi Earle
Book design by Laura Berry

COUNTERPOINT
2560 Ninth Street, Suite 318
Berkeley, CA 94710
www.counterpointpress.com

Printed in the United States of America

1 3 5 7 9 10 8 6 4 2

For Elisabeth, James & Ethan

But suppose that the intelligible world is "the city of words," say Utopia; and suppose that the world of that city is not a "something" that is "outside" (i.e., beyond the world of sense) but is, as it says, "no place," which perhaps suggests no place *else*, but this place transfigured.

—STANLEY CAVELL

I Dream

with

Open Eyes

· Prelude ·

Part of my mother's family came over on the *Mayflower*, and there's a story that one of this branch—a girl named Mary Chilton—was the first of the Pilgrims to set foot on the ground of the New World. She was still only a child, just twelve years old. I like to think of her springing off that boat where they'd been confined for sixty-six days. Whatever apprehensions the adults may have been freighted with, despite the exhaustion they were certainly laboring under, I want to imagine that in the moment of watching the girl leap from the frame of the vessel, they soared through the air with her. Winged and uncontainable. This grave assembly had made the astonishing, fanatical decision to abandon civilization in order to follow commands they'd scoured from their old holy book. They were staring out at a lonely strand bordered by dead trees and harsh tangle. But the instant of absorption in that child's flight to freedom transformed their consciousness. They saw the world through her eyes, recovering a sense of unknown, boundless prospects.

———

The manuscript in which my mother's mother painstakingly recorded the tales of our family history vanished in the course of my journey from America. On arriving in England, I worked my way through stacks of boxes, month after month, certain that I must be on the verge of finding the slender brown volume in which she'd kept the fruit of her researches, but over and over I slit open cardboard flaps to discover with a pang that it was still missing. At last I was forced to try and reconcile myself to the absence. Perhaps the chronicle had never come with us to begin with. Lost, having been set aside for safekeeping, in the last frantic phase of packing when it had seemed the task of preparing to move from our large, overstuffed house couldn't be finished, though we were on the verge of having to vacate the premises. Those days laced with little nightmares of departure: the disappearance of a beloved animal who never strayed; the discovery of a ruinous "ghost mortgage" taken out on the house before we acquired it; precious objects suddenly gone missing; copied identity papers found to have shed their originals. As if America itself had kept a grasp on some vital part of my being, which would mean that I'd have to go back again, or would learn that I'd never really left.

Sometimes I feel I've spent my life fleeing the United States, then being swept back into the country's wide, pillowy, warm, hot, flaming, writhing embrace. Long before I could knowingly escape, I was propelled from the place by main force. Born in Grand Junction, Colorado (I treasure that town name, evoking a theatrical crossroads, brashly colored light bulbs sizzling on and off around a cosmic marquee), I was barely six months old when my father gave up prospecting for uranium on behalf of the Atomic Energy Commission in the Southwest to try his hand at diplomacy with the State Department.

He landed a post in Edmonton, Canada, after the station chief there succumbed to drink. We returned to the U.S. a couple of years later, only to leave again almost immediately for Santiago, Chile. This post lasted longer, but my mother finally put her foot down against that whole career track; fed up, my father later said, with the fuss of being a diplomat's wife: all the hostess duties, twinkling in high heels and Marilyn lipstick between swells of laughter and fragrance.

"It just wasn't her," my father would say with a slightly bemused shrug, arching his heavy brow.

But I see now how she couldn't stop turning her gaze back over her shoulder for the United States, all the time we lived abroad.

What was it she pined for so inconsolably? The crisp promise of real fall? A handful of chatty, eloquent friends in New England and New York whose drawling, smoky voices and dauntless, sly grins I remember rising over glasses in which the ice clacked like dominoes? A certain strain of decent gaiety? Impregnable optimism? The English language, to which her letters and speech bore such a lyrical, shape-shifting relationship—marbled with cadences from her Bostonian mother, her Carolinian father, Edwardian children's literature, and peak Golden Age Hollywood? Her gentle parents in their white, columned house on Main Street in Cooperstown, where she'd grown up sailing turnabouts on the Glimmerglass, skiing woodland trails named after characters from the *Leatherstocking Tales*, going to elegant dances in technicolor dresses at the country club that I picture from her albums like a lush Douglas Sirk set? The whole storybook upbringing: true-blue beaux, ice cream socials, bonfire sing-alongs, and self-sacrificing, self-realizing charity—one endless Fourth of July firework bouquet of earned freedom, which she spoke about matter-of-factly as a slice of paradise lost: *All That Heaven Didn't Quite Allow*?

Did she miss America when she longed to return, or her early history in the village—a past that was anachronistic even as it was happening? Or was she just fleeing the foreign-ness of other parts? Those subtleties of everyday being in faraway places that continually divert the heart's search for an echo? Unfamiliar materials. Wayward plants in the garden. The manner in which things open and lock. Anomalous ingredients of ordinary recipes. What morning means. When night begins. The way the walls of your new residence never quite seem to enclose you.

And have I now left America because the country became alien to me, or because I believe that somewhere out there in the great beyond I might still find a place that sings *home*?

By the time I was six, my father had taken a desk job with the Department of the Interior and we'd moved to a suburb of Washington, D.C. My first memory of living in that development is of getting lost, over and over. Staring helplessly down the ranks of homogeneous dwellings lining blank streets. It wasn't that our house was very distant from the school, or off on some tricky cul-de-sac, but I remember the façades multiplying as I walked, becoming ever more indistinguishable, as if I were caught in a bad dream. Sometimes I recalled the street markets in Santiago: enormous, light-spangled fish and bunches of bright, scented blossoms like the frills on the dresses of women who'd come down from the Andes to trade—something festively disordered, unpredictable—and felt a sadness that I couldn't put words to.

As soon as I was old enough to leave home, I started traveling whenever I had means. By the time I was in my early twenties I'd begun spending longer and longer interludes in Europe, followed by almost ten years living in Jerusalem. And now this. Once more across the Atlantic, to the country my mother's family fled almost exactly four hundred years ago. November 1620 ... November 2016. The dates of the Pilgrims' arrival and of the election that launched our departure have a strange symmetry. After all the other moves, some ebb tide of circumstance and homesickness drew me back again. This passage out feels different—it was born of a homesickness that has never relented—but we'll see.

The world falls apart—what do we do?

What should we do with our physical beings? With our minds, our loved ones, our former cares and belongings? Falls apart how: storms, disease, fires, war, bankruptcy, social mayhem? A change in leaders? Crumbles to what degree? How far gone must the world be to qualify as fallen? Which world? Where do we start or stop drawing its circumference out from the needle of our individual selves? And why begin revolving the spread arm of the compass out from the axis of our own persons—why not from those who've inspired us, those we care for, who cared for us, our most significant institutions—a promise, a memory, an irreducible ideal?

Our reality collapses—what do we do?

Where do we turn in space? What if we turn only to find we then must simply keep turning again and again? Should we instead remain exactly where we were until the earth beneath our feet gives way entirely, our own flesh dissolves, or we find ourselves returned to the place we began? How can we know, before it's too late, whether we're being histrionic in deciding the crisis must impel us to action, or stupidly blasé in determining that the event should be stoically endured without changing anything personal? This last question can't be answered without examining the confidence we felt about the way we'd been living before the disaster. For there's no reason— even resolving that a given event must drive us to do *something*—that the something we do must involve transforming our individual existence. That's obvious. There's no inherent reason whatsoever. No reason . . . Irrational. Unreasonable. But suppose what we call reason really has failed us? Was our understanding of the term flawed, or did the concept itself prove illusory? And what then, either way? *What now?*

After the 2016 presidential election, my wife, Rebecca, and I began debating whether to leave the United States. Not questioning our life in New York exactly—we'd been doing that intermittently, more or less rhetorically, for years, in the parlor-game fashion many people with options, or who imagine that they have options because they are not destitute and know they do have advantages—of education, of experience, of class, race, and connections—periodically ask themselves whether they ought to leave New York or Los Angeles, London, Paris, Hong Kong, Tokyo, or some other global metropolis, in order to start life again somewhere simpler or more exciting—somewhere more beautiful affordable, authentic, or just *different* from wherever they've been eddying in the same stagnant life patterns for years.

This current questioning was unlike that pastime, however, because of the specificity of the dilemma we posed ourselves: Should we go into exile? We were asking if what had happened politically, whether understood symptomatically or as the illness itself, meant that an irrevocable change had occurred in America—one that would determine the country's character for, at the least, the better part of whatever life remained to us. We were asking whether, in consequence of a singular event, we ourselves could not continue living in the country as we had been. For a long time after the election, the precise nature of what we would do in response to this change was uncertain. But from then onward, when we spoke about leaving New York, our dialogue carried an edge of emergency.

As the direction of our thinking began to gain definition, friends we respected would say to us, "But you're not actually going to *leave America* because of *Trump*, are you? Come on. You're not going to dignify that garbage con man with power over your destiny, are you?"

We didn't like how the question made us feel—weak, incoherent, or just patently wrong. But we would end up shrugging, compressing our lips, opening our hands, and helplessly nodding. "Well, kind of. Partly. Yeah. Truthfully—yes."

He was indubitably the match to the fuse. The gilded whip. The Primetime Mover. The symbol that signified an actual, irreclaimable loss. And certainly also, I knew, the excuse.

When people would say to me, "But he's a joke, a clown, a narcissistic pig, a nothing," I would find myself remembering the moment in 1932 when Klaus Mann, Thomas Mann's son, happened to find himself seated near Hitler's table at the Carlton Tea Room in Munich. Mann described watching Hitler cram his mouth with strawberry tartlets. He was "much more vulgar" than Mann had anticipated. "Why and how did he manage to make people lose their minds?" Mann wondered. Hitler looked like "a gluttonous rat. He was flabby and foul and without any marks of greatness, a frustrated, hysterical petty bourgeois. It was a most unpleasant experience to have him so close to me, but at the same time it meant something like a relief." The sight of Hitler in the flesh made plain that this man could not possibly conquer Germany, Mann decided, let alone the world. Hitler was "just a louse with a bit of magnetism."

Mann understood too late, he confessed, that his mistake wasn't that he'd underrated Hitler, but that he'd overrated his fellow countrymen. "They were smitten with his grammatical howlers and brassy lies, his slimy humor, his illiteracy, his bullying, his whining, his nervous fits, his half-crazed megalomania. Everything that made him revolting to me beguiled and inspired them."

What is wrong with my compatriots? Mann asked himself, deciding that they were "mangled by resentments and foiled ambitions." He could see the "swollen Philistines, neurotic demagogues, hard-boiled intriguers" and so on, but "did not perceive the tremendous challenge all those pitiful characters collectively represented." When it finally struck him that Germany's new leader was not a "problem," but a "plague," Mann was among those who left home voluntarily, or rather "were forced away by our own disgust, our horror, our forebodings," he wrote. "We left because we could not breathe the air," and "the fear of suffocation is a plain, cogent reason for any preventative action."

That resonated. For all the ways that Trump was no Hitler, the two men occupied analogous positions in a roiled substrate of the popular imagination. When Mann described how people's thoughts had become "profoundly muddled" by arrogance and bad conscience, causing them to spy conspiratorial encroachments on the nation's honor and true interests in every aspect of modern civilization, from trade unions and contemporary art to the League of Nations and Black music—investing all such heralds of a new age "with the diabolic design of insulting and impoverishing the valiant folk" in the country's heartland—it was easy to feel tremors of vertigo.

I thought from time to time of Mann at the Carlton, and also of a party in Manhattan I'd been to during the summer of 2017 in the company of an older, eminent sociologist who, when the subject of Trump came up (as the subject invariably came up), abruptly remarked, "You know, I bet there are more people talking about Trump right now all over the globe than have ever talked simultaneously about another individual in the whole of human history."

We all fell dead silent. "My God, it's probably true!" someone cried at last, horrified by the contribution our own conversation had just made to that triumph—by the complicity of the entire world in Trump's spectacular omnipresence.

On the one hand, one couldn't possibly overstate his boorish, vacuous absurdity. On the other hand one couldn't overstate his world-historical significance. *These and these are the words of the living God.* It was as though humanity at large had become hypnotized by the idea of its own fascination with someone they knew to be a bottomless void. The man might have been just a bad joke, but he was an *infinitely* bad joke nonetheless.

Yet if all this suggested that on some level it was impossible to overreact to the news of the election since—however long his presidency lasted—he'd already infected the atmosphere to the point where it felt asphyxiating, there was, of course, another side to the issue: the question of how one's response affected others. We could not lose sight of the ways we were embedded in a larger fabric of family, friends, and community that would remain, for the most part, geographically stationary. To what extent can any of us pretend—especially after a certain age—that it's possible to take the future into our own hands and run with it as if we were free agents of a giddily independent fate? To what extent do we even *want* that abstract, total liberty except in fleeting gusts of adolescent nostalgia?

This bind was brought home to me one spring day in 2019, almost a year after we'd left America, when my phone rang as I was walking down a sweltering street in Berlin. I moved into the shadow cast by a sleek design studio and answered to hear my father in Fairfax on the other end of the line.

He rarely contacted me out of the blue—I could count on one hand the number of times he'd done so since my mother's death four years before—and my first thought was alarm, that he was having a health problem and I was far away. But in fact it emerged quickly that he was calling simply to hear my voice. He missed me—and I was far away.

Going through some old papers, he'd come across a cache of photographs of myself and my siblings when we were kids clambering around a dramatic rock formation in Canyonlands National Park. He said he wanted to know how best to send me copies, even though he knew perfectly well that he could have done so digitally. He asked me for my best mailing address, as if by invoking the postal service he might restore us to a time before our electric emanations would have to suffice for all intimacy. "Now that you live *overseas*," he said mockreproachfully. Now that you've become a *Brit*, he sighed, "I want to make sure these reach you safely. I feel like nothing I send through the mail ever gets to you."

"I'd love to see the pictures," I said.

"Frankly, I got quite sentimental going through them. We used to have such a great time on those trips. God, I love that country!"

My father's discovery, as a young geologist, of the American desert was emancipatory. His Viennese–Jewish family had barely escaped the Nazis when he himself was only eight. He'd spent the latter part of his childhood in Boston in a solemn, cramped apartment that I never heard him mention affectionately. Having been forced to abandon their prosperous existence in Austria, the family became poor in America. For a long time, they survived only with the help of a Jewish welfare agency. My father's mother never got over the loss of their past life near the Belvedere Gardens, with its musical soirées and vibrant circles of friends. His father, a doctor, worked tirelessly to rebuild a medical practice in their new home, but never attained anything close to the success he'd enjoyed as a gynecologist in Vienna. My father hated Boston's cold—both the bitter weather and perennial mean-spiritedness. ("I got beaten up all the time by Irish kids for being Jewish! God, the wind *blasting* down those streets off the harbor!") His face still scrunches up when he speaks about the city. But once he went out west for the first time, the horizons opened wide and he found his America.

When I was hunting for my grandmother's account of her family's Puritan ancestors, I came upon some letters my father wrote my mother from Utah when he was courting her at the end of the 1950s. They buzz with conviction that he's experiencing real wilderness, but in a uniquely American idiom, at once topographically so alien as to appear almost extraterrestrial, and populated by a companionable mix of exiles from diverse societies in disarray. In one note, composed somewhere near Hanksville ("which, as everyone knows, is situated at the junction of the Dirty Devil River and Stinking Creek"), he promised her "this time I am really out in the Boondocks. This region is one of the most desolate and remote in the whole US. More than arid, most of the country is bare rock and those 'shifting, whispering sands' one hears about." He describes monstrous vertical mesas erupting out of flat desert, "all very much like a Dali painting were it not for the incongruous snowcapped forests just a few miles south in the Henry Mts." My father called the camp itself, with its centralized water system piped into trailers, "a typical product of American ingenuity." But the appeal of this location at the back of beyond was compounded by the surprisingly cosmopolitan cast of characters he shared it with. He wasn't just getting away from the landscapes of urban civilization, he was also recovering some flash of the theatrical, polyglot culture he'd left behind in Vienna. "The camp chief is a tall rangy Henry Fonda type whose father fled Spain during the Civil war and whose mother is Polish, seems like a hell of a nice guy," my father wrote. "There is a Frenchman and a German. Strangest of all, there is also a young man who was born in Russia and raised in Detroit with the fascinating name of Isadore Million. He has just married a local Mormon girl who is not only damn attractive but has a sophistication and polish that would be unusual in New York."

If, during my father's years with the Foreign Service, my mother had yearned for the homey contours of a snow-globe, small-town America, my father's first American passion was roused by the promise of the country's still nominally unsettled frontiers. It would be easy to suppose that she yearned for the clasp of an intimate past while he longed for the open-ended future, but the future my father rhapsodized was also nostalgic: a mythic cowboy spirit charging out the gates of three thousand years of claustrophobic Jewish history on the back of a Yahweh-bucking bronco.

I could recognize the allure of both Americas, the infinitely cozy and the sublimely undomesticated—I was, after all, theoretically their genetic confluence. But they seemed, in their own ways, equally distant from our current moment. Both presupposed the existence of an established social order, which it was possible to define oneself against. When everything is in flux—past, future, and present—the terms of rebellion and conformity alike grow ambiguous.

On the phone that June day, my father kept pressing me to tell him how we were *really* doing in London—wanting, I think, at once to hear that we were finally happily settled and to learn there was still a chance we'd throw the move over as a botched experiment and return. To all his prompting, I found myself able to give only vague, banal answers—not wanting to disappoint either of his wishes, and realizing also that my true feelings were too tangled to communicate.

At some point he veered course and asked me whether I ever found myself missing New York. I answered, as I'd done often before, that I missed people there all the time but did not miss the city itself, although what "the city itself" was, apart from its people, I found hard to articulate.

"You guys were so happy there for such a long time. What happened?"

I mumbled something about how the attractions of New York had come to feel subordinate to its money and aggression. Many people I knew would agree that the entitlement, agitation, and envy that were always part of the place's identity had magnified to where they signaled a paradigm shift. Big money, or the lack thereof, now seemed to dominate everything—which aligned the city all the more closely with the values being promulgated by the New Yorker in Washington.

I recounted the moment in an expensive supermarket the last summer we lived there when a tall, toned man with a burnished tan advanced down the aisle of products in which my wife Rebecca was standing and, finding less room to pass than he liked, had lifted her up like a box, moved her out of his path, then kept walking without breaking his stride. She simply did not exist, except as a trivial interference with his shopping agenda. And I told the story of a young woman I knew who suffered irreversible harm while waiting for hours to be seen in the ER of an understaffed, miserable public hospital in Brooklyn across the street from blocks full of multimillion-dollar brown`stones. When I'd walked in to visit her, there'd been people moaning, sprawled up and down a large, dim triage room with not a single doctor in sight. If it's a cliché to deplore the juxtaposition of great wealth with wretched poverty, that hospital floor still shocked me—all the more so in 2017, when the Trump-engorged stock market was daily hitting new peaks and the churn of fortunes being generated all over the city was viscerally tangible.

How much does such one-off, anecdotal evidence count for? But what if numerous such events occur within a tightly compressed period of time? At what point in our individual experience does the accumulation of stray observations attain a critical mass that enables us to say, *This place has gone past the bounds—become pathological*?

I knew how my father's father had struggled with such questions in Vienna after Hitler's ascendancy. How he'd come within a hairsbreadth of waiting too long. In my grandfather's case, my father said, it was only some while after the Anschluss, when he saw an elderly man down on his hands and knees being forced to scrub the sidewalk with a toothbrush by a couple of jeering brown-shirted officials, that he'd come home visibly shaken—and *still* he'd lingered on, clutching to the hope that things might yet ease off, recalibrate. It wasn't, in fact, until he'd been informed by a Nazi ex-patient that his name was actually on a list for arrest the next day that he'd realized there was no choice but to flee.

I knew all the ways that what I saw happening around me after 2016 was nothing like Central Europe in the 1930s—and also the ways the news uncannily imitated that era, simultaneously mocking and multiplying history's horrors through the funhouse mirror of new media. I saw how slight most of the dangers rattling my social circles were compared to what my father's family had faced—and also novel forms of jeopardy that threatened to extinguish what lay behind people's eyes while leaving the façade of their existences intact. All around us dark moments of history seem to be suggestively, not quite intelligibly echoing. What are we to make of that creepy soundtrack, like the squawky, crepuscular, electronically produced bird chorus in the final scene of Hitchcock's horror film?

Shortly after coming to London, I met an actress from New York who'd also just moved to the city. *"I left America because I needed to remember what it is to be human,"* she announced. I found her comment at once affirming and appalling. Of course we all want to feel justified in making a major decision. In those first months away I clutched at any wisp of evidence indicating we might have been right in acting on our own fears and longings. Yet even had her offhand remark been revealing, wouldn't such a rationale be spurious in light of all the others who were compelled to remain behind?

When does a political reality that's obviously "wrong" threaten something integral to one's being, whether that hazard is to the physical self, psychology, or spirit? Even at that point, what gives you, individually, the right to remove yourself? Then again, what if it isn't about any "right" but the question of finding where and how *you* can be most effective—acquire the distance necessary to get perspective on the crisis and start trying to carve a path to some broader deliverance?

At a certain point in my conversation with my father, I remember swinging my gaze up from the shadowed sidewalk to a grassy patch across the street where a young mother, slumped over with heat, was wearily pushing a small child back and forth in a rickety stroller while speaking Arabic into a flip phone wedged between her cheek and shoulder. What passage had brought her to this place? I wondered. Over how many generations, through the prism of how many different cultures and conflicts? How freely determined my own passage appeared in the scheme of things. If I couldn't make the violence of leaving "right," at the least it was incumbent on me to find more illuminating words to communicate what I'd done than those I'd just stammered to my father.

By the time we hung up, I found myself only able to repeat how glad I was that we'd spoken, how much I missed him apart from any question of the relative merits of one place or another, how much I looked forward to finally taking that trip back west together that we were forever inconclusively plotting. We wished each other "lots of love," then touched the red buttons on our respective glass rectangles and were divided by 3,600 miles again.

The day after my father called me I went to an exhibition at Berlin's German Historical Museum about the struggle for democracy during the Weimar Republic. The show had been explicitly designed to engage with the challenges of our own time, opening with the declaration that at present support for liberal and representative democracy had become seriously endangered by a combination of factors. "Authoritarian and anti-pluralistic political parties are gaining strength not only in countries of the former Eastern bloc, but also in nations in which democracy is upheld by centuries-old traditions," wrote the curators. What can we learn about the fight for democracy in that earlier, frighteningly volatile moment that might help us today? they asked.

It was an ambitious exhibit that looked at everything from the arguments of Weimar-era legal theorists striving to establish the constitutional framework for a more just, inclusive society, to the development of new communication technologies, the rise of a proto-feminist sensibility, revolutionary art projects, the pursuit of sexual freedom, and the surging appeal of fascist and far-left political parties.

I wandered from room to room looking at posters of joyful naturists disporting themselves by the sea, and at newspaper photos of bloody street brawls. I read reports of advances in progressive education, and of increasingly virulent anti-Semitic propaganda. Groups of women organized to demand emancipation, while others formed to advocate for greater domestic dedication, in protest against what they saw as a new, selfish zeal for personal fulfillment.

While I passed between the display cases, I followed a group of university students being lectured by a handsome young teacher who spoke in a terminal monotone that suggested all knowledge of the period had been thoroughly digested and compartmentalized. "On the one hand this. On the other hand that. On that hand this—but also that and this as well . . ." By the time he was done and the students began respectfully clapping, it seemed that everything there was to understand had been squeezed from the era, and now everyone could go off to rinse their slightly sticky fingers.

But I found myself only more in the dark the deeper I wandered. When I'd finally passed out from the last room, I felt numb and demoralized. Yes, there were innumerable parallels with our own age. Yet how few lessons any of these resemblances seemed to offer, and how rudimentary they appeared! Mostly, the explanatory labels kept reiterating: *It's very important for politicians to compromise.* Fair enough. However, much of what was actually on display suggested that the era had been rife with groups and ideas that needed to be un-compromisingly, even violently repudiated if civilization were to survive. The exhibit asked, "What is the nature of democracy?" But this question seemed frequently to blur with another, unacknowledged mystery, "What is the nature of human nature—of nature as such?"

What kind of life are we really struggling to create once we mute the grand, bland choir of social pieties and crank up the outlaw symphony of our hearts?

There's a pub, not far from where I live now, on a heavily trafficked road with a small area out front enclosed by a low, flaking black wall, spray-painted with skulls, in which people gather to smoke and lean over the sidewalk, watching the passersby with bored menace. Mostly long-haired, tattooed men in leather with coiling, tufted gray beards, jostled by a few tough-looking women whose bangs are dyed arcade slot-machine shades. The underworld burlesque of their looks makes me smile and appears emblematic of human impulses that a rational democracy based on mutually beneficial, commonsense values can't quite assimilate.

It's the old problem Dostoevsky illustrated through the crystal palace, touted by its planners as the supremely logical architecture for organizing humanity—a design which even the most irreverent naysayers would never be able to ridicule. Precisely *because* it's intended to establish a perfect, indestructible collective and he won't be able to stick out his tongue at it, Dostoevsky's underground man recoils from this transparent structure in terror. He anticipates the day on which "in the midst of this future universal good sense, some gentleman or other with an ignoble or, better to say, with a reactionary and jeering countenance" will rise up and remark, "Hadn't we better kick over all this good sense and send it flying at last into the dust solely so as to toss all these logarithms off to hell and begin again ourselves to live according to our own stupid will?"

I walked out of the museum feeling most struck by the dizzying contradictions of the Weimar years, when good and evil traded places like cards in a frenzied gambling den. Significant numbers of Germans resisted the worst tendencies of their society in the 1920s and early 1930s, often eloquently and passionately. Sometimes they seemed to be prevailing. But ultimately, although the most abhorrent elements were a minority, there were still too many of them, and their tactics proved too vicious. The left was willing to fight back with physical force, but the right killed and brutalized more people. So the right won.

It was difficult, in fact, not to come away thinking that the real message of the exhibition was that shameless lying and unbridled savagery are excellent techniques for destroying democratic institutions and getting one's own rabid way.

Was there anything fruitful we could take from studying this period with one eye toward our present-day debacle? Along with that question of historical relevance, I found myself wondering whether there was anything we could do as individuals in opposition to such massive anti-humanist forces. The exhibition made clear that sometimes a society can simply become trapped, spinning in a noxious whirl of powerful interest groups exploiting economic and technological change for private gain, yet person to person we still long to fight back. We still have our own lives to lead, and can't wait for a generational change to reprieve us.

I saw the persistence with which activists in the Weimar period kept mobilizing joint endeavors against the mushrooming power of the nationalist right. However, all these groups also foundered in the pitch of the fray, and the people who'd participated in their marches and strikes were yet compelled to keep responding to events one by one. The refrain is drummed into us: *No single person can bring change*. On one level, of course that's true. But sometimes democratic alliances can crumble under the pressure of ruthless party strategies before individual resolve breaks down. And even when the liberal institutions remain at least vestigially intact, most of us, nonetheless, spend considerable time by ourselves, mentally if not literally, and what happens then? How, as individuals, do we imprint our ideals on the world—or at least create a space in which those ideals might gestate?

The fact that both historically and in our own time single individuals had succeeded in stamping their ghastly visions over enormous modern states offered a kind of negative proof of the potentiality I wanted to explore. Not by projecting any one person's illusions over society but rather by conjuring the potential for a shared, imminent elsewhere—what Camus called humanity's "living transcendence," the origin point of rebellion and art.

As I walked down a boulevard lined by monumental, sternly collectivist gray buildings, deeper into what had been East Berlin, I found myself recalling a line ascribed to the nineteenth-century revolutionary poet Heinrich Heine, who'd struggled to envisage a way forward in his own era of murky rebellion and bestial regression. "I dream with open eyes," Heine declared. "And my eyes see."

What would it mean to really live in that spirit of double consciousness—both steadfastly absorbing the reality before us, and unleashing our imagination's capacity to conceive other worlds? Heine felt that in drastic times one had to resist a binary approach to perceptual modalities, instead making lucid observation conjunctive with the prospect of our most ardent fantasies. He saw unbounded reverie as central to this project—the wellspring of humanity's miraculous creative ability. "Thought wishes to become deed; the word wishes to become flesh . . . The world is the signature of the Word," he announced. As for "the proud men of action," he warned them that they were only tools of the people of thought, "who, often in the humblest silence, have prescribed all your work." For his own part, Heine resolved to let his thoughts run free, taking on "whatever terrible forms they will; let them storm through all the lands like a frenzied troupe of Bacchantes . . . let them break into our hospitals and drive the old, sick world from its sick bed!"

This image comports with the idea that if we can't change anything systemic by ourselves, perhaps through our words and dramatic gestures, we may yet project beyond ourselves a kind of infectious presentiment of radical transformation, one that reorients the gaze of someone watching toward a vision of the future that's not mere reduplication—toward hope. We have so much guidance about group activism, but little attention is given to the idea of cultivating our inner revolutionary spirit. Yet mightn't such development be instrumental as a step toward conceiving an uprising that turns out differently from the failed collective revolts of the past?

There was one object from the Weimar show that lingered in my mind as an oddly inspiring work, though it didn't fit easily anywhere on the conventional political spectrum. It was a portrait from 1927 entitled *The Radionist*, by the artist Kurt Günther. The painting depicts the upper half of a middle-aged man with fiercely pronounced bony features and huge, deep-set pale eyes behind rimless spectacles. He's dressed in a natty brown suit and is planted before a table beside an ashtray, a bottle, and a glass. A thick cigar is jammed between his thin lips. But what grabs the attention is the pair of headphones he's wearing, with long, spider-leg antennae jutting out from his skull at sharp angles; a large wooden box with lots of silver dials looms nearby on a second table. In one hand the man holds a small book from which he appears to have just glared up at the painter with an expression that suggests he's taking offense at an intrusion.

The startling image became well known and a topic of conversation. Looking back at the picture over time, people saw the work as an indictment of the privileged middle classes: *Aha*, they said. *A selfish bourgeois with his radio, cutting himself off from the real world and the miseries of the people.*

In fact, however, the subject was a neighbor friend of Günther's, a paraplegic, crippled in the Great War. Beneath the table, his legs were powerless. The radio was providing him access to cultural life, along with a live pulse of contemporary events that would otherwise have been unavailable to him. He was defiantly refusing to let his physiological confinement sever him from the world.

One truism that bears repetition in times of raging confusion is that the actual situation rarely matches our reflexive judgments, and we would do well to pierce through these to a more personally discomforting perspective. Sometimes, as in the case of *The Radionist*, reality not only belies appearances, it's the reverse of what first seems to be the case: What looks most removed can prove to be the most engaged, while that which seems most plugged in may be hostage to the clamor of the times and, effectively, the most cloistered.

The limitation or lag in our capacity to appraise what we see need not be taken as a strictly negative phenomenon, however. We know so much about the world today that conduces to a petrifying despondency—political, cultural, and planetary. Sites of the unknown might be approached as a forensic challenge for those of us in quest of fresh prospects, not simply the ratification of facile denunciations and blind fear. "In times of terror, when everyone is something of a conspirator, everybody will be in a situation where he has to play detective," Walter Benjamin once wrote. If we pause long enough to bring the requisite layers of context to what we're looking at now, we may discover clues that can help us begin tracing where to turn next in our search for answers.

Recalling her experience of analysis with Freud, the poet H.D. remarked that it wasn't the case that Freud summoned the past "and invoked the future. It was a present that was in the past, or a past that was in the future." The notion evokes the quasi-kabbalistic approach to historical materialism espoused by Benjamin, who wrote of the imperative to "blast open the continuum of history." Thinking comprises "not only the flow of thoughts, but their arrest as well," he proposed, calling for a new type of historian who would cease "telling the sequence of events like the beads of a rosary." Instead, he challenged historians to grasp the constellation that their own era formed with an earlier one. In this way, they might establish "a conception of the present as the 'time of the now' which is shot through with chips of Messianic time."

Benjamin implies that history, too, possesses an unconscious and that—as with the individual—it's possible to develop a more constructively dynamic relationship with this realm than the one we typically, passively accommodate.

This idea leads back to the question of my own self-expulsion from America, with its commingled public and private dimensions, for one thing I knew as the move began happening was that I didn't fully understand what I'd done. Sometimes I wondered whether the words I did find to talk about it might not have constituted an elaborate evasion of some more chthonic explanation for this decision to abandon a life rich in family and friends, in an objectively beautiful, socially congenial, progressive, leafy Brooklyn neighborhood—along with an awfully nice home near Fort Greene Park, all those great theaters, restaurants, and the ebullient, multiethnic swagger of urban America—for the ever more dis-United Kingdom of Brexit, morose public resignation, and a profoundly disembodied body politic.

Moving to Jerusalem in my twenties might have been mad, but at least one could discern the shimmer of high ideals: Jerusalem is a perfectly reasonable place to go if you're delusionally seeking to track down God at the source. But try framing some such project with England in the place of the Holy Land and I can hear the explosion of laughter through my hammering keys.

Yet had the move, in truth, been quite so mundane or arbitrary? Lines from the last stanza of an Elizabeth Bishop poem tolled through my mind: "Continent, city, country, society: / the choice is never wide and never free. / And here, or there . . . No. Should we have stayed at home, / Wherever that might be?"

Perhaps there's a different understanding of place and home than that conveyed by the names flag-pinned across the maps of our stories. If there were a more fertile approach to thinking about this decision, I came to suspect that its secret lay precisely in the difficulty I encountered in trying to explain myself. For the way I would invariably find my voice stumbling and subsiding toward silence when people asked why I'd moved came to seem symptomatic of the degree to which I'd acted unconsciously. I would need then to turn back to the figure who remains the most evocative explorer of that realm in modern times. For all that I'd delved into Freud's work and life story in the past, for all the flaws in his arguments and the problems with his handling of specific cases, I knew there were truths in his vision that I'd not yet plumbed the depths of, and I sensed a new urgency in the pursuit they impelled.

This return to the unconscious was surprising because the plan to leave America had been born out of what felt at the time like such an abundance of conversation repetitively analyzing our situation that the vessel which brought us away might have been assembled from verbal self-consciousness. Yet in truth my unpremeditated outbursts on the subject were often the most telling.

I remember being at dinner at an apartment in Chelsea with a couple of friends the week before we left New York. A livid thunderstorm rumbled and snaked behind the rooftop water towers perched outside the windows. One of my hosts asked what I felt like now, on the eve of the event, whereupon I exclaimed, "Somewhere between a rat fleeing a sinking ship and a monk setting himself on fire!"

The answer just came from me, cast up from the depths.

My friends broke out laughing—a little too hard, exchanging uncomfortable glances.

The moment also laid bare another element of the decision to leave America, one of which I'd been initially oblivious: For all the gravity with which we felt we were acting, there was also something performative about it—a flamboyant quality that, looked at in certain lights, might be taken as comic. We'd made a spectacle of ourselves!

To whatever extent we'd acted unconsciously, this also meant there was still a great deal to learn about the whole escapade. Perhaps our state had parallels with those pregnant spaces of the unknown I invoked earlier. Having finally settled in London for "the foreseeable future," it seemed as if over the past several years we'd been acting as if in a dream. Spinning Marx upside down, I found myself thinking that hitherto we'd only changed our world; the point was to interpret it.

The process of transferring our lives had often felt as if we were winding our way through a labyrinth. Different texts and artworks gleamed along the way like strands of the thread Ariadne gave Perseus to navigate his return from the Minotaur. Indeed, like my God-haunted, radical ancestors who'd sailed away from Europe, the idea struck me that in some manner I had yet to reckon with, I too had acted in response to the urgings of old holy books, even if my own gospels were written by profane artists, philosophers, and poets. It was in some fashion their call that I'd heeded when we packed up our American life. To reflect on what we'd done meant to contemplate afresh the lives and works that composed my cultural pantheon.

Gershom Scholem, the humanist scholar of Kabbalah, described periods when the elements of the old order become unfixed as history's "plastic hours." For all the danger of these times of disorienting flux, they are also "crucial moments when it is possible to act. If you move then, something happens," Scholem wrote. By his criteria, we inhabit one of those hours now, and cannot be certain of its outcome, in part because we ourselves might abruptly elect to do something wholly unexpected. Deprived of the familiar economic and political superstructure, we are cast back on ourselves for the conception of promise.

Yet this need not be a solipsistic endeavor. Writing about the philosopher Karl Jaspers as an exemplary figure in dark times, Hannah Arendt asserted, "He need only dream himself, as it were, back into his personal origins and then out again into the breadth of humanity to convince himself that even in isolation he does not represent a private opinion, but a different, still hidden public view—a 'footpath,' as Kant put it, which someday no doubt will widen out into a great highway."

On a blustery, gray September morning more than a year after we'd left America, something compelled me to open the very last of the boxes we'd brought with us across the ocean. Why had I kept that solitary box untouched for so long? What urged me at that moment to tear it apart?

I can say only that, overcome by despair as the slide toward chaos accelerated on both sides of the Atlantic, I felt as if I were physically seized and led to this act. There, inside the final container, wrapped in white paper, was a light-brown volume with the words *Work on Ancestors (Beginning only)*" written in my grandmother's spidery handwriting—the manuscript I'd been searching for all these months. Pure coincidence? A glimpse into some occult order? Whatever the process, I surrendered my conscious search for the object, and the record of my family history rematerialized.

That autumnal day, I read again my grandmother's opening words, dated March 1937, in which she described how changes in the conditions of church and state under the Empress Elisabeth's reign dramatically unsettled the living conditions of the "less well to do people." Together with this destabilization, there arose a new curiosity about the world across the ocean. "These conditions combined with the discontent of many of the people caused them to consider getting out," and the consequence of this was the start of the migration to America, she wrote.

I traced my finger once more over her words about our ancestor,

Mary Chilton with her "lively personality," and about Mary's tailor father, James, a separatist, who'd sold everything the family owned to make the arduous journey, then had died on board the boat after it dropped anchor, in sight of land. Later that same morning, I came upon a nineteenth-century etching made of "Mary Chilton's Leap," which I'd never seen before.

In this image, the girl stands at the prow of a skiff that's been rowed into Plymouth Harbor from the *Mayflower*. One foot remains on the boat, the other hovers in midair. She leans forward, braving gravity, while a man gripping the sides of the boat behind her stares on, mesmerized. The next instant it appears the girl must either fall, or spread her arms and be airborne. It's as if we the onlookers can determine by force of vision which it will be; her act may yet become ours. What choice have we but to leap, seeing where we stand now?

I

· Furies ·

How has it happened that so many people have come to take up this strange attitude of hostility to civilization?
—SIGMUND FREUD

Our house in Brooklyn was a gathering place, and on election night we invited a number of friends around to watch the results come in. Another get-together of dear companions in our tall, ember-orange brick home, with its treasures and clutter, its old shadows and tree-filled windows. The building on Cumberland, right next to the derelict little car service place with its worn notices soliciting drivers and welcoming corporate accounts, almost directly across the street from the residence that Marianne Moore moved into in 1929, and where she lived for many years in what Elizabeth Bishop, a frequent visitor, described as a narrow, cramped apartment arrayed with books and pictures of birds done by friends.

While occupying that fourth-floor flat, Moore crafted a distinction between the work of "half poets," whose verse was important only on account of the "high-sounding" gloss that could be put upon it, and those whose words mattered because they were "useful." We will only have poetry, she wrote, when the poets among us "can be / 'literalists of / the imagination'—above / insolence and triviality and can present / for inspection, imaginary gardens with real toads in them."

The staircase railing outside her front door held a deep scorch mark that Moore's mother blamed on Ezra Pound. "He came to call on Marianne and left his cigar burning out here because he knew I *don't like cigars*," she said; though when Bishop queried Pound long afterward, while he was incarcerated in St. Elizabeth's Hospital, after being taken into custody in Italy by the Allies for his radio broadcasts praising Mussolini and the Fascists, he laughed loudly and said he hadn't smoked cigars since he was eighteen. Pound was a poet who placed actual toads in imaginary gardens, and sometimes I pictured him with his long razor face shambling along Cumberland Street toward Moore's place in the 1930s, quoting Yeats to himself, "Byzantium"; hard, skeptical eyes shifting right and left, dreaming of ideal, ruined civilizations and a world without Jews. A reminder that art is no amulet against moral atrophy. "I hail the superhuman; / I call it death-in-life and life-in-death," Yeats had chanted.

We'd slid several bottles of champagne into the refrigerator; they lay wedged along a narrow middle shelf, sleek, algae-green fish with gold snouts and no fins. But the bubbly was ritualistic, not festive. It would be a poignant milestone to have a woman in the White House, yet she hadn't been our choice among the Democratic contenders. Her politics presented no challenge to the American economic model, hinted at no need for a reassessment of the country's bigger-and-more-of-everything-is-better ideology, with its flip-side theme of snuff-the-phantoms-who-preach-otherwise-before-they-can-singe-you.

Below the bottles was a shelf of food bowls covered with cellophane, and on the silver refrigerator door were silly magnets stuck to curling photographs of our life through the years here. My three older children, now grown, who'd left home long ago. Parents beaming, who'd left the world altogether. Backgrounds of flowers and faraway oceans.

Beyond the symbolic triumph of a female presidency, what we were preparing to celebrate was the release her administration promised from the nightmare circus of the election. She would return the country to business as usual. If it wasn't what we wanted, we just might find we'd get what we need. The livid throng of leering ghouls unstoppered in the race would slither back into darkness. Our private, inner tour guides could still point to a vague, sloppy arc of national progress, indicating the sights that made this place home, despite everything.

This confidence in the U.S. elections had been bolstered by the Brexit referendum a few months earlier. We'd seen the dazed grief of people we knew in England after that vote was tallied. People walked around London as though they'd been punched in the face, someone told us. Overnight, everything switched gray, another person said. Surely no one would want to repeat that kind of mistake. We looked at the colorful mix of people on the streets of our own neighborhood and felt twinges of good-humored pride. So much style and self-possession radiating in these expressions of identity. Even the boom cars thumping by, blasting their staccato anthems to a life of Midas luxury with Glocks cocked and loaded, seemed part of that spirit of indomitable freedom. And wasn't the whole country becoming more exuberantly heterogeneous? In the end, America would swing back from its nasty spasm of monoculture nostalgia. The lightning of blatantly mendacious demagoguery couldn't strike twice in the same year among kindred populations.

I'm sure everyone who turned up at our house that night—writers, academics, artists, along with one lawyer working on justice system reform issues—felt more or less as we did. Our friends came from different places and disparate personal circumstances, but we shared a belief that this fever would break, even if that wasn't the same thing as thinking the sickness itself was about to be cured.

We took vegetables out of the refrigerator to warm them. We put glasses in the freezer to frost them. Hollow-stemmed champagne glasses that had belonged to my mother, which she'd inherited from her own mother, Elizabeth Cabot Putnam. *ECP*, in ornate curlicues, was engraved on the set of old silverware we kept wrapped in gray velvet cloth. My grandmother spoke with an elevated, quavery Boston accent so antiquated that to my ears it sounded English, not American. The formality of the society she came from was such that I almost never heard her refer to my grandfather by his given name, Monroe. He was always "Dr. McIver" in our presence at the dining table. Though when he died we were told that she'd cried out, "*Oh, Monroe, Monroe, don't you know, a gentleman always lets the lady go first!*"

In truth, however, my grandmother's cloistered world had been breached before she turned thirty, during the First World War, when she volunteered to serve with a medical corps in France. On her overcrowded boat across the Atlantic, she shared a cabin with three young Frenchwomen who taught her to apply rouge and false curls and helped with her French. She said she'd never felt better in her life. Evenings she sat "in a perfect hullabaloo," in a dining room "full of men (except for one unbelievable siren) smoking, singing to the ukulele, and shouting generally." In France, she witnessed terrible suffering, but life ran at a high pitch and her spirits flagged only when she felt cut off from the action. Even bombing raids on Paris while she was based there, in which the whistling and shrieking of falling munitions made her feel she was "surrounded by a nightmare mob of howling banshees," didn't faze her. Theoretically she felt she must be afraid, she wrote people back home, but in practice fear just wouldn't come. In the midst of one prolonged, heavy attack, she went out onto the balcony to watch. A bomb dropped just down the street and she studied it for a time, deciding that it resembled a small sun on a foggy day. Then she walked back in, resuming the task of taking dictation from a colonel. She knew she was helping in the best way that she could, both nursing and keeping journals on the progress of her patients (she referred to them there in French, as her "blessés"), while off duty she explored the pleasures of art, nature, and conversation in a new world. As time passed, she found herself wanting to convey to her family what it was about her injured men that made them "so utterly different from Americans and so thoroughly charming." First she attributed the allure to their "great abandon and responsiveness . . . no pent-up, restrained, self-conscious emotions." Then she decided this wasn't quite right; it was rather that "their touch is lightness itself." That, along with the way the men would "suddenly say something that makes you want to cry," such as the morning when one talked to her sweetly of having woken from a dream in which his mutilated body was whole again.

Some nights she and her fellow nurses went dancing, or to the theater. Coming home late she would whistle "La Marseillaise" for "Monsieur" to unbolt the window shutters and throw down a huge bunch of keys to her. Other evenings she and her circle held "Emerson parties," reading aloud essays such as "Fate," "Power" and "War," then plunging into "hot discussions" about their ideas. Her letters home were almost unfailingly ebullient. Taking part in an international relief effort, my grandmother saw and did things that enlarged her individual identity, even as the experience intensified her allegiance to a certain strand of American idealism. The work by Emerson which she decided was the best of the bunch opened with the declaration that "life is rather a subject of wonder than didactics." There was "so much fate, irresistible dictation . . . and unknown inspiration" involved that it was doubtful whether we could relate anything from our own experience that could help another person. What we have to say to one another "is rather description, or if you please, celebration, than available rules."

Most of the correspondence was addressed to her father, James Jackson Putnam, to whom she was overwhelmingly attached. When she'd left him on the dock the day her boat sailed, she thought she'd "certainly burst; I never felt so awfully in my life." He died shortly after she returned to Boston, one week to the day before the Armistice, and I've often wondered what the homecoming then became for her, recalling, along with her kindness, something sad and remote in her bearing, passing slowly in her blue dress before the French glass doors looking down into the garden of the old house she eventually moved to in Cooperstown, with its tall, tapering junipers and violet beds of iris.

In 1909, when Putnam, a distinguished psychologist and neurologist, was sixty-three years old, he'd met Sigmund Freud on Freud's visit to America and turned, virtually overnight, into a passionate advocate for psychoanalysis. His conversion to a system foregrounding the role of the unconscious in mental life damaged his professional standing and the family's social status in Boston. His wife, Mary Cabot, never understood the decision to adopt the foreign doctor's graphically immodest views, and grew embittered. But to Putnam, the chance Freud's work offered to substitute knowledge "for unreflective emotional reaction," and thereby to diminish human wretchedness and misunderstanding, had to be embraced.

Even so, the self-awareness Putnam valorized was not identical with Freud's ideal of classical stoicism. Though his family roots extended back into the depths of the Puritan past, Ralph Waldo Emerson had burst into his family's philosophical-spiritual landscape like a flaming meteor, illuminating features of character and purpose that the older theology left in darkness, and which the Viennese doctor's psychological insights could not supplant. (Putnam wouldn't have known how core features of Freud's vision of the mind's dramatization of its own history had been adopted from concepts in Nietzsche that were themselves heavily indebted to Emerson, whom Nietzsche called the author "richest in ideas" of the century. "Never have I felt so at home in a book, and in *my home*," Nietzsche wrote of his encounter with Emerson's essays.)

The messianic force of Emerson's teachings in the life of my New England ancestors was heightened by a personal connection— Putnam became a close friend of Emerson's youngest son, Edward, and the many hours he spent at "Bush," the Emerson family home in Concord, together with his reading, helped shape his greater metaphysical worldview. "The secret of culture is to learn that a few great points steadily reappear, alike in the poverty of the obscurest farm and in the miscellany of metropolitan life," Emerson had written in the essay my grandmother so cherished. These few

considerations alone were to be regarded: "the escape from all
false ties, courage to be what we are, and love of what is simple
and beautiful; independence and cheerful relation," these were the
essentials—together with the desire "to serve, to add somewhat to
the well-being" of others.

Along with its clinical utility, Putnam thought psychoanalysis
could become a tool to help deepen people's understanding of what
connected them to the creative energy of the universe, which in turn
would heighten their commitment to public service. Short-term, at-
tainable goals were insufficient, he felt, to inspire the sense of obligation necessary to advance civilization. He liked to cite the biblical
sentiment that "the people who do not see visions shall perish from
the face of the earth."

This notion has haunted my thinking about the contemporary
quandary. Our failure to find a way of reconciling Enlightenment
values with that simultaneously elemental and transcendental hunger evoked by the prophets has left us politically vulnerable. We seek
to hold back the tides of feverish conviction while watching a mortal
vacuum yawn wide in faith's absence. Putnam arrived at his insight
through a mix of personal proclivities, family traditions, and observations made in the course of decades of work as a doctor of nervous
illnesses for patients from all social classes. It's the side of him that
refused to consign all our impassioned, quixotic dreams to the realm
of childish wishes—that recognized their role in sustaining the vitality of civilization—that made him so beloved of those he cared
for, and makes me continue to feel sympathetically attached to his
work. Freud's more theoretically profound grasp of humanity's predicament never quite extinguishes Putnam's relevance.

———

I wheeled from the refrigerator, to the big old gas range, to the sink, to the low window looking out over the back garden. Generic techno pulsed from the patio of the neighboring house. Until recently the domain of Kevin, who held late-night crap games *cum* barbecues there, blasting hip-hop, laughing loudly, and squirting lighter fluid into the grill to make atomic plumes flame up over the cracking clatter of hard dice throws, it now belonged to Eric, an independent trader who'd added this large property to a portfolio of homes he rotated between in the United States, the Caribbean, and beyond. He was a self-consciously chill single guy in his thirties, polite and jumpy, with sunglasses that seemed to darken the harder one looked at him. The house was quieter with Kevin gone, but I missed his roguish smile and the sparkle in his eyes as he tried to sell me scalped Knicks tickets. I missed his gusto for life. Eric's fortune, amusements, and demeanor seemed congruently phantom-like. Notwithstanding his courtesy, he seemed a stray apparition from some denatured future, casually dissolving the local realities he passed through. Not long before, having gone out for a bit of night air, I'd caught sight of him alone in the park down the street, chasing a digital cartoon avatar on his phone. He didn't see me and I watched him for a moment in his bright white polo shirt, gliding through the dark trees, holding the little screen close to his face as he crisscrossed the paths below the monument to the Prison Ship Martyrs, in the space Walt Whitman had first conceived as a park for the multitudes, where they could breathe the sweet marine breezes and let their young gambol over the grasses.

At some point I wandered upstairs and switched on the black panel television, which stood on a wooden cabinet beneath a Japanese scroll depicting a mountainous landscape. Though it was still a long while before the first results would come in, election-night programming was already in progress. The screen was spewing garish colors across a large map of the nation, before which a cheery man was pacing, swiping his hands east, west, north, and south, making vectors and statistics appear and disappear with facile sorcerer gestures. The contest for our next leader was a big, bright game resembling the splashy packaging of cheap children's toys.

Rebecca came up beside me carrying a bowl of black olives while I stood fiddling with the remote.

"What's he saying?"

"Nothing."

"Why are we watching?"

"No reason."

I pushed a button and the zippy man with his psychedelic America collapsed back into blackness.

Our voices were sober, though the note of caution was more a superstitious prophylactic than an indication of real anxiety. How much would she win by? We wanted a landslide. I'm sure all those we'd invited did, although the Democrats as an organization provoked a spectrum of responses. Most people we knew expressed at least mild disappointment at the arrogance of the party leadership rolling out its canonical, neoliberal platform, like a thick, sticky layer of tarmac, overtop all the youthful enthusiasm for the improbable, older socialist candidate. But even a close friend who'd experienced firsthand the harshness of Obama's policies toward Muslim populations, and who felt certain the new administration would only harden those stances, had voted for Clinton. We all understood that the ringmaster of this infernal campaign had to be hustled back into the darkness. And he would be. After I turned off the television and followed Rebecca downstairs, I muttered again that he'd lose, repeating it several times like a spell, my thoughts drifting back to a few hours earlier when I'd said the same thing to my friend Adam, a painter.

"Yeah . . . I'm not so sure about that," he'd responded, taking a last drag on his cigarette before stomping out the butt on the curb before my stoop and preparing to unchain his ramshackle old bike from a NO PARKING sign. Adam wasn't planning on coming over that night, but when I'd seen him in the afternoon, he'd sounded the note of skepticism I'd heard from him before. "We'll see," he said. "Hope you're right."

That very morning *The New York Times* had placed the odds of a Democratic victory at 85 percent. This was the same number at which Planned Parenthood rated the effectiveness of condoms. Of course I was right.

Adam was the only person I knew who'd voiced occasional doubts about the election over the past several months. One person in a social life built up over more than twenty years in the city—I might not have bothered paying any heed at all, except that Adam was my oldest friend in the world. Our mothers had known each other since they were girls at school together in Cooperstown during the Second World War. We ourselves became friends in Rhode Island, at the home of my great-aunt, Molly Putnam, a child psychiatrist who'd known Sigmund and Anna Freud through her father, and who helped her mentor Helene Deutsch find sanctuary from the Nazis in Cambridge. My connection to Germany and Austria's rupturing embrace of modernity didn't come exclusively through my father's experience of persecution. Not only had James Jackson Putnam befriended and supported Freud's efforts to introduce psychoanalysis to America, as a young man he himself had studied in

Leipzig and Berlin (rooming in the latter city with his pal Edward Emerson). Later, he led sing-alongs of Wagner's *Tannhäuser* at Putnam Camp, the Adirondack retreat he founded with William James and to which he took Freud, Carl Jung, and Sandor Ferenczi during their visit to the United States. These disparate lines of culture were entwined in my mother's New England character, just as Adam's maternal roots in colonial American history were braided with the Austro-Serbian heritage of his own father, who was also driven into exile by the mid-century cataclysms, first to Paris, then to Cambridge, Massachusetts, where he became a protégé of the Bauhaus architect Walter Gropius.

Adam and I shared the occasional holiday throughout childhood. Later we lived together in New York. I married Anne, a painter, who was also Adam's cousin. We'd collaborated on many ambitious, fantastical art projects over the years. Our lives were as entangled as old vines in the hinterland of some estate lost in time, but my interest in Adam's opinion about the elections wasn't motivated only by the length of our friendship. He had a knack for coming at political questions from unexpected angles, reflecting his autodidacticism and singular visual perspective. I couldn't lightly dismiss any of his opinions, even when I disagreed with him, and in this instance, I knew his doubts arose from personal experience.

Adam had married a woman of Italian descent from New Jersey with ties across the central townships of the state. The two were forever heading off there to family reunions. Holiday barbecues, birthdays, anniversaries, they went to all of them. In July 2016 he told me he'd begun to notice a curious thing.

"There's a civil war going on out there in the middle of Jersey," he announced one evening, when we were also standing out front of my house while he smoked a cigarette. I frowned. "No, I'm not kidding! I've seen fights over dinner tables where you start getting nervous when someone picks up a steak knife. One of your journalist pals should be looking into this."

"These are arguments about the election?"

"Yeah, but they're not arguments. They're just people shouting their heads off at each other. Whole branches of Julia's family that used to see each other all the time have completely stopped speaking," he said. "There're like book clubs and Pilates classes and I don't know what that people have been going to for *years* that've totally collapsed in the last few months. It's like all of a sudden her whole family's gone into combat."

I asked him whether the fights were provoked by resentment on the part of family members who felt left behind by the economic changes of recent years.

"No!" He shrugged. "That would make sense." With a couple of exceptions, he went on, the different branches of her family were all doing okay financially, more or less on a par materially. They were Catholic, but few were religious enough for abortion issues to dictate their politics. They followed the same sports teams, went to the same supermarkets, and were instilling basically the same middle-class values in their kids.

So what was fueling the support for Trump?

"Hillary!" He shook his head. "They just fucking *hate* her. Totally corrupt—evil." Adam made an exorcist's cross with his index fingers.

The answer disappointed me—one heard it everywhere then. I'd expected something more original. I looked at him skeptically. "So you mean the corruption, misogyny—all of that?" Corruption was so endemic to politics that this explanation for the animus didn't seem to go far, and as for the rest—but he broke in over me.

Sure there was misogyny at work, he said, but some of the most virulent denouncers in his wife's family were women, and it seemed condescending to assume that their femininity had gone somehow unrealized, or that they'd just haplessly internalized the attitudes of men in their lives. As for the endlessly reiterated stories of the Clintons' financial corruption—yes, that was part of it, but no one was even pretending that her opponent wasn't more venal.

What was it, then, that so maddened these reasonably well-to-do, proudly "average Americans" about the Democratic candidate to the point where, in his telling, they began foaming at the mouth on hearing her name? "Why do they make it sound as if she's done something unforgivable to them personally?" I asked.

In the midst of the litany of charges Adam began ticking off, certain words kept repeating: *Hypocrite. Phony. Fake.* Even if she couldn't conceivably merit such monumental revulsion, it seemed worth considering what these terms signified in the equation. If the rage fomented by their news feeds was consistently expressed through accusations of falseness, maybe what Adam's relatives were bewailing was a loss of the real. And perhaps this deprivation *was* genuine, even if she weren't its cause. She had become a smiling, bright-eyed, pantsuited figurehead for the nebulous carpetbagging of their core identity—not just putting a face on the expropriation of masculine potency, let alone the violation of some traditional female identity, but personifying the loss of the public's internal wilderness as such. Something in the impression of her perfectly standardized personality, all those pre-scripted responses and carefully curated positions, replicated the experience of life at an unbridgeable remove from the realm of felt being—which is to say the *surrealism* of life as it assails our psyches and bodies.

I remembered being at a party earlier that summer when some breathless former professor of literary theory began rambling about how on the one hand people now felt they weren't really supposed to complain about anything since everything humanity had ever dreamed of—beauty, wealth, tropical retreats, cosmic adventures, banquets, orgies, invincibility—was lurking a few finger-clicks away in one's own private screen cave. But on the other hand, of course, none of it was ever really quite all the way there, and somehow this disjunction—the omnipresent pseudo-presence of every hedonistic wish come true, the paucity of what actually came through the sheets of polarized glass—had effaced the epidermis of what *was* around us.

These sorts of hazy metaphysics about new media were largely old hat by now, but perhaps not as a premise for political mutiny. Whether one thought of it as a digital version of soma, the pleasure drug from Huxley's *Brave New World*, or a new model of the universal temple to self-interest conjured in Dostoevsky's crystal palace, this idea of the screen cave as a space supplying everything humanity could desire, which yet somehow left one feeling even more empty, cheated, filled only with itchy malaise, seemed to resonate with what Adam was saying.

"They keep blabbering about the damn deleted emails!" Adam exclaimed, as if the void made by those thousands of erased messages were the repository of our country's stolen reality. Listening to his account of the fights in New Jersey, it was as though Hillary were being held individually responsible for so much of life having moved online. But it went further than this: it wasn't only the theft of sensorial presence they protested in the form of her person, it was also the loss of some infinite, nameless possibility. Hillary personified the sterilization of the American unconscious.

The question of *how* she'd been saddled with a crime of such proportions seemed less puzzling. One point brought home by my reading of despairing Central European authors from the first half of the twentieth century was that, consumed in sufficient quantity, propaganda *works*. I told Adam how a journalist friend who'd traveled around with Hillary's campaign had been stunned, as she drove from small town to small town, that in every place she entered—stores, bars, restaurants, municipal buildings, sports facilities, and doctors' offices—Fox News was constantly playing, endlessly reiterating the same messages about Hillary's pernicious falsity and her designs on the real America. I'd seen how that intraneural drip of cable news had begun to degrade the political acumen of my own father—himself a former refugee!—on questions of immigration. Not to the extent that he'd speak positively of Trump. On this subject he would concur with my criticisms, but then out of nowhere he'd begin scoffing about some lie Hillary had been charged with—this somehow segueing to a censure of the Democrats' larger failure to reckon with the fact that there was a genuine problem with uneducated people pouring over the southern border. I'd counter with a story disputing this. He'd rehash another old indictment of Hillary's character, and finally we'd just sit together in dull, aggravated silence.

The Viennese author Stefan Zweig, who'd been caught in the whirlwinds of both world wars, detailed how the effect of propaganda, beyond promoting the position of a particular party, was instrumental in exhausting and rinsing out the moral conscience to the point where nothing anyone said could make a real difference.

At the same time, the other candidate, the one who made no

pretense to truth-telling—who was flagrantly a fantasy screen fabrication—contrived to be simultaneously all carnal and pure unconscious: Trump was the unconscious made flesh. Capitalizing on his instincts as a developer, he'd seen how reality had become a distressed asset that he could grab up on the cheap and rebrand in his own image. *My opponent says at night all cows are black. But in the night of my mind all cows are red meat*, he proclaimed.

Whereas Clinton's messaging consisted almost entirely of variations on "stronger together" and "it takes a village"—riffs on the notion of empowering a sacred, self-sacrificing collective—the other campaign's point of departure was that people's integral selves had already been sacrificed against their will, for the sake of a sanctimonious, ostensibly selfless community, which they, in fact, were burning to secede from. They wanted their own ancestral selves back, with interest. Lacan, according to one philosopher, perceived the function of politics as creating "an imaginary hole in the real." But under the guise of salvaging reality, it seemed now the case that politics was being employed to puncture a real hole in the imaginary.

Reality has been snatched from you by the elites, *with Crooked Hillary at their head*, Trump announced. *You have no reality of your own left—No wonder no one respects you! Henceforth reality is what I say it is and I say it will be what you wish, so long as you say that I am what I say I am. That is the* Shahada. *So unleash your most lavish material fantasies. I am obviously unreal, yet here I am before you and look at me, I have it all. Obviously I have no reality, yet I will soon become the most powerful reality on the planet if only you swear to have no other realities before me. Imagine how easily I can then fulfill your own piddling dreams. Unless you eat the digitally enhanced wafer of my bloated flesh and drink the golden rain of my blood, there is no life.*

We're all inside the screen now, lock her up for pretending there's a key.
We're all inside the glass now, nothing matters except what I feel.

Of course different factors played roles in different parts of the country, and the economic abandonment of certain regions triggered more traditional forms of populist resentment, but a recoil from this simultaneous sucking away of the palpable and the potential was what Adam saw driving Trump supporters in the suburban civil war he'd stumbled upon. In addition to the real hypocrisy of Hillary's multi-hundred-thousand-dollar speeches to big banks—along with the loss of rust belt industries and middle-class economic security, together with the nostalgic racism and revanchist nationalism—a more elusive, interior sense of dispossession was at work, which comprised the shuttering of individual dream factories.

I still didn't fully understand why Adam thought this situation increased the odds of a Republican victory, but he kept repeating that these were just not the people who were supposed to be voting for Trump and, furthermore, that the lot of them was fired up beyond the reach of reason.

We returned to the topic every so often in subsequent weeks, but our conversations didn't really advance much. What could one do about such a diagnosis were it correct? I got so far as to wonder how one might even talk about restoring a sense of radical mental freedom that had only ever been make-believe, but I didn't press on from there.

On Election Day, when Adam pedaled off down the street, lanky, bearded, and paint-spattered, looking like an Eastern Orthodox icon on wheels, I chose to discount what he said about the New Jersey Furies. Deferring to the statistical experts, I went back inside to finish preparing for our guests.

2

· Vocabulary Test ·

"*I know words. I have the best words.*"

"What?"

"Someone's just retweeting their favorite Trump lines."

"I don't want to hear them right now—it's like we're snickering our way to the apocalypse. Do you know where the big ceramic bowl is?"

"I think it may be near the cooking pots. You're right."

"What?"

"The absurdity's a distraction—but he won't win."

"We need to get another chair down from the bedroom."

"The thing I can't stop thinking about is when he said he could shoot someone in the middle of Fifth Avenue and not lose a single voter."

"Did you see the grater?"

"Near the toaster."

Rebecca and I paced the nubbly, peeling linoleum of the kitchen floor. Put down as a stop-gap when we moved into the place in 2003, which we'd replace with something fine when we finally had means to redo the whole room, the money never came and the linoleum remained. The cream-colored, slightly rusty tin cabinets stayed, as did the cheap vinyl countertops. The tall bookshelf kept overspilling with children's literature, cookbooks, stray works of social commentary, an unpolished silver kiddush cup, and several broken geodes picked up who knew where with my older children, along with a few fossil trilobites from my father.

We didn't change anything after we moved in; we just kept acquiring more bits and pieces. The present kept interrupting, like a clamorous child—in the person of that child—over our misty aspirations to more thoughtfully mold the shape of our life together. But with this, there'd also been so many warm, voluble conversations in these rooms that if all the words spoken there still hung in the air, the walls of the house would give way before them and the exchanges would fill the sky over Cumberland Street. I pictured the dialogues swirling and streaking—black, red, verdant, and coruscating. And even when everything inside fell silent, every room of the house still overflowed with books. All those calling voices and verbal visions lay in wait for any hand that reached out to them. We'd fallen in love with the place for the old, dark mahogany shelves built into a big wall of the parlor. We'd put up new bookshelves in the dining room, the halls, our studies, and the bedrooms. It was a house made of language, and though when I reread these words I hear their ring of vain romance, the sentence nonetheless keeps repeating in my mind— louder than any trepidation is my persuasion of their truth. We'd talked about everything here—everything. Only now it occurred to me that I couldn't recall a single discussion of what we would do in the event that the demagogue actually won. As if before that contingency, all this verbal architecture simply went blank.

Looked at more coldly, there was another unacknowledged gap in this fairy-tale image of a house made of words: We knew by now that the content inside the multicolored covers of those thousands upon thousands of books surrounding us was already as good as void in the eyes of many present-day beholders. Recognizing this development had begun to subtly change our relationship to our own living space—to historicize it.

When we'd moved into Cumberland Street, books were still (if just barely) "part of the larger conversation," as the phrase goes. Cultured people with even a little money invariably had lots of them—as many as possible. But over these past thirteen years, there had ceased to be any definite correlation between the presence of books in a house and the conceit of cultural relevance, let alone relevance of some other variety. How many times recently had I heard one of my educated peers say, "It's awful but I just don't have time to read books anymore"—or "I don't have the concentration," or "I can't remember the last time I read a book all the way through." Wistfully, matter-of-factly, or sardonically. And these sighs were paltry compared to the lamentations over young people's refusal to read *anything*. Indeed, the presence of large numbers of books in a house no longer even signaled education so much as being "of an age," of maintaining an antiquarian interest. Whatever it now meant to "be civilized," if anything, books had lost their safe seat in the construct.

It had been three or four years since we'd begun to notice a sharp uptick in the numbers of books being laid out on the streets of our neighborhood in boxes marked FREE—PLEASE TAKE. These objects had not simply lost all economic value, they'd become oppressive orphans. *Please, please take us!* Even finding thrift stores that wanted them, let alone libraries, was almost impossible, as we discovered when it came time to move. I'd often pick up a few volumes instinctively from the lineups we walked past along Brooklyn's sidewalks. We joked that we were running a rescue shelter for forsaken books, but really that wasn't so far off the mark. Or if not a shelter, perhaps a shrine for these cultural artifacts. There might not have been anything intrinsically wrong with such a project. But we hadn't set out to create a Museum of the Book, like the mythical Nazi Museum of the Extinguished People! We'd just wanted to read and write! Books were the medium through which we made our living, literally and figuratively. In the years of our life in this house, our passion had transformed into an archeological discipline. This latest period had seemed to culminate that process. Pulling a volume off the parlor shelves, I felt like a tomb raider.

Of course the paleo-ization of the book, together with the decline of reading, was a subject that came up frequently among our writer friends, though rarely with real bitterness by the summer of 2016. What was the point? Mordant humor sufficed for such talk. The more philosophically sanguine among us might occasionally note that this was all just a natural, evolutionary shift consequent on the arrival of new technologies and lifestyles. Creative narrative forms were thriving, after all. With television, podcasts, and short-format video, storytelling was arguably flourishing as never before. Why fetishize the book?

There were moods in which I went along easily with this notion of an essentially indifferent transposition of media, even merrily. Though inside I felt qualms about the casual way the word *fetishize* was bandied about, so crudely did it short-circuit discussion of the idea that there might be an integral value to particular mediums of expression. It all felt somewhat as if a person attached to walking were being mocked for not grasping the fact that cars were demonstrably a faster means of getting between places. Nor could I ever quite shake the sight, the previous summer, of two children nearby each other on the couch of a friend's place, one with an iPad, the other with a book. Watching the former impatiently tilt and swipe the glass of his device, I'd thought how what he clutched opened out in a great *V* for victory to the cosmos—and the cosmos of consumerism in particular. Whatever book he might have been reading at any time, the porosity of that text to the larger material world was literally embedded in the "page." His social media apps and shopping preferences shared the space of the words and expanded the premise of any story they told to include all those nascent acquisitions barraging his algorithmically customized mall-of-being. The girl next to him, with her book spread open between her quiet hands, seemed encircled—entirely contained by the volume in a way that seemed to mirror the enfolding embrace of a parent. I knew the analogy was romantic, but her clasp nonetheless seemed a material echo of that older, warm crescent. None of the other vehicles for narrative bear this intimacy of simultaneously cradling and being cradled by a paperweighted world of still words. And the idea that this intimacy (from the Latin *intimus*, "inmost, innermost, deepest") has no clear successor does seem an occasion for mourning, however inevitable the change, howsoever futile the regret. Is this mourning a species of fetishization? Or nostalgia? Or is it simply the muscle memory of a certain act of imagination? "Human lips with nothing more to say / Retain the shape of their last uttered word, / And a sense of heaviness stays in the hand / Though a jug being carried home has half spilled over," wrote the poet Osip Mandelstam.

People sometimes bemoan the loss of a capacity for critical thought consequent on the collapse of older literary habits, but that linkage is undermined by all the accessions of false consciousness in eras when the book was glorified. Yet a type of intimacy may, indeed, be endangered now, and what this means sociopolitically we can't yet determine. Several years ago, one of my older children took part in a volunteer project in Tel Aviv, working to assist undocumented migrants from Eritrea and South Sudan. On returning to New York, he spoke about how, spending days with individual asylum seekers and other volunteers, he'd realized it was the first time he could remember ever engaging in conversation with groups of people in which there wasn't one screen or another—phone, television, computer—displacing the experience. More than this, he said he couldn't actually recall situations in New York where people even looked directly into each other's eyes the way they'd done in those stark rooms sheltering the refugees. For my son, this open-eyed engagement with other individuals and worlds was electrifying.

The intimacy offered by books nurtures its own form of political consciousness. Reading Carlo Levi's *The Watch*, an Italian novel from the post-Mussolini era this morning, on a day when Extinction Rebellion protests were blocking traffic in Central London, I came across a passage beginning, "The question now was whether that extraordinary popular movement called the Resistance would actually develop further, remolding the shape of the country, or would be pushed back into historical memory, disavowed as active reality . . . like a spiritual experience without visible fruits," and felt myself profoundly stirred. Enlivened for our own struggle, just by virtue of feeling my own urgent questions inscribed through another consciousness. More than any particular political message, reading imparts a sense of solidarity in solitude across time and cultures that can strengthen our courage, even when it validates our foreboding.

One problem we face now is that those who would resurrect wholesale a former golden age, with all its rancid inequities, are counterbalanced by those who seek a future in which the slate is finally wiped clean—whether for the sake of sanitizing the moral landscape to protect fragile inheritors of trauma, or in deference to new technologies that promise to mold reality afresh in ways everyone can buy into equally.

Something in the ecology between past and present has gone awry. The imbalance distorts our judgment not just on what's happening now, but also gazing forward in time. We've lost our temporal demarcations, as if these were the stilts of wooden piers swept away by a superstorm. News comes to us continually. There's no anticipation of a rich weekend paper, let alone the next morning's edition. There's no Sabbath to our work, since in America almost everyone makes themselves constantly digitally available. (Surely one of the great silent coups in the annals of business management is the unheralded transition to the expectation that ambitious employees in white-collar jobs will append off-hour contact information to their work emails—as if every job required the vigilant responsiveness of doctors on call for a hospital emergency room. Then again, with the unassailable excuse of being always partly at work, each individual has been gifted by their company with an ever-ready escape hatch from the discomfiting immediacy of family intimacy.) The electronic mailbox never ceases delivery. The online store never shuts. The virtual entertainer never stops dancing out for our private delectation. We live in the perpetual twilight smear of casino time. Forever awaiting some jackpot of news—personal, professional, or global. Forever hunched before our screens, rattled and ravaged as a sclerotic, zombie-eyed smoker staring at the spinning symbols on the slots in Las Vegas.

Even if we cast aside the haptic model of the physical book as no longer culturally or environmentally viable, the practice that used to be referred to in schools by the acronym SSR—sustained silent reading—holds off this subjugation to incessancy, allowing the mind to simultaneously focus and drift across time zones without the gambler's agitation. In so doing it too becomes a form of resistance to the corrosive hysteria of the hour. "Philosophy is a battle against the bewitchment of our intelligence by means of language," Wittgenstein wrote. The purpose of this struggle, others have glossed, is deliverance from a kind of idle fascination, which is to say the liberation of consciousness, the inception of freedom as such.

"I know words. I have the best words." Trump's riff in Hilton Head on the penultimate day of 2015 continued: "I have the best, but there is no better word than *stupid*. Right? There is none, there is none. There's no, there's no, there's no word like that." And the crowd burst with hilarity. Detonations of laughter that blur into explosions of gunshot. Gag and MAGA. Gog and Magog.

Perhaps the world ends neither with a bang nor a whimper, but with gibberish.

In the final moments of clearing up before our guests arrived, I found myself arranging some of the artworks we'd come into possession of over the years: the exquisite, old miniature oil painting of Archimedes planting a compass across an open book. A tiny, ancient Medusa's head. Silk magic lantern screens depicting silhouettes of brownies swinging through a filigreed forest made by one of my grandmother's cousins. The polychrome Chinese lions from my great-aunt; a Persian rook; Roman dice. A small black wooden hand clutching a scroll from ancient Egypt. Drawings, photographs, and conceptual pieces. Detritus of diverse dreams of civilizations, fallen, superseded, forever obscure or now forgotten, I reencountered them then in ways to which I was inured most days. Many of the objects were fragmentary. Almost all the older ones had originated with my mother's family. Few had real monetary value, but they each evoked a different world, and possessed beauty autonomously. Lately, however, I'd begun to think of the collection of objects in our house, like our books, as finished.

My mother had died the previous summer after suffering for several years with dementia. The process of accruing these old objects in our house in Brooklyn had sometimes appeared conjunctive with the disassembling of her mind. She'd lose another block of her memory; my father would disperse another cluster of family heirlooms. Together with my great-aunt Molly, she'd taught me to read, imparting her belief that some residue of magic still clings to creation, the dew of a morning which has yet to dawn but which we might wake to at any moment. Her love was an earnest of that prospect. And she'd died in unspeakable grief, pain, and humiliation in Willow Lane, the locked unit in the Virginian, a "continuing care" facility a couple of miles away from Embassy Lane in Fairfax, the suburb where we'd moved after coming back to the United States.

Throughout the election period I'd had the uncanny feeling of being returned to the Fairfax of my adolescence. A recording of the wild pounding and shrill, roaring chants from the bleachers at an old Fairfax High pep rally could be substituted seamlessly for the rabidly gleeful cheering at a Trump rally. The voices might have aged, but the bellicose, vapid, self-congratulatory elation was the same. "We're from Fairfax, couldn't be prouder. If you can't hear us, we'll chant a little louder! WE'RE FROM FAIRFAX, COULDN'T BE PROUDER . . ." Over and over, louder and louder, while the broad-chested coaches with silver whistles around their necks scanned the crowd with searchlight glares for shirkers like me who displayed insufficient pep.

When my siblings who were on Facebook informed me that many of our former high school classmates were boasting on their feeds about how great a Trump presidency would be, it seemed that a direct vein did indeed run from my experiences in that suburb to the national mood making the America First candidate possible.

Across the street from us on Embassy Lane during the years of my youth lived a family in the grip of a father who abused his three daughters for years, until the police arrived one evening and the whole family disappeared. My brothers and I didn't know—the children were our friends. Sometimes in search for them, we'd come upon the man out back by the basement steps, with his balding, bulbous head, pencil mustache, and pale skin, gripping the green snake of a watering hose, his eyes narrowing interrogatorily at the sight of us. We'd move quickly on, looking for our sweet, dreamy, lost friends. Just up the street from them lived a family of xenophobic fanatics belonging to some offshoot of the Christian Scientists, yelling shrilly from their doorway about UNICEF and communists; on the corner of Embassy and Colony lived a quiet family who, on failing to make their mortgage payments, set their house ablaze, then drove off into the night; two streets over on Queen Anne Drive, a friend of mine shot his abusive father in the heart with a rifle; minutes away, near

Pickett Run, another friend was butchered by a motorcycle gang over a drug deal gone bad. Closer to the Army-Navy Golf Course, the father of a classmate, a vet, beat his wife senseless, again and again, until a heart attack killed him; while the tall, bony father of another friend, who played Uncle Sam in the Fairfax Fourth of July parade, was accused of molesting the girls he lured to his house with offers of babysitting work. Mapping my subdivision, with pins for murderous domestic violence and random sex crimes, the neighborhood would look like an old horror-film voodoo figurine bristling with needles. And down beyond the dead end at the bottom of the street, in the tract of woods where we went to drink and stare up at the stars from the wooden plank bridge spanning the creek with its brown water skimmed rainbow shades by runoff from the oil tank farm, psychos hung cats from trees after gouging their eyes out.

Oh, the scar-spangled cruelty of our American suburb. With its high school mascot of Johnny Reb, a Confederate soldier clutching his saber-hilt, and the Confederettes as the cheerleading squad— where Rebel Run bordered the school on one side and Old Lee Highway on another, where racism was the ground and sexual abuse the figure, and Tysons Corner Shopping Mall the closest thing to a commons—how eerie it was to feel the spirit of that place resurrected and projected over the national psyche in the form of the politically weaponized Trump Organization.

Throughout the campaign cycle, whatever horror one family member or another might have been feeling about some new vile development, one of us had only to say, *Thank God Mom wasn't around to see this* for the rest of us to break into exclamations of relieved agreement. "Can you imagine what she would have thought?" "Thank God! That's one thing to be grateful for anyway," my brother

Ethan exclaimed on a video call from his home in Los Angeles. "Just imagine." "I can't," my father said.

For despite all her years living in Fairfax, where her values had found so little sanctuary, my mother's quaintly formal manners and generous, instinctive pluralism had remained strangely intact. She'd just kept on cheerily, doggedly *giving* to her extensive circle of friends, neighbors, charities, and liberal causes.

In the 1970s slideshow, there my siblings and I are, wearing big red, blue, and white "McGovern for President" buttons at a forlorn foldout table in the middle of nowhere, battling a flappy wind that keeps tangling the balloon strings and wreaking havoc with stacks of brochures we can't find takers for anyway; and here we go, neatly combed and brushed with shirts bunchily tucked in, off to sing carols at the area hospitals where our mother volunteered. That's one of us knocking on the doors of leery-eyed strangers up and down the cookie-cutter streets of our neighborhood to get names for her petition to integrate the local swimming pool; oh, and this picture was taken a little later—here we are helping her polish the silver tea service for a party she hosted to celebrate the graduation of a drag-queen refugee from the Khmer Rouge, whom she'd befriended while teaching English as a second language.

"Your mother is the dictionary definition of a bleeding-heart liberal!" my father would groan, but the chuckle that followed was affectionate and tinged with something like awe.

"Sticks and stones may break my bones but names can never hurt me," my mother chimed back, with a little jiggle of soundless laughter.

Like her own mother, her speech and manners were a time capsule of an earlier era in American history. Good news was "swell," "grand," or "the bee's pajamas." She invariably called our refrigerator the "icebox." The phone was the "horn." The television was "the idiot box." Reflecting back on her language, I thought of something else Elizabeth Bishop had said about visiting Marianne Moore's place. Its atmosphere "was of course 'old-fashioned,'" Bishop wrote, "but even more, otherworldly—as if one were living in a diving bell from a different world, let down through the crass atmosphere of the twentieth century." The encounter on Cumberland Street with Moore's stories and phrases, "the unaccustomed deferences, the exquisitely prolonged etiquette," produced "a slight case of mental or moral bends" when one got back on the express train to Manhattan. That's how I always felt leaving my mother behind, inside her little quarter-acre moat of lawn before our ranch-style tract house with its picture window looking out at the crabapple tree.

Standing now before our parlor bookshelves in Brooklyn, I drew out the forest-green volume of my mother's grandfather's psychoanalytic essays with its introduction by Freud, in which Freud wrote of the boon it had been to have a man "of Putnam's lofty ethical standards and moral rectitude" ranged among the supporters of the new movement.

With my mother's death, I'd lost the last threads connecting me physically to that America of old New England, with its heritage of Transcendentalism, arduous public service, and honorable civic pride. No doubt this heightened my awareness of the absence of her sensibility from the landscape around me. Paging through Putnam's work, I came across his plea to fellow doctors to look upon all their patients as motivated in some measure by their "self-foreshadowing best." Whether working with neurotic conflicts, willfulness, or regression, by seeking out these signs of promise, doctors would learn to identify more and more of such harbingers, just as closer examination of the seeds of different plants would reveal myriad dissimilarities— evidence of different possible outcomes, which could then each be nurtured toward their most hopeful fruition. His injunction seemed the reverse of the find-the-worst-in-everyone-to-eviscerate-them mania in which we were now gripped.

The last thing I remember thinking on election night, before guests started arriving, was that though the GOP would lose, something in the national discourse had coarsened sensationally, perhaps irretrievably. So far from grappling more effectively with Trump's words over time, as the space for reflection shrank and reactive language amplified, it seemed increasingly the case that whatever repugnant comment he made, people floundered to respond in any other way than by flinging his insults back at him. It was all a variation of "You're the same only more so." "We may have done X, but you did X times X!" Everyone had begun playing his numbers-based language game. The spiral just kept sucking downward. At one point, when he launched an attack on the city of Baltimore, saying there were rats running all over town, the local paper of record published an editorial that began with its authors declaring they would "not sink to name-calling in the Trumpian manner" and ended by saying "Better to have some vermin living in your neighborhood than to be one." Apparently unconscious that over the course of one brief opinion piece, they'd lost track of their own vow of decorum and dropped straight into the pit of his mocking lexicon, a triumph for the debaser-in-chief.

But this wasn't really the editors' fault since the grammatical trap of the big lie is that any direct riposte broadcasts and amplifies the liar's discourse. If I say to you, "Look at that gorgeous blue sky overhead," and there are actually a number of clouds floating above, we might have a reasonable conversation about what degree of cloud cover disqualifies a sky from being classified as gorgeous blue. If, on the same day, I say to you, "Look at the fires in that solid gold red sky," there's nothing you can answer back directly that won't enter into my matrix of madness or deceit. Even to say, "No, that sky's not on fire. No, that sky's not gold or red" is already to employ my lexicon with the fig leaf of a negative prefix—giving "equal airtime" to terms that bear no relation to reality outside the babble of this exchange.

Language has been a principal tool in our corruption, and we must create a new vocabulary of opposition. Part of what made this political moment possible was the ingrained poverty of our defini- tion of success: loud, rich, stuff-glutted, powerful, massively popular. The language of response we need to develop would give prominence to silence, receptivity, self-doubt, and relinquishment; the inspiring failure, the profitless beauty, the heroic loser, and the abiding sub- limity of certain lost causes: the articulation of what exists outside this hour's vortex, and the verbal rediscovery of the natural world as a counterweight.

I put down my great-grandfather's essay. I set the head of Medusa back in place. I'd finished with our old mementos. Even ritual- istically re-constellating the objects from my mother's world felt stale now: they were where they should be and there was no room for more. The whole project of the house seemed complete. We'd gotten our life to where things ran smoothly enough. But I kept recalling another observation from Gershom Scholem, who'd con- sidered Walter Benjamin his best friend when the two were young men in early-twentieth-century Berlin: "It is a profound truth that a well-ordered house is a dangerous thing," Scholem wrote. Such a house would be susceptible to messianic apocalypticism, which he described as "a kind of anarchic breeze. A window is open through which the winds blow in, and it is not quite certain just what they bring in with them."

The doorbell rang.

3

· Cartographies of Need ·

The eleven-year-old girl who burst into tears on our living-room couch that night later said she'd started crying because she'd never before seen a group of adults lose control of themselves and begin simply to panic. She looked in our faces and found nowhere to anchor. I remember her sobbing in the center of the room. I remember pairs of eyes either side of her, open wide as the moon. I remember all the food going cold. I remember feeling something in the space had moved, but not being able to decide what that was. I remember all the curtains being drawn, as if we were observing a blackout. I remember going to the bookshelf at a certain point, drawing out Stefan Zweig's war diary, opening at random, and reading his entry in choppy English for the third of September, 1939: "I am expecting everything from these criminals. What a breakdown of civilization." Then, turning to the final note scrawled a few months later: "I am really afraid that all this is but a prelude. Always the same default in mankind, a thorough lack of imagination! . . . This power of destruction has made such terrific progresses, that even one year would impoverish the whole world."

I remember closing the book, its pale yellow cover the color of lemon meringue from my childhood in Cooperstown. I remember the girl folding herself, weeping, into her mother's arms and no one speaking a word.

I remember after everyone left, well after midnight, picturing all the old champagne glasses, which had been forgotten in the freezer, shattered—littering the frosty interior like broken windowpanes on an icy sidewalk. I remember thinking how it was now November 9. *November 9 . . . 1938 . . . Kristallnacht.* Ridiculous. These were old champagne glasses, for God's sake. Don't listen to the seductive sirens of historical double-exposure. But I felt my lips shape the silent scream from the Munch painting, right before someone showed me that same image animated online; old icons of angst ushering in our reception of present-day catastrophe. I knew that the invocation of such revenants was histrionic, but this awareness only seemed to make them come faster. Had we become so gorged on specters of past disaster that we could no longer see clearly the contours of what lay directly before us?

Go back . . . reel time from the opposite direction.

Projected in reverse, one would first see a semicircle of adults frozen before a bright flickering rectangle—the screen on which Trump was concluding his victory speech, standing in a dark blue suit, white shirt, and blood-red tie against a battery of giant American flags adorned with gold tassels, at a podium emblazoned with a red, white, and blue sign. Five red stars above the name TRUMP in bright white letters, over the name PENCE—smaller—in white letters; above, smaller again, NEW YORK, NEW YORK in white letters; above, smallest yet, MAKE AMERICA GREAT AGAIN! in white letters. Framing the stage, right and left of the lectern, two small pedestals, both draped in glisteny dark fabric, topped by an open-sided black box containing a scarlet MAKE AMERICA GREAT AGAIN hat, like relics in a sacristy, or Vuitton purses in a Fifth Avenue display window.

One would hear him pronounce his last sentence: "*And-I-Love-This-Country.*" Each word punctuated by a forward jab of his right hand: three fingers up in the air, thumb pressed against index finger to form a little hole, like a coded symbol of the abyss, ultimate nothingness. The crowd breaking into roars, hoots, then chants of "*USA! USA!*" All that golden hair. The president-elect clapping for himself, yanking Pence to his breast, shaking his right fist in the air, clasping one beaming blonde after the next. And the campaign theme song breaking forth: the high-pitched London Bach Chorus piping the overture to the Rolling Stones' "You Can't Always Get What You Want."

Rewinding through the hours leading up to that moment, the adults in the house would show more and more animation—shifting places between couch, chairs, and floor, standing on the carpet moving their lips, clacking glasses down on mantels and tables. Early in the film there'd be so much motion between dishes, bottles, and different rooms that it would appear almost as if the adults were dancing. We'd see the front door opening and closing, shutting and opening again, as more and more guests came in smiling, taking off their coats, dropping bags. We'd observe the slightly twitchy good-humored greetings of old friends—children racing everywhere. The cartoon speech bubbles would be filled with stock pleasantries, tense expressions of relief that the election was over, inquiries about schools, parents, trips, work. Speeding ahead, we'd watch the bubbles begin shriveling, popping into blankness, while things start to slow, as if a paralyzing toxin were being emitted from that shifting glow on the rectangle propped atop the cabinet beneath the Japanese scroll.

I would like to go back and chart the paths carved by our feet moving forward and back across the floorboards and rugs over the course of that night. I would study those lines. I'd graph the vectors made by our arms and fingers. The trajectories of stares. The morphology of mouths. The instants of contact between hands and bodies. By mapping the physical impact made by the news on all these human beings, perhaps the event itself would become legible. Perhaps I could grasp it negatively—the way one might resurrect a potter's fingers from prints left in clay, or reconstitute the contours of an object fallen from space by studying the cavity left behind in the earth's surface after the object itself had decayed.

I would like to go back and sift through everything that was said then, because perhaps somewhere in the vast wreckage of words there's a clue to the meaning of what actually transpired that evening. For if there's no mystery, nothing more to decipher, then there are only the rites of cessation. The president-elect descending the stage into the crowd, into darkness. Moving heavily against a backdrop of fluted midnight-blue curtains while Mick croons, *You can't always get what you whahh-haunt. You can't always get what you whahh-haunt.* Trump passing with his entourage across the faces, devices, bald crowns, red hats, mousse-quilled hair and signage until, at 25:59 in the full thirty-six-minute ABC recording of the victory speech, Mick begins to snarl, *She was practiced at the art of deception / I could tell by her blood-stained hands*, whereupon Trump bends to the charnel glow of a screen held between the fleshy fingers of a man in a scarlet MAGA hat, in a clump of other figures and floating glass panels, then rears back, mouthing a kiss to the air, to his adulators, to the mirrors of all media everywhere, while his bodyguards glare desperately at the flock of phones straining to be blessed by his image, trying to determine whether one might hide death.

I know these traces are meager: the pageantry of that satanic Camelot on the screen; the dim, sociable disarray in our home; but they're what I witnessed of the new leader's arrival. I would compile every piece of evidence I could find—if not to understand, then to diagram; if not to accept, to make the totality of refusal fuel the determination to revolt.

I don't recall any of the chit-chat at the beginning.

I don't recall our responses as the night wore on except for the rote conjugation of despair and disbelief.

"Oh my God,"

"My God."

"God damn it."

"What is happening?"

"Is this really happening?"

"My God, I can't believe this is actually happening."

Rewind.

Guests trickle into the living room, filling the couch and arc of chairs before the screen. One or two curl on the floor. Children bob in the background. I can see Rebecca and myself weaving between people, smiling, reaching out to touch and hold them.

I can make out the newscasters sitting and standing, swirling in space, while their fingers stroke curvy arrows and numerological horoscopes from the atlas of digital maps fluttering across different channels.

I can see us pouring wine at different points along the wall of bookshelves filled with brightly colored volumes. My hand tilting over the big red copy of Allen Ginsberg's collected poems ("Moloch!

Moloch! Robot apartments! invisible suburbs! skeleton treasuries! . . . invincible madhouses!"). Twisting across the black-and-white Library of America edition of the constitutional debates ("Justice is the end of government. It is the end of civil society. It ever has been, and ever will be pursued, until it be obtained, or until liberty be lost in the pursuit."). Rotating above the cracked brown binding of Cavafy ("Above all, don't fool yourself, don't say / it was a dream, that your ears deceived you: don't degrade yourself with empty hopes like these.").

Jeff rested his fingers on the curve of the love seat that came down to us from my great-great-grandmother. Dominque and Nancy sat with folded arms on the flowery couch. Nina sat cross-legged on the dark red carpet, leaning forward, arms crossed over her torso, hands rubbing opposite upper arms. Sina stood by the angular brown secretary which had been Helene Deutsche's gift to my great-aunt Molly, on top of which stood an old Chinese silver opium pipe, the tall stem of which rose to just beneath an icon of the Annunciation in which the blue-robed Madonna's eyes had been scratched out by time or some unknown vandal.

Numbers began coming in from a handful of tiny, sparsely populated districts, and Trump won them easily. The victories were meaningless and entirely expected, and when the children said that Hillary wasn't winning much we chuckled reassuringly, condescendingly. A bit later on, when there was still little good news, my son said what was happening wasn't good. We assured him that the count continued to be statistically innocuous and did our best to explain why this was the case, gliding superficially through the complexities of the Electoral College and other idiosyncrasies of the American democratic system. Hillary still had an 80 percent chance of winning—that was what mattered.

At 9:30, the odds turned to 50/50.

And then there was that extraordinary moment, like the nose of the *Titanic* dipping into the black sea, like the first World Trade Center tower falling, when the lines on the bar graph crisscrossed, and Trump's jagged red vein began to climb over her sky-blue contrail—then to surge higher and higher, while hers plummeted lower and lower.

The faces in our house withered; the screen people in GOP campaign rooms inflated with mounting, flush rapture.

My son repeated that he'd known it hadn't been good when Trump kept winning all the little places, which we'd told him meant nothing. Nothing would come of nothing, we'd told him, speak again.

I remember that a little after ten the doorbell rang and I flew to answer it, like a child. Our friend Natalie was there, tall, bundled, fresh from the street and late hours at work, buoyantly questioning.

"It's a disaster."

My voice must have been electric with incredulity.

"What do you mean?"

"He's winning. He's going to win. The electoral map is becoming impossible for her."

"No . . ."

"All the numbers are wrong. Every prediction was wrong." I was shaking my head.

"Is it true?"

She was taking off her hat and gloves. We were moving into the living room.

His odds were now soaring higher every few minutes, like watching a military rout—the battlefield transforming from an intricate configuration of tactical retreats to a cascading, pell-mell abandonment.

"My God . . ."

"What!"

And then the contest was done.

Those of us who were left descended to the lower floor, where the dining room was, and sat around the dark table where the real food was meant to have been, conversation trailing like poorly stubbed cigarettes. We looked at the wood of the table, at the brick of the hearth arrayed with old pictures, at the shelves lined with books. I saw flames rising. The country in chaos. Everything we had reduced to nothing. Markets crashing. Bloody clashes in the streets.

"We'll never be able to get out of here now," I blurted out. "No one will want this house. Everyone will be trying to leave. We'll be stuck."

Rebecca snapped at the fatuousness of this reaction. And she was right to do so.

I didn't know how to explain that after so many years studying the lives of people who during the 1930s had—in that terrible phrase—found themselves "trapped by history," I felt that all of a sudden it had happened to us. We'd become those doomed procrastinators I was forever writing about. It was all the more shocking because part of the reason I kept reading and thinking about that era was the parallels with our own situation, which kept rearing up at me, and which it seemed vital to learn from. But—once again—learn what exactly?

Recently I'd come across a *Times* editorial from 1944 by Henry Wallace, Roosevelt's first vice-president, in which Wallace wrote of the combination of intolerance with lust for money and power that defined American fascism: "The American fascist would prefer not to use violence. His method is to poison the channels of public information . . . The American fascists are most easily recognized by their deliberate perversion of truth and fact. Their newspapers and propaganda carefully cultivate every fissure of disunity . . . They claim to be super-patriots, but they would destroy every liberty guaranteed by the Constitution. They demand free enterprise, but are the spokesmen for monopoly and vested interested."

It all read like yesterday's op-ed.

Just that week someone had sent me Lewis Lapham's essay from 2005 analyzing how far down the road to fascism America had gone since Umberto Eco's 1995 address on Ur-Fascism, in which Eco spoke of a coming "TV or Internet populism in which the emotional response of a selected group of citizens can be presented and accepted as the Voice of the People." Eco had cited Hermann Goering's alleged quip, "When I hear the word culture, I reach for my gun," but it was no longer necessary to incinerate books, Lapham argued, since although more books were being published than ever before, "to people who don't know how to read or think, they do as little harm as snowflakes falling on a frozen pond." Nor was it necessary to suppress oppositional media, since "People trained to the corporate style of thought and movement have no further use for free speech, which is corrupting, overly emotional, reckless, and ill-informed, not calibrated to the time available for television talk or the performance standards of a Super Bowl half-time show." Secret police weren't necessary either, since "The society is so glutted with easy entertainment that no writer or company of writers is troublesome enough to warrant the compliment of an arrest or even the courtesy of a sharp blow on the head."

How much further things had gone in the eleven years since that admonition. How many boxes was it necessary to tick before realizing, *Yes, it has happened here. Why are we waiting?*

Then again, *had* we been waiting? If so, for what sort of systemic indictment or relief? What was "it"? What would "not waiting" have looked like? We'd tried in our way, with written words and ordinary kindnesses, to build little dams against the dark floodwaters. Even supposing that American fascism had now finally arrived, the recognition didn't come with a kit prescribing what to do next. I didn't seriously imagine there would be roundups of the unwanted in Fort Greene. Of course not! Yet if some recent analyses were correct, the roundups of our psyches had already happened—concentration camps for the citizenry's attention were open for business and ubiquitous, headquartered right inside what used to be called "the privacy of one's own home."

Among the problems with studying the lessons of history is that they're printed upside down in multiple versions, one scribbled over top of the next. The chilling déjà vu tingle of recognition is balanced by bewilderment at how different things really were in the past. We're constantly amazed by the way everything has happened before and the fact that our situation is entirely unprecedented. Both A and B are true. Keep circling all of the above, then drawing spirals across the page and table surface.

I thought of the clouds that seemed to shroud the heads of people we knew in post-referendum London, and of a friend in Israel whose pacifism and promotion of Palestinian rights had left him enclosed in steadily contracting coils by the state's expanding nationalist aggression, and who now lived entirely cut off from the news, from society. He was marooned within his own country, a sadder, wearier, increasingly remote version of his former self. Perhaps that was what one would end up having to do—living the "inner emigration," as some of those who'd stayed in Germany during the Third Reich claimed to have done. Would we now fight our way to some little refuge—probably, realistically, somewhere upstate—subside in our own private, blandly pacific cul-de-sac? Or commence a just slightly emptier, uglier, meaner shadow-life of our current New York City existence?

Not until the moment of my outburst before the grim crew at our dining table did I realize how, for all my effusive criticism of different aspects of the country, I too had preserved a sense of American exceptionalism. Later, in London, I had a conversation with a thoughtful young man from Athens, who'd been living and working in England for the past decade. I asked him what he'd felt on hearing the results of the Brexit vote. The man had preserved a close relationship with his family and I expected to hear him say he'd been horrified to find his adopted country cutting itself off from his European roots.

He looked away from me. "To tell you the truth, I felt a certain *relief*," he said.

I stared at him, brow furrowing.

"I know one shouldn't say that," he went on. "But I was so tired of the condescension toward the situation in Greece. That attitude of *Silly little pigs—they're at it again.* The sneering about our dysfunctionalism and foolish emotionalism. Suddenly it was like, 'Guess what, you're not immune either.' The same with the Americans and Trump. It's not just the 'stupid Southern Europeans' who are susceptible to this political breakdown—this *moment.*"

If nothing else, my own sense of American exceptionalism must now be dispelled, I reflected. But what then was left of my sense of America as such? A few weeks earlier I'd been with Adam in our garden, discussing some news story that made me abruptly wax lyrical about America's unbound horizons, geographical and metaphysical. I acknowledged how callow I felt praising this amplitude, in the midst of the upsurge of violent prejudice and blindness, but still the place kept reawakening in me an exhilarating feeling of wide-open vistas. Adam countered almost gruffly that I'd damn well better hope I held on to this faith because "the whole thing's finished if you lose it." I hadn't pressed him to elaborate on what he meant by "the whole thing"; but now the scene returned to me as a question: Could there be places whose operative identities were *dependent* on the conceit of a special destiny, and wouldn't such states then be especially vulnerable to the moral rot that ensues when the venial compromises that accompany realpolitik attained some critical mass? I'd felt the same tension in Israel. And what happens to individuals who inhabit such societies while attempting to hold them to their original, empyreal standards?

It had been driven into me since early childhood that I was linked to the country's founding fantasy: the creation of a holy nation in the wilderness—the novel experiment in civilization that would also constitute a return: the New Jerusalem! Sitting between my grandmother and mother in my youth, I would page through photographs of old paintings and busts of our early ancestors in the family album and the endless lists of compiled names in my grandmother's book of genealogy, suspended in the spell of their voices slowly weaving the long lines of history. I would tell myself, *This is my family. I am descended from these people.* The phantom faces bobbing in succession all the way from an imposing, high-towered church in England to the brick rectangle with a picture window of 3624 Embassy Lane in Fairfax. Just think of that. *Think about it . . .* But think what? What on earth did "it" mean? I didn't yet fathom that we might strive to make aspects of our predecessors live again through our actions—the idea of substantively honoring a memory. Not taking unctuous pride in some prominent ancestor, but heeding their summons to an unful-filled calling. At the time, I just felt myself tugged back to the limbo they floated in on those black scrapbook pages resting flat across my grandmother's knees.

My mother's ninth great-grandmother was Anne Hutchinson, the fearless Puritan matriarch, who's been claimed as a proto-feminist on account of her commitment to the transmundane potential of her entire community and her willingness to defy the Massachusetts Bay patriarchy—despite the fact that her egalitarianism was in thrall to a fanatical piety that drove her to promulgate the most stringent inter-pretation of the faith they had left England to live by. Anne categori-cally denied the existence of free will and the notion that any human action could influence the work of salvation. She exalted the doctrine of predestination professed by leaders of the Calvinist movement back home, before they discovered that to establish a functioning society in the New World would require some judicious pruning of their orthodoxy. If everyone's fate were entirely predetermined, how could you motivate anyone to contribute to society's betterment?

And my mother was the eighth great-granddaughter of John Cotton, the English minister who'd embraced the conviction that personal metamorphosis through the advent of grace at the moment of spiritual conversion was the central event of Christianity. From his pulpit at St. Botolph's in Lincolnshire he'd brought Anne to dedicate herself to the Puritan mission, promising that those whom God elected to save would experience direct communication with Him, and that the Massachusetts Bay Colony represented a crowning wonder of the

Reformation. One might say that in compensation for the loss of free will, Cotton held forth the prospect of a heavenly intimacy.

After listening to Cotton's sermons, Anne heard God prophesize to her in the words of Jeremiah: *I will make a full end of all the nations whither I have driven thee, but I will not make a full end of thee.* She followed Cotton over the ocean to the New Jerusalem. At first the two worked in tandem there as allies, but Anne's insistence that she possessed unimpeachable knowledge of God's will, combined with her efforts to make the community adhere to its foundational theological precepts, led to frequent tussling with the authorities. Eventually, her belief in the nonhierarchical dispensation of grace led her to challenge the very possibility of human magistracy, at the same time as Cotton was placing ever greater emphasis on law and the obligation to address the community's pragmatic needs. Despite the fact that she had never lost faith in him, Cotton at last joined the other Puritan elders in finding Anne guilty of sedition and contempt. She, her husband, and their seven surviving children were sent into exile. Anne's courage and conviction that she was the vehicle of a transcendent truth were impressive, even though what she actually believed in was for the most part antipathetic to the values that inform the social visions we're inspired by today.

In the bronze statue of Anne before the Massachusetts State House, she gazes up implacably toward heaven, a book propped in the crook of her left arm, a fist clenched against her heart, while a child nestles in the folds of her skirt. Something in her attitude of dauntless faith did remind me of my mother, suggesting the way character traits gesture backward through time, even when everything around the marked features may alter so dramatically that the scene resembles a slow-motion version of a myth out of Ovid.

Though vastly less judgmental than her Puritan forebear, my mother had tried to hold herself and her family to an exhaustingly higher set of old-fashioned, formal standards, which made my siblings and me freaks in the Fairfax vernacular. My mother too believed in assurance through revelation, "an inward conviction of the coming of Spirit," though in her case that took the form of non-doctrinal telepathy and communication through dreams. She was continually having presentiments about the circumstances of loved ones—fuzzy intimations that coexisted with outbursts of adamant conviction about the task of those wielding power. To this day I can hear her inside me, speaking out with Anne's passion against the dereliction of America's duty to give refuge to the world's needy, as this country had once done for her husband's family when they arrived on these shores as indigent refugees.

"How *could* you be so rude and inconsiderate!" she'd exclaim if she stood before the ranks of those entering the White House in 2017. "You *must* learn to stop thinking only about your own selves. It's just *Me-Me-Me* all the time." Opening and closing her hands by her cheeks while speaking, as if these were tiny mouths whining. "Frankly, I think you're behaving like big bullies and you should all be ashamed!"

I still recall when our parents drove us all into Washington in the spring of 1968 to see the Poor People's March camped out on the mall, thirteen years before Reagan cheerfully revived the Protestant view of poverty as divinely punitive, a visceral emblem of the needy's moral deficiency. I remember the sagging tents and stinking churn of yellow-brown mud as we threaded our way between the cramped shelters and wide, hopeful, hurt faces in the wake of my mother's firm steps. I remember the concentration and sympathy in her gaze through which, even as a child, I could see we were being shown a great wrong that demanded our attention.

My mother moved through the police standing watch at the edge of the Poor People's encampment as if she were Anne Hutchinson walking out from the meetinghouse in Boston where the judges were gathered, with her stare focused beyond worldly authorities. Just as—in a manner my father never ceases to retell with wonder and pride—when she'd later accompanied him to China on a State Department visit during the Tiananmen Square demonstrations, my mother had unhesitatingly walked up to protestor after protestor to express her admiration for their bravery, earning their trust and encouraging them to tell their stories. All these sorts of actions on her part could be understood as variations on the ethical imperative of finding intimacy with those under duress. A sense of obligation that went beyond the contours of any particular crisis to embrace her reflexive commitment to making manifest our commensurate humanity, an idea driven by instinctual empathy at odds with all varieties of exceptionalism—save the principle that inherited privilege confers a greater responsibility to help others less fortunate.

Yet how isolated she became at the end in that miserable brick box near the bottom of Embassy Lane. Her constitutional inability to associate monetary success with greater merit or personal interest embroidered her breast with a kind of scarlet *A* for *Alien*. The neighbors could not understand her, neither her speech nor her etiquette. How privately she kept her small notebooks filled with fragmentary poems in bedroom drawers that she refused to open for anyone because she so disbelieved in the grace of her writing. I longed to know what she wrote because those lines were the only things she'd made for herself, mementos of impressions that didn't find expression in her household labors or acts of charity. When I saw a few pages once, I discovered brief, poignant descriptions of natural phenomena. Seasonal changes and the flitting passage of wildlife seen through the window above the kitchen sink where she stood endlessly toiling. I knew she wanted to make more of her literary voice than her life had conduced to. Sometimes out of nowhere she'd begin quoting "The Love Song of J. Alfred Prufrock," humorously announcing that she should have been "a pair of ragged claws scuttling across the floors of silent seas." I think of the lurid scenes she stumbled across constantly in that suburb, cracking against the glass of her old New England bell jar upbringing. My sister told me just the other day that before going into the Virginian my mother was always saying that she hadn't wanted to end up in Fairfax, that she'd never imagined the family would live there so long, that her closest friends were always elsewhere, that we lived too far from the museums and theaters, that she'd always wanted to leave, but could never overcome the argument with my father, or her conscience, that doing so in a manner that might bring on the changes she pined for could only be financially imprudent. Yet whatever renunciations she accepted, she never surrendered her positive spirit, while continually giving money and other forms of assistance to everyone in want she came to know, along with the representatives of a larger, international assembly of causes.

However frequently my father might have clutched his head in a kind of caricature Old Testament outrage at her wantonly inclusive politics, he revered my mother as an infallible moral paragon. How often in her final years, after she had moved away from our house to the Virginian, did his eyes well up as he toasted her extraordinary selflessness and uncompromising ethical wisdom at one gathering or another. He'd start remembering their first home together, the caretaker's cottage on a peach orchard in Grand Junction; salt-of-the-earth neighbors; camping trips deep into the red sandstone operatics of Arches National Park. Stargazing at night in the desert when the fire was extinguished and not a whisper of haze lay between them and the constellations whose myths she knew in such detail. "God, she *loved* it out there!" he'd cry. "And when I think of her ending up in that *hell* in 'Willow Lane.'" Then he'd turn away so hard it was as though his face were a door shutting into a mountain.

After the court pronounced Anne Hutchinson guilty and banished her for pretending she could know she possessed such intimacy with God, she left Massachusetts on foot from the farm near the sea to which she and her children had taken their belongings. It was the first of April, but the snow was still so deep she sank to her thighs when she stepped into the drifts. John Cotton must have felt stricken with remorse at the thought of her expulsion. The two of them had nurtured a vision of the New Jerusalem for decades. They'd shared one of the original dreams of what America could be. And now he was part of the tribunal sending her alone into the wilderness.

I imagine he rode down from Boston to the farm in modern-day Quincy early on the day she was leaving, tortured by the thought that she'd never stopped believing in him. Perhaps they spoke together one last time in the doorway while her children finished loading what they could onto the carts, and she gathered herself for the trek to Rhode Island, where she hoped to find refuge in the settlement of Providence Plantations, founded by Roger Williams in the name of freedom of conscience, though in the end she proved too radical even for that community and struck off once more into the forest.

Cotton stood by helplessly as she completed her preparations, portly and woeful, his fleecy curls billowing out from either side of his brow like miniature wings on children playing angels in nativity scenes. At last he murmured some kind of reassurance. He expressed his sorrow. She didn't pass judgment on him. He'd been her guide in the discovery of God's light, after all; how could she turn against him? He tried to press her hand. She gave him her blessing, then strode resolutely out the low doorway into the deep snow. She walked forward into that white blankness without looking back, because this was her fate now and she had to live it. That movement into the unknown is the physical action I would memorialize. While Cotton stood looking after her, biting his tongue to prevent himself from calling after her. Wishing everything were different. That he could somehow still save her. That she'd not placed him in this irresolvable conundrum: torn between his duty to maintain the law of the colony he'd become so invested in and his responsibility to her and the sense of radiant purpose they'd conceived together when they were still dissenters in the Old World, dreaming of the freedom to establish a sacred commonwealth on earth.

Watching her diminutive figure in broadcloth trudging through the snow, becoming smaller and smaller until she vanished completely between the scrawling black branches at the boundary of the cultivated land, Cotton must have asked himself what would become of her. He must have tried to tell himself that she would be better off where she was going, even if where she was going appeared, from his vantage point, to be nowhere. He must have remembered the last feeling of her palm in his. And the moral clarity of her voice. He must have wished he could see her pale face spin back to him once more—and must have been glad to be free of her righteous purity at last. My mother kept telling my father that she *wanted* to go into the Virginian up to the last moment. Over and over she promised

him that she needed to be some place where he didn't have to worry
about her. She wanted him to be free to live his own life, she said
repeatedly, as if either of them knew what that life was without the
counterweight of her society. Ravens pecked at the white crystals for
invisible seeds. She'd consoled *him* when she stepped into the void.

A year after Anne and her children left Williams's colony, traveling to what is now Pelham, New York, she and her family were
scalped and burned to death by Native Americans. Dutch soldiers
had recently made a surprise assault on members of the Siwanoy
Nation living in the area, killing eighty men, women, and children.
Anne died in one of the raids meant to avenge that massacre. My
last sight of my mother was at the long table of the Virginian's bright
dining room, with its elevated television perpetually chanting, the
gaudy colors flickering like flames, her poor white-haired figure
shrunken there amid the other residents lolling backward and forward as though they'd been hatcheted, mouths gaping open, limbs
flapping, disconnected. Weeping and shrieking.

I know it's only a crude visual stutter across the centuries, yet I
can't stop striving to interpret these hieroglyphics of the body, twitch-
ing under the shock of different socio-historical circumstances. And
perhaps somewhere there's a key that reveals the meanings are, after all, cognate. "Just like our residents, we embrace the future every
day," says the Virginian's online prospectus, adding that that the facility stood on land once belonging to Native Americans and that
the first generation of senior residents was called the Pioneers.

After my eruption at the table, one of my friends made a comment
to the effect that he thought I was trying to say something about our

larger situation, the sense of our all being caught now in a national upheaval of unknown dimensions. This was generous of him, and true—up to a point. For what I was even less able to delve into at that moment than my conceptual horror at the idea that we'd become characters from the historical annals I was forever brooding about was my fear that we'd now never muster the material or mental wherewithal to leave New York, though I'd been longing to get out for years, apart from any particular cataclysm. All my close friends knew of this wish (many shared it), which sometimes felt like lyric *Wanderlust* and at other moments like dull malaise. I short-handed the urge by saying I no longer felt "creatively nurtured by the city." Not that the city had any obligation to provide this. But I meant by that phrase—oh, a slew of things having to do with the cultural fallout of its soaring costliness—the homogenizing corporatization that shrank and quarantined the space for eccentricity, severing all interplay between those whose existences were ordered for victory and those wayward souls with unproductive lives—between ambitious realists and those who dreamed impossibilities alone. I couldn't say just why the loss of lost, discursive characters seemed so corrosive to the metropolitan ecology, but now I think it had something to do with the disavowal of the variegated social fabric in which other people's humanity enlargingly surprises our private life.

I could walk down Cumberland Street toward Fort Greene Park one minute and see nothing but brusque, buffed, ear-budded go-getters, carrying commuter cups and smartphones, walking hard straight toward me and seeing nothing before them but their coming day in tech, marketing, or busy-ness as such. I could walk down Cumberland Street the next moment and see nothing but the left behind: huddled, lame, obese, ill, addicted, impoverished, or just

unknown, staring from steps and behind windows no one thought
to look through. The two Cumberland Streets would not merge if
you viewed them through some sociological stereoscope. They did
not reflect a layered community. They were two entirely different
Cumberland Streets that could not be perceived at the same time,
although they occupied the same spatial outline, like the duck-
rabbit illusion Wittgenstein writes of: "I see two pictures, with the
duck-rabbit surrounded by rabbits in one, by ducks in the other. I do
not notice that they are the same. Does it *follow* from this that I *see*
something different in the two cases?"

My mind drifted all the time to dream lives in other places and
eras, where I fantasized that these divisions had not been so imper-
vious. I wanted to believe Andy Warhol's portrait of the Lower East
Side in the early 1960s, in which "everything was low-budget to the
point of no-budget," and you could rent whole floors of buildings
with the savings from minor scraps of work each month. It was a very
peaceful neighborhood then, he wrote, "full of European immigrants,
artists, jazzy blacks, Puerto Ricans—everybody all hanging around
doorsteps and out of the windows. The creative people there weren't
hustling work, they weren't 'upwardly mobile,' they were happy just to
drift around the streets looking at everything, enjoying everything."

The ecology I was romanticizing was grounded in empathetic as-
sent to convivial idleness, the ideal Whitman sang of when my house
on Cumberland Street was being built in the mid-nineteenth century
and he lived nearby: "Loafe with me on the grass, loose the stop from
your throat . . . Only the lull I like, the hum of your valvèd voice."

But the new economic landscape had erased the space for that
invitation. The night of the election made clear, whatever else, that
the prevailing vision was one in which there were only mutually exclusive categories of losers and winners, the damned and the saved.

The last embers of conversation dwindled down. The last guests embraced us at the door.

We moved listlessly through the paces of setting the house back to its everyday order. We weren't speaking much by then. The occasional reiteration of shock or agitation like the last, stray sounds in a forest after most of the wildlife has settled for the night.

When everything was put away I went to my computer and watched the end of the victory speech again. Heard once more the opening of "You Can't Always Get What You Want." Then flicked to a recording of Mick performing the song in a white suit on an English television program in 1969. Hunched, leering, and rocking on the studio floor: *And we went down to the demonstration / To get our fair shares of abuse / Singing, "We're gonna vent our frustration"*— which comes at 23:10 in the ABC election night tape as Trump grins with his eyes shut, reaching up to clutch the gold-ringed fingers of an unseen man. Whereupon Mick, in the studio, rises to his feet, twirling, clapping, and pivoting, doing his totemistic weave and kick. *You can't always get what you want, but if you try some time, you just might find, you just might find you get what you nee-eed.*

Mick said the Stones had tried to get Trump to stop using the music because they didn't endorse him, but he kept playing it anyway. Mick said it was weird that the song had become the emblem of his campaign: "A doomy ballad about drugs in Chelsea." Though some people said the song was really about the end of sixties idealism, before capitalism, dope, and violence co-opted it.

But this was the beginning of the criminal Lacanian presidency, in which what would prove most unbelievable was the way that nothing was hidden. The parable of the Emperor's New Clothes falls apart if the Emperor gloats at the chance to parade in the nude while his subjects applaud his revealed obscenity, stripping off their own clothes to join him. This was, in other words, before people's realization that Trump had been right to use precisely this song. In time we would discover that though his sentiments, values, and convictions might not have been what we wanted, he would nonetheless give us what we needed: money and ceaseless, cheap, bumper-car volts of sensation. As for what we'd ostensibly wanted, those ideals of the sort Whitman invoked when charting his Democratic Vistas (the truth, justice, and compassion he extolled when declaring that "of all dangers to a nation . . . there can be no greater one than having certain portions of the people set off from the rest by a line drawn— they not privileged as others, but degraded, humiliated, made of no account"), these would be stirred up online with their antitheses into primeval gobbledygook.

So that sometime later, when one read stories of another migrant child dying in the desert custody of ICE—parched, disoriented, crying in pain—the news would be irksome, but no longer capable of wrenching us from our lairs. What was there to do except tweet our hearts out? The economy kept doing better than it ever had before, and if that was the price, lo and behold, we found we'd already paid it.

Rewind:

25:57—*I saw her today at the reception / In her glass was a bleeding man*, at which instant Trump's face is blinded out white by someone's camera-flash to thin eye-sockets and mouth hole—he becomes for that instant a glowing skull.

Rewind:

22:13—*I knew she was going to meet her connection.* Having crossed the stage, Trump pivots again to the crowds, raises his shaking right fist in the air, then turns to the stairs. Little doomed Barron trudges after his father. Silent Melania in a fluttery, silky white pantsuit follows, trailed by sunny Ivanka, in a short robin's-egg-blue dress, followed by sharp-suited Jared, face split in smiles.

Rewind:

00:00—Crowd shots of men and women shaking their red MAGA hats in the air, chanting "U.S.A.! U.S.A.!"

2:19—Pence squinting from the podium: "I come to this moment—I come to this moment deeply humbled. Grateful to God for his amazing grace."

3:33—Trump and his train move onto the stage against red and blue-lit curtains. Trump clapping. Jerry Goldsmith's brassy, triumphant instrumental "The Parachutes" from Wolfgang Peterson's *Air Force One* booming while he walks to the lectern—a film in which Harrison Ford plays a U.S. president who, after collaborating with the Russian president to capture the communist leader of a former Soviet Republic, delivers a speech in Moscow in which he swears he will never negotiate with terrorists, then ends up being hijacked on Air Force One by communist terrorists disguised as journalists, whereupon the president proceeds to kill the fake journalists. That's the music playing as Trump marches to the stage to deliver his first speech as America's president-elect.

Perhaps the most desperate need made manifest in the election was an end to the dream that there was any solution to reality except flat-out rejection—the smack of pure wish-fulfillment mainlined, for all the blood-stained ugliness of the needle that delivers it. *If you try some time, you just might find, you just might find . . .*

Cocky Mick slip-sliding, sashaying in his white suit, bending and straightening, moving forward and back, aqua scarf flying, hair tossing behind him, leaping and slapping his hands together high over his head, thrusting groovy, plump lips to the camera almost exactly one month before Altamont, where he would rooster-chest in his red shirt above the crowd like a flame dancing at the end of a fuse.

Please allow me to introduce myself, I'm a man of wealth and taste.

"Sympathy for the Devil" was another standard at Trump rallies, where the entrancing chaos, crackle of danger, and promised mass catharsis was repeatedly likened by reporters to the savage, treacherous delirium at the Speedway concert, after which the Stones would gather around a little monitor to watch and rewatch the instant during their performance when, in a great arcing trajectory, one of the Hell's Angels hired by the band to provide security but enraged by the battle to preserve the sanctity of their motorcycles against the drug-addled crowd would lurch up from the mass of lost souls to stab eighteen-year-old Meredith Hunter in the back—the gray phallic shank plunging over and over into the young Black man in the brilliant green suit, until history itself seemed caught in the carnival ecstasy of American violence.

When all the devices were finally shut down and Rebecca and I were upstairs in our bedroom, we looked at each other in the house where we'd been living for thirteen years, where a child was now sleeping, where our eyes would not close, and realized we no longer knew where we were.

4

· Place & Time ·

Not long after I moved to London, my sister, Elisabeth, came to visit us. I took her to the Freud Museum, which she'd never seen. I thought it would interest her, not only because of our family history with Freud, but because she'd been trained as a social worker and began her career as a therapist in a psychiatric hospital. Since then, the winds of economic pressure had carried her into the private sector, where the company she now worked for collaborated with pharmaceutical firms on clinical trials of new drugs, many of them targeting mental illness. Her employer promoted itself as the first to introduce a new methodology for interviewing subjects in these studies: *All* exchanges were to be conducted remotely (indeed, staff weren't allowed to interact with patients in person). This ahead-of-the-curve policy was intended to allow researchers to stage interviews with total objectivity, which was impossible at live research sites where one invariably formed personal relationships with study participants. The approach of course presupposed that a remote interaction wouldn't have biases of its own, say, toward the kind of de-individuation that bleeds into dehumanization, while assuming that a personal relationship can't reduce biases favoring a narrow, generically pathologized interpretation of patient narratives—opening through intimacy to other dimensions of identity, perhaps even socioeconomic context.

A corner of my sister's rental apartment, in a nineteenth-century brownstone elegantly ornamented with decorative moldings, a couple of blocks from my home in Fort Greene, had been converted into a nondescript video set intended to represent a normative office environment—desk, filing cabinets, houseplant, no mementos of any kind—which framed her while she conducted interviews. The premise being that American office space is neutral and could therefore facilitate the process whereby patients verbalized symptoms exclusive to their interior agons, though to some people that infinite nowhereness might in fact trigger nightmares more horrifying than those provoked by a space swarming with imagery from Bosch's *Last Judgment*. The former's scrubbed nothingness, prefiguring death without god or interruption of any kind, inducing a state of mind that might make the advent of even the most hideous devil welcome, simply for its disfiguration of sameness.

But leaving this aside, the blank setting is yet a carefully staged space, and I was sure the contrasting, anthropologically dense environment of Freud's consulting room would intrigue her by virtue of its strangeness, if nothing else.

For a time, we wandered the large house in silence, moving through still rooms hung with long burgundy curtains, where Freud's belongings had been transported by Princess Marie Bonaparte and re-constellated as they'd been in his apartment at Berggasse 19 after Freud's escape from the city which he'd called home since he was four years old. Stepping through the twilit spaces, I found myself remembering our father's flight from Vienna and felt as if we were Hansel and Gretel, going into the forest of our own ancestral history. Yet we had no crumbs to scatter. How would we find our way back again? I looked at my sister, and the long ovals of her eyes, which, with their dark humor, resignation, and refusal, have always evoked for me our father's mother, seemed to tremble with emotion.

I thought again, as I am continually thinking, of our paternal grandparents at the table of their apartment near the Belvedere Gardens after the Anschluss, trying to determine what the vast political changes meant for them personally—knowing that what they did next would cast the die for their children's future. I see their hands clasped across the dark wooden surface and hear their low, rushing voices. But perhaps they were dead silent and sat opposite each other without seeing anything. Perhaps the smoke from his pipe filled the room as she quietly wept. Perhaps neither of them could stop moving. Pacing the rooms, tearing their hair, and clawing their breasts. How unassimilable it must have been after a lifetime of saying, in one context or another, "Our home is Vienna," to realize they'd lost the right to exist there.

My sister and I walked past tall, dark bookcases filled with thousands of polychrome volumes, and tables crowded with antiquities. Framed photographs of friends and loved ones hung from the shelves. Yellow lamps reflected off the glass doors of vitrines lined with heads, vessels, and figurines. A number of statuettes posed rigidly with scepters, while a winged Eros appeared to spring into thin air. Our feet sank into the deep oriental rugs as we paused before painted amphorae and clay deities. Freud remarked to visitors that he felt a greater kinship with his classical predecessors than he did with his contemporaries. On one occasion, he gestured to a row of the classics bordered by idols of Athena, Eros, Osiris, and Amon-Ra and declared to a guest, "Here are my respondents."

At last we entered the large room where Freud practiced analysis. The poet H.D. observed that its dimness made it resemble an "opium dive," while the precious objects appeared to her as architectural elements in an edifice made of time. "Length, breadth, thickness, the shape, the scent, the feel of things. The actuality of the present, its bearing on the past, their bearing on the future," she wrote of this place.

Freud's desk is arrayed with an assembly of figures, mostly gods and kings, which counterpointed the words he was reading or composing on its flat surface. During sessions with patients, he stepped from the desk to a green chair behind the head of the famous couch draped with a dark red and indigo Ghashgha'i carpet woven by female members of a nomadic Persian tribe. From their recumbent position, patients couldn't comfortably see Freud, but by twisting right they would confront the idols on his desk, which thus became, simultaneously, a silent chorus bearing witness to the tragedies being narrated, proxies for the analyst, and evocative compatriots of patients' dreams. Part of what Freud was doing in this space was projecting patients' recollections and fantasies into the immemorial theater of culture—dignifying them as artifacts in the entablature of our common civilization.

H.D. likened Freud to a museum curator. Surrounded by his "Greek, Egyptian, and Chinese treasures; he is 'Lazarus stand forth,'" she declared.

I wanted to speak about the poet to my sister—I saw affinities, as well as provocative discrepancies, between their characters. Both women were fiercely independent and sustained a youthful curiosity about the outer edges of worldly experience. My sister spent much of her free time tenderly, unflinchingly photographing the life she encountered as she moved through the city. H.D. took snapshots of bohemians cavorting in the woods that made Marianne Moore's prim mother cry out, "I'd adore to run through the hedges . . . under the big trees, in the deep snow—alone,—or with just a few."

Moore and H.D. had known each other since their college days, and the two were in close contact throughout the years Moore lived in Fort Greene. She and Elizabeth Bishop overlapped at Cumberland Street, and H.D., from her various Manhattan addresses, would have echoed Bishop's "Invitation to Miss Marianne Moore": "From Brooklyn, over the Brooklyn Bridge, on this fine morning, / please come flying, / In a cloud of fiery pale chemicals, / please come flying / . . . We can sit down and weep; we can go shopping, / or play at a game of constantly being wrong/with a priceless set of vocabularies, / or we can bravely deplore, but please / please come flying." H.D.'s connections to Ezra Pound ran deeper still. He'd made her his protégé when she was still an adolescent, dubbed her a "Dryad," made her the ambassadress of Imagism, and become engaged to her—though the marriage never happened and H.D. later wrote of how, with his unreliable character and eyes like gambler's gems, Pound left her feeling "smudged out," his kisses smothering her "clear geometric thought." He viewed her later attachment to Freud as a self-defilement symptomatic of Western culture's overall decline, writing her at one point of "vile Freud all bunk." The foolish Christians should have stuck to the reading list bequeathed them by Dante, not buried all their good authors. "You got into the wrong pig sty, ma chère," he chided her.

She'd gone into analysis with Freud early in the mid-1930s, attending her first session a month after Hitler was appointed Germany's chancellor, at a point in her life when she felt enslaved to empty compulsions, which seemed to mirror a larger malady of the age. There was something "beating in my brain," she wrote, which needed release. "I wanted to free myself of repetitive thoughts and experiences—my own and those of many of my contemporaries . . . I knew that I, like most of the people I knew, in England, America, and on the Continent of Europe was drifting. We were drifting. Where?" I could imagine my sister exclaiming something comparable—albeit with a wry laugh rather than H.D.'s occasionally overwrought gravitas.

The poet's question was magnified by the omens accumulating in Vienna during the period when she was walking six times a week from her rooms at the Hotel Regina to lie on Freud's couch. Right in front of the hotel she occasionally witnessed "coquettish, confetti-like showers from the air, gilded paper swastikas and narrow strips of printed paper like the ones we pulled out of our Christmas bon-bons." When she picked up the thin papers they revealed short, bright mottoes, HITLER GIVES BREAD and HITLER GIVES WORK. After the tinsel, there were swastikas chalked on the sidewalk, death-head marks, some leading straight to Freud's door. And then there were neatly stacked rifles in bivouac formations at street corners, reminding her of pictures from the American Civil War. The soldiers, too, "were out of a picture or a film of a reconstructed Civil War period," she wrote. Everything seemed performative, replicated, while the Viennese themselves appeared under a spell. She felt as if she were the only person in the whole city who bothered to actually peel up the shiny scraps from the pavement and read their printed messages. Among her acquaintances elsewhere in Europe and the United States there was a parallel sense of somnambulant helplessness. For years now she'd witnessed a "growing feeling of stagnation, of lethargy." Half her friends couldn't acknowledge that the deluge was coming, while those who were cognizant "were almost too clever, too politically minded." While the first group denied the flood, the other half "counted the nails and measured the planks with endless exact mathematical formulas," but had no clue how to assemble the Ark. She wanted to scream at them all, "Where is this taking you?"

Before the stream of events swept her into the cataract, she meant to take stock of herself and her possessions, she announced. Her lover Bryher was forever going on about the threat of impending catastrophe and sometimes it needled her. Like many of us now, there were moods she got into in which she couldn't "give a damn who goes and who doesn't to war. All I want is to pick up the pieces, to know how I feel, not to be badgered by conflict," she told Bryher. *God, what we wouldn't give today for a clear view of our path forward—free of this interminable, bloodthirsty discord!* She and her peers were surrounded by a "great forest of the unknown," H.D. wrote, a supernatural current that was building in force—and she sought out the "old Hermit" who lived at the margin of this realm to help her interpret the thoughts collected inside her, so she'd know how to navigate her course.

Sometimes it would happen that their exchange veered into contemporary questions. H.D. said that she couldn't believe Hitler would dare the great powers as Germany had done in the last war. "Yes," Freud replied, but "before he has time to think many many people will be murdered." By "people" he meant Jews, H.D. explained in a letter to Bryher (who was herself assumed to be Jewish). "I said I didn't think massacre was possible, there was still open sympathy in the world . . . he gave a flea shake to his shoulders and said, 'well we had better go on with your analysis. It is the only thing now.'"

I don't know when it was that I realized my sister was no longer beside me. I twisted all the way around, but she'd left the consulting room and library. Perhaps she'd found people elsewhere in the house whose appearance had spoken to her and she was taking their photographs. She was always breaking away to take portraits of those who arrested her gaze. How many times had I halted on the unruly boardwalk between Brighton Beach and Coney Island while she cut off to engage someone! Nobody intimidates her, and she makes everyone splendid—heart-rending, seductive, or fantastical. She's ordinarily so self-effacing, so endlessly diffident, but I've seen her shamble up in her boots, jeans, and brown leather jacket to gigantic, crazy-eyed gang-bangers, extending a gently sparkling smile, and the next moment they're posing with elaborate dignity for her lens. H.D. told the poet William Carlos Williams that her sympathies were "with those people that feel themselves apart from the whole—that are somehow lost and torn and inclined to become embittered by that very loneliness." This description would accord with that of the individuals my sister is most drawn to in her street photography. But there's a sense in which for H.D. people were most interesting as potential conduits to some trans-sensory revelation, while for my sister these people's realities delineate her own horizons for the time she's absorbed with them. They are her "respondents," in Freud's terminology. I thought of something Diane Arbus once said about why she photographed "freaks." A freak is like someone "in a fairy tale who stops you and demands that you answer a riddle," Arbus observed. "Most people go through life dreading they'll have a traumatic experience. Freaks were born with their trauma. They've already passed their test in life. They're aristocrats."

That perspective helps explain why it is that, by and large, my sister is someone who remains where she is. She's not *waiting* for anything. Yet within the ambit of her circumscription, she roams with a gypsy freedom that I, in my geographically far-flung rambling, don't approach. She doesn't endlessly question everything, asking herself and others whether the whole paradigm ought to change. Or she knows it should change, and knows it won't change, and contents herself lighting matches in dark corners, glimpsing, revealing, then quickly blowing out the flames again so as not to hurt the eyes of life's nocturnal aristocrats. To her, this place and time must be home.

Conversely, when H.D. began seeing Freud, she was struggling to integrate an interest in the scientific potential of psychoanalysis with her faith in the reality of magic, which encompassed an ongoing quest for immortality through the original thaumaturge, Merlin or Theseus, who would enable her to dispel the material world altogether. My sister disbelieves in immortality. Asked how she feels about the prospect of a clean break from being, she would likely say something along the lines of, "Thank God for that anyway." But she would do so without bitterness. She takes the world as she finds it, as complete in its brokenness. The form American civilization has assumed in her lifetime is the shell to which her life must adapt, she's concluded, which has impelled her to discover instances of the subtle poetics underlying that façade—and is also part of why, notwithstanding her subversive heart, she's been able to endure in the corporate sector. Spending endless hours on conference calls, in excruciatingly dull meetings, at conventions, and on retreats with aggressively up-beat people whom she describes as living in perpetual dread of being made redundant, of failing, of being found out, or of simply being swept away by some massive, faceless, financial convulsion—people for whom employment comes in tandem with fear of losing their positions; forever awaiting new drug-trial results, new investment, new management, new market conditions, new team goals, new titles, new payments on new purchases, new relationships formed on new online platforms, new children, new side effects, new crises, new deaths: polar opposites of Arbus's freak-aristocrats. These are the people tasked with finding elixirs for America's epidemic of depression and anxiety.

My sister's rejection of the supermundane, in any case, aligns her with Freud's attitude, while H.D.—who wrote that though she never argued openly with Freud about the great, transcendental subjects, yet knew there was an "an argument implicit in our very bones"—was nearer to our great-grandfather, Putnam. Like him, she refused to fully grant Freud his own professed atheism. He was "midwife to the soul," H.D. wrote, was indeed, "himself the soul." While as for me . . . Well, my sister had moved to Fort Greene in part to be closer to me, and I'd left her there while I went off in pursuit of some otherworldly fantasy.

I remembered sitting across from her in the living room of her second-floor apartment, by the exquisite marble mantlepiece lined with photographs of our family, telling her in a long, winding way that we were moving. I remember her staring at me, looking away, staring at me again—and then her gaze falling irretrievably to the hardwood floor, while muted screeches of braking buses rose from the street below.

"I knew this was what you were going to tell me," she said.

"But—" I sputtered and hawwed about how often we'd still see each other, how much I'd be back, how often she'd come to visit me, how perhaps I'd find something in this next life I was embarking on that she'd come to value for herself—something to share. But her eyes did not lift. In place of celestial prophecies, she had absolute knowledge of earthly ruthlessness.

"I'm sorry," I said.

"It's alright." She shrugged. "I'm sure things will be great for you there. I totally get it."

"I'm so sorry."

"It's alright," she repeated, laughing; her eyes flung with tears like raindrops on windowpanes. "I knew it's what you were going to tell me when you said you wanted to speak."

I did not repeat, "I'm so sorry." Nor did I say, "I can't bear to live here any longer. I feel I have to try something new. I'm so stuck in my empty routines and circular thoughts I feel I'll burst my skin." I didn't wallow or go melodramatic. But my lips kept parting, and I could feel air pushing and pushing to form words I knew would only make things worse, for there was no palliative to the message that I was renouncing our life in common.

She forgave me for leaving. Of course she forgave me. She's my sister and we love each other. Yet it was unforgivable and we both knew that, and she forgave me no more than I forgave myself. How could she? It was not a matter of forgiveness. Forgiven or not, I no longer lived around the corner from her. We no longer walked down the wide, uneven sidewalks of Lafayette side by side, trading sardonic remarks about ourselves, our family, the world, and reality. We no longer bumped into each other accidentally on our separate paths, going to work, or a shop, or to run around the park. We no longer said, "Goodbye, I'll probably see you this weekend." We no longer made tentative plans. An ocean lay between us, and the oceans were rising.

Before my sister's trip to London, Rebecca and I had schemed to give her an experience so rich that she wouldn't only see why we'd moved—she got that—but might somehow start thinking she had to move here herself. Because here we were in the fall of 2018, living a novel existence in a gigantic new city where she could find everything she delighted in. Yet really, I could not imagine my sister leaving America. It was as if the expatriate fate line were simply absent from her palm.

But then again, I thought now, staring at three impassive Egyptian coffin masks hung along the vertical axis of one bookshelf, it was also true that my sister's professional life was not the life she'd imagined for herself—she said so repeatedly, even while she drove herself relentlessly at work. From time to time, she spoke of how she missed doing therapy with human beings in real rooms. She was part of a business world that was fundamentally antipathetic to her sensibility, which she saw no clear escape from, even while it continually monitored and evaluated her. Part of me felt a responsibility to fire up a flare from the great elsewhere, if only to remind her it existed. "What is called resignation is confirmed desperation," Thoreau wrote in *Walden*. When I thought of the tense, repressed environment she described at her company, I remembered Emerson asking, rhetorically, whether it was truly strange that a society posited on self-denial should be "devoured by a secret melancholy." Partial conformity to a society's notions of justice might be felt not as a distancing of oneself from the system, but "as a sense of compromise by it or conspiracy with it," the philosopher Stanley Cavell wrote in his gloss of this notion. "Silent melancholy may be taken as a sense of political depression," he concluded.

I found myself whispering this sentence over and over. But there was too much to keep inside. I had to go find my sister. I spun from the twisted cord separating the public from the foundational set of psychoanalysis, and went off in search of her.

She wasn't in any of the downstairs rooms. I hurried up the white staircase. She wasn't in the video room watching the haunting, grainy, amateur footage of aged, ill Freud in the garden of this very house with his legs under a blanket, shot in 1938 just after he'd arrived in the sanctuary of London. She wasn't in the exhibition area inspecting paintings from the show *Freud, Dalí, and the Metamorphosis of Narcissus*. At last I discovered her standing motionless near one wall of the Anna Freud room. Initially, she didn't realize I was nearby, and watching her from a few paces away I could tell that she was deeply affected by what she was seeing. The encounter with the phantom topography of Freud's life, overlapping as it did our own family history, had moved her in ways she hadn't been prepared for. When she became aware of me, her head began slowly shaking.

"I can't believe it," she said.

"What?" I asked quietly.

"I can't believe how much you modeled your whole place in Brooklyn on Freud's house."

"What . . ." I said, more stupidly.

"All the bookcases . . . The little archeological bits and pieces you had everywhere, the old furniture . . . even the friggin' color of your curtains!"

I was completely discombobulated.

All the while I'd thought my sister was having a poignant time-capsule experience of our European prehistory, she'd been staring in astonishment at elements of Freud's interior decoration that corresponded with the settings she'd been surrounded by for years at my house in New York. The tone of her voice suggested that she felt tricked. As if the whole time I'd appeared to be living on Cumberland Street a few minutes from her apartment, I was actually already thousands of miles away in the spectral chambers of Freud's life.

"It's not really all *that* similar—" I began.

"Oh please." She turned to me. "This is exactly your house."

I stepped back, involuntarily. The displacement she identified was only the first in a series that now seemed to be piling up before me, physically propelling me into the past. For of course Freud's house on Maresfield Gardens was itself a reconstruction. Having spent so many hours in his apartment on Berggasse, when H.D. visited Freud in England she exclaimed at how difficult it was "seeing the familiar desk, the familiar new-old images on the desk there, to realize that this was London," just as the antecedent Viennese rooms, in her account, had suggested a vision of some age-old, Near Eastern pantheon. More personally disorienting was the truth that if my house *had* reproduced the atmosphere in Freud's rooms, I'd made that recreation largely unconsciously. The glass slides of memories from Cumberland Street and my perception of the room we were standing in slid across each other, coalescing and diverging, reversing and merging.

I acknowledged to my sister that, yes, there were large, full bookshelves and little clay antiquities and oriental carpets in both places, but that could be said also—

"No." Her head was shaking again. "It's the whole *mood*."

"The mood? I didn't know my house had a 'mood.'"

She wasn't amused, and I swallowed, trying to decide the degree to which I was being archly disingenuous.

When Rebecca and I first moved into Fort Greene, two years after I'd been displaced by the September 11 attacks from an apartment on Lower Broadway with skylight views of the Twin Towers—after I'd seen that glass buried under gray ash, while the little balcony off the bedroom, instead of confronting a perpendicular superhighway of silver metal and glass, became a frail perch over a smoke-heaving pit of monstrous dimensions—it's possible I was yearning to conjure the historically remote, contemplative world I remembered from visits to Freud's house. I suppose that longing could have played into how things began to be arranged, but after a while the project took on its own momentum through dialogue between Rebecca and myself—following a kind of internal, connubial logic, like the mutual analytic project of mapping psychic landscapes.

Furthermore, as I've said, the majority of old things in our house on Cumberland Street in fact were inheritances from my mother's family: the graceful, yet heavy dark furniture, large libraries, and collections of classical remnants found in cultured late nineteenth-century homes in Boston was not so distant from their Viennese counterparts of that era, demonstrating how the moment in which we live often proves a more reliable predictor of our stylistic choices than geographical location. In truth, if there were a model in the recesses of my memory for the spaces we made in Brooklyn, that had been the amber parlor and living room of my grandparents' home in Cooperstown, where I'd spent so many enchanted hours reading and daydreaming, and which had largely been a reproduction of interiors my grandmother recalled from her childhood in Beacon Hill and on Marlborough Street, combined with an admixture of Persian furnishings and bibelots that my grandfather acquired after falling in love with Iran while serving as an army surgeon there during the Second World War.

He himself was not from New England, but rather rural North Carolina, where he'd been raised mostly by Black women, employed after his own mother became an invalid. His father, who'd been among the attendants on General Robert E. Lee at the Confederate surrender in Appomattox, shut up inside himself after returning from the Civil War, spending his days in devotional labors as a ruling elder for the Euphronia Presbyterian congregation, refusing ever to say a word about what he'd witnessed on the battlefield—refusing almost to speak at all. It was those unknown women, with their histories of slavery and exile, who'd helped mold my grandfather's sensibility, his vision of good, evil, home, and culture. Unknown to me, I mean, except that when my mother sang her favorite lullaby to us, "Swing low, sweet chariot," in a low voice that captured her father's honey timbre, I'm sure the cadences of the spiritual were those he'd learned from the women who'd rocked him to sleep. I'm sure it's some reverberation of their voices that is rising now in my mind in London, as I stare out a long window at a dense cloud of green leaves. *I looked over Jordan, and what did I see / Coming for to carry me home* . . .

Our voices are never all our own, which is why they have depth and may resonate. There are dreams, or dream sequences that will trace "a line like a graph on a map or show a jagged triangular pattern, like a crack on a bowl that shows the bowl or vase may at any moment fall in pieces; we all know that almost invisible thread-line

on the cherished glass," H.D. wrote of the process of analytic exposure. There was a whole ensemble of "shapes, lines, graphs: the
hieroglyph of the unconscious, which Freud had been first to system-
atically explore," she declared. The southern side of my own family
history has remained largely repressed, or at least tacitly neglected,
another formerly nearly imperceptible thread-line, which had come
to feel jerked into sight by the unraveling dream sequence of the 2016
election.

Just after my mother died, I came upon an oval half-portrait of
her paternal grandfather in the 1860s, dressed in a gray Confederate uniform with a high, stiff collar and buttons down the front like
bullet slugs. His gaze is aimed far away from the camera. He has a
loose, off-kilter mustache and dark, deep-set, lonely eyes. His lips are
sealed and the edges of his mouth fold down. He looks like a young
man who has yielded up all life's expectations. The miniature is set in
a metal frame embossed with bristling rifles, flags of the Union, can-
nonballs, clipper ships, and wheels. I've learned that this border was
added later, attached by someone trying to frame the image as the
portrait of a patriot in service to his country rather than a traitor to
the united republic. Such revisionist efforts were common from the
1880s until the First World War—the same period in which American cities were freighted with many of the statues of Confederate
leaders that have become rallying points for white nationalists today.

I wonder when my own grandfather acquired the picture,
whether it had been a keepsake bequeathed while his father was alive
or a posthumous inheritance. When my grandfather came of age,
he walked out of the family home and traveled north from Raleigh
to Cambridge to attend Harvard Medical School, almost without
looking backward—leaving the South with the kind of implacable

determination of some character in Faulkner. My father remembers seeing this intensely peaceful man shuddering with horror when images of racist attacks on civil rights–era protestors came on the news in the mid-1960s. But that portrait was with him at the end. Perhaps he was the one who reframed it. His family was of Scottish descent, emigrating from the country that gave romantic inspiration (especially as filtered through the writings of Walter Scott) to numerous revolutionary projects, liberal and reactionary, all across Europe as well as the United States. Who knows what he saw in that image? The original setting, or its democratic recasting? Or solely the apparition of his silent, dead father?

All our houses are irreversibly drawn and quartered across time and space. An archeological rendering will expose geographical as well as temporal displacements that undermine the grounds of our attachment to any particular place as exclusively our own. How then do we choose to present these inescapably trespassing montages to ourselves and the world? How much of the past do we imagine we can stake a proprietorial claim to? The hill at the top of Fort Greene Park had been the site of a Revolutionary War fort designed by and first named after General Rufus Putnam, another ancestor of my mother's. In what sense does that tie make me *belong* in the neighborhood more than any another resident, or transient? If my family lived in the neighborhood for centuries, perhaps this meant I'd genealogically enjoyed more than my due and it was time to let someone else take over my space there. So far from justifying resentment at the arrival of strangers, why shouldn't greater length of habitation reduce one's private hold on a place? My connection to American history reverts to me as a debt, not a property deed. In the course of an argument my family was having about the current refugee crisis,

I remember Rebecca saying, "I don't see why the fact of being born somewhere should give you any greater right to live there than a person born someplace else." Legal convention, certainly, but morally? How *does* the pure chance of birth location confer proprietary territorial legitimacy?

Yet the ways our homes are temporary, metamorphic collages, so far from diminishing our hold on the world, might also be seen as expanding the grounds of experience, unfixing the imagination's frame of reference just as, in the labile realm of analysis, both analyst and analysand shape-shift through a gamut of disparate characters. (Freud, for H.D., in her transference, became everyone from the Old Man of the Sea, to Hermes, to Janus, to her father, to her brother, while also—in the dual identity of father and brother—evoking a female-male character from Goethe with whom H.D. had long associated herself.) So the embodied conversation we have with our homes makes them transferential effigies, calling forth a tangle of wishes and relationships, even if we occupy their premises only briefly.

I'm sure I'd never really been trying to recreate Freud's rooms on Cumberland Street, yet my sister was responding to something real nonetheless, for, above individual memory, the interiors of the former space shared with rooms from our family history an enduring common vision of what civilization looks like. Half knowingly, half unconsciously, I'd sought to conjure a domain of books, art, and dreamful reflection from remnants of my father's lost Viennese world and my mother's past. However, until my sister made the comment about the resemblance to Freud's house I hadn't been aware of the degree to which our home on Cumberland Street had itself been an expression of homesickness. And perhaps finally there'd grown to be just too great a disjunction between our rooms and the surrounding environment.

Was that the reason why the whole model came to feel exhausted—it had failed to open itself far enough to be fed by exterior reality? Yet what would doing so have meant in practice? Open to which people? To what aspect of the street? Who lived on Cumberland by the end? Perhaps we mean something else by the idea of receptivity than simply opening our doors to the neighbors at large—something more conceptual, or socioeconomically particular. As the air up and down our streets fills with information en route to our myriad devices, might the whole distinction between outside and inside be anyway collapsing? Imagine if all the words, pictures, and sounds traveling in the air we walk through abruptly became visible—the sheer vibrating, violent, muddy glut of it all. Emerson deplored the assimilation, the "maudlin agglutinations" that went on between people "of one town, of one sect, of one political party . . . the ideas of the time are in the air," he lamented, "and infect all who breathe it." But today we literally inhale the ideas of the moment in great clouds of wireless transmissions.

What *should* our spaces look like in relation to the outside world? Is there a model of living we're trying to cultivate behind doors for ourselves, our children and our visitors, which we see as ideally communicable to the larger environment? Should the rooms be harmoniously consecutive with what lies outside? Or, on the contrary, do we want our interiors to appear in sharp opposition to exterior reality? If the latter, is that stance inherently politically suspect, or can the disassociation itself become an act of resistance? Perhaps we should just let our spaces more or less naturally happen, evolving like sleeping animals into the forms prescribed by their architectural genealogies and our instinctual habits? To the extent that the project of shaping our inside spaces is intentional, isn't it always to some degree a proposition about what civilization itself should look like? (Imagine a new, more nuanced protest chant: *Show me what civilization looks like! This is what civilization looks like?*) Yes, we also desire worlds very different from those of our own domiciles, but our choices within still offer a discriminating commentary.

Foucault reflected on how political literature in the eighteenth century began to concern itself increasingly with questions of what form the constructed environment should assume so as to promote order and nurture a moral family life. How might the development of cities and their collective infrastructures be most productively organized? What pattern should houses take? Treatises on government, often incorporated within police reports, became forums for exploring architecture and urban planning. By the mid-nineteenth century, the primacy of the architect in this project was being challenged by the technicians of new economic processes concerned with communication and speed. In tandem with these advances, the model of muffled, middle-class domestic space began to crystallize, contrapuntally.

On the one hand, what could be more quintessentially bourgeois than the curtained, carpeted, stuff-laden interiors of Freud's homes in Vienna or London, or my great-grandfather's townhouse in Back Bay? On the other hand, the model of materialized learning and interplay with the past they presented was intrinsically subversive of the political order that enabled their construction. The libraries they contained were replete with volumes about liberty, injustice, rebellion, and the impassioned pursuit of a more true society—along with individual experiences of a socially disruptive Eros—while the artworks they displayed awakened visions of siren worlds beyond their insulated walls. We're cautioned against indulging any nostalgia for such edifices since their construction was invariably predicated on structural exploitations, which fatally taint their finished form. Yet the admonition, in its more extreme iteration, itself seems indebted to a narrowly Protestant reading of Original Sin. As if there were no personal agency involved in the perpetuation of evil. As if the shape into which the manure-flower of money blossomed never cast a shadow that helped blight the filthy root.

Viewing our homes as simultaneously refuges from the outside world and open-ended portals to the Zeitgeist, what balance might nurture a revolutionary imagination?

There's a letter I cherish that my great-grandfather Putnam wrote to his daughter Molly from Paris in 1911, en route to the Psychoanalytic Congress in Weimar, at which he would embrace the opportunity to have Freud personally analyze him. He was sixty-five that year. Molly had just turned eighteen. But he began writing her after midnight, his mind racing with "café au Pré Catelain," as he wrote, and exploding with visions of the European cosmopolitan ideal. London and Paris made Boston seem tiny for reasons beyond physical scale, Putnam noted. It was the traces of monumental battles for "the people's progress" embedded in their stones that made these two cities monumental. What we want to get hold of when we travel is the true life and inner history of the places we see, he declared. "Real history, whether of individuals or nations, means the series of efforts through which men have, half blindly, tried to find freedom and express love." As the letter continued, Putnam began projecting over the contemporary streets of Paris images from books he'd read of the barricades erected by the poor with "extraordinary courage," during the "great, if terrible Revolution." This process of psycho-historical reconstruction revitalized his feeling of commitment to the charitable and therapeutic endeavors he'd already given much of his life to in Boston. "I throw in my lot with the radicals and the reformers," he vowed, adding that he'd become far more supportive than formerly of all socialistic endeavors. "*Institutions*, and the evidences of the *struggles of the people;* those are what we really want to see—whether at Versailles or Chartres," he concluded.

The economic underpinnings of the cultural tableaux Putnam assembled on Marlborough Street didn't lower the political ceiling of his thought. To the contrary, it was the vantage point he attained through his intellectual expeditions there which blew the roof off his townhouse altogether, enabling him to look up in awe at the universe, and down in horror at the abiding misery on the streets.

Emerson opens his essay "Experience" with a question: "Where do we find ourselves?" By this he meant where are we now, and where is the place where we discover our true nature, where shall we found the project of our renewal? "Our life is not so much threatened as our perception," he observed. No less than H.D. in Europe in the 1930s, Emerson diagnosed his contemporaries as sleepwalking and adrift. "Viewed from any high point, the city of New York, yonder city of London, the western civilization, would seem a bundle of insanities," he wrote in 1850. "We keep each other in countenance and exasperate by emulation the frenzy of the times." The consequence of this conformity was anaesthetization of the soul. The question then becomes, what can awaken us? Is it still possible for society to be healed? How do we draw nearer to that universal promise Emerson invoked when he cried out, "I am ready to die out of nature, and be born again into this new yet unapproachable America I have found in the West."

It was when I thought of this enigma of approachability that I recalled the clue linked to our ancestors that lay hidden in plain view in Freud's house, the sign that might finally help us find our way back again.

I reached out for my sister.

"Come back downstairs. I want to show you something."

I led her once more into Freud's consulting room, brought her to the edge of the divider, and directed her attention to the desk. There, amid the idols, old receptacles, and writing tools, I pointed out a metal animal about the size of a fist, with long, sharp metal quills and a fierce snout—the farewell gift our great-grandfather had given Freud after his visit to the Adirondacks.

"Oh my God—that's really it?"

I nodded.

"That's the porcupine from Putnam Camp?"

"The very porcupine."

She drew her camera forward and began taking photographs. For a moment then, as we stood side by side, it felt as though I must not have left America without her after all, since the two of us could not be separated: our eyes opened through the lens and language onto the same mental pathways etched by history and wonder.

I ran quickly through the object's provenance, explaining how Freud's interest in porcupines derived from a parable Arthur

Schopenhauer had written about the predicament of porcupines in winter. Schopenhauer described a group of porcupines on a cold day who crowded very close together so as "to profit by one another's warmth and so save themselves from being frozen to death." But soon they felt one another's quills, which induced them to separate again. And thus the porcupines were "driven backwards and forwards from one trouble to another," until they discovered the "mean distance at which they could most tolerably exist."

Freud cited the tale in his *Group Psychology and the Analysis of the Ego* to illustrate the "sediment of negative, hostile emotions" appertaining to any close, long-lasting relationship, a phenomenon that evades attention only on account of repression. But the allegory resonates also with Freud's larger, abiding concern with the problem of intimacy—how much is necessary, how much proximity to others can we bear? This, in turn, recalled Freud's vexed relation to the idea of America, and ultimately to the prospects of civilization as such. How close can we come to other people in our efforts to protect ourselves and build something larger than our isolate beings before the collective itself begins to pose a hazard to individual survival?

Prior to leaving Vienna for the United States in 1909, Freud explained to his followers that when one faces a major task, it's useful to have in mind a secondary goal as a means of deflecting tension from the main challenge. So, in this instance, Freud explained that he'd resolved to go to America to see a wild porcupine, and to give some lectures. He didn't, however, divulge the philosophical backdrop to his interest in porcupines, as if resisting the propinquity even of that group expressly dedicated to building his movement.

The invitation to the Adirondacks, which came spontaneously from Putnam after he'd heard Freud lecture at Clark and craved more conversation with him, seemed Freud's best hope for spotting the physical porcupine that had eluded him thus far on his American tour. When he arrived at Putnam Camp and other guests learned of his wish, they told Freud they knew where a porcupine had its dwelling not far above the cabin he was staying in. One morning two giggly adolescent female relations of Putnam's showed up at his door and led Freud off on a hike to find it. Contrary to his expectations, the climb was long and distressingly arduous. At last, approaching the site of the lair, a terrible odor began to assail them—and then the party came upon a motionless, swollen animal covered with flies.

Freud stepped forward after a moment and poked it with the end of his gold-headed cane. "It's dead," he remarked. Then he turned back down the path.

The discovery could only appear ominous, but Putnam attempted to reframe its significance. Just before Freud's departure, he presented him with the porcupine icon as a compensatory souvenir. (After reading Putnam's most ambitious book, a psychoanalytically inspired study of the wellsprings of human action, Freud marveled to Lou Andreas-Salome at Putnam's insistence on perfection having "not only a psychic but also a material reality. That man can't be helped, he must become a pessimist!") The origins of this object, produced rather magically on the spur of this moment, is mysterious, but Freud in any case treasured it, granting the artifact a prominent place in his collection.

For years, I've pondered the question of what exactly it meant to him. In the past, I'd wondered whether the porcupine served Freud as an emblem for the "new yet unapproachable America," or the irreducible, bristling dark wildness at the heart of the psyche—for the Id and the greater wilderness beyond the borders of society. More recently I'd thought the porcupine might be understood as precisely the opposite: a symbol of the work performed by culture on nature, transforming the mysterious, savage unknown into a representative figure one could mount on a desk. Perhaps, in other words, the porcupine represented for Freud the ideal of what civilization does with the terrifying mystery of nature—reproducing and interpreting it, critiquing and sublimating.

But standing now at this hour of crisis beside my sister in Freud's last residence—not far from the room he'd actually died in—the porcupine seemed rather a strange kind of fetish object, and in this guise to formalize a problem that had haunted us since the election: What happens when civilization itself forges the beast? Were the terms of the traditional division between culture and nature reversing? Had savage nature become sanctuary, while civilization took on the predatory character of a primal wilderness?

I felt a sudden urge to leap the crimson cord, rush up to the desk, and grab the porcupine back for my sister to take home with her to America. Then she sighed and I gently squeezed her arm in a gesture meant to be solacing. I think we both knew by this time that it was too late for a talismanic restoration of anything.

5

· Future Forecast ·

I remember the moment when the question came home to me.

The morning after the election it was raining, and this felt symbolic, just as the deep blue warmth of Election Day itself had seemed preternaturally still, as if nature itself were being held in suspension pending a verdict. It had become perfectly ordinary to hear people everywhere speaking in terms of archaic omens and portents.

Rebecca and I walked our son to school. Despite the grim drizzle, everything was placid. It was a calm life we led, I reminded myself, notwithstanding the furor of the previous night.

The buildings are still standing, a voice in my head said. *The trees are all there. Dogs are frolicking in the park. People are drinking coffee. Driving to work. Trucks are making their deliveries. The new condo towers are still rising downtown. Yellow leaves are still patterning the sidewalk. The world has not stopped. We'll muddle through in one piece after all. Did that victory even happen, or could it still be a dream? Doors are opening and closing. People are walking wherever they please . . .*

The little voice in my head mumbled on, until, reaching the playground of the school, we saw a large-eyed, skinny girl eight or nine years old, with long braids, the only child in sight, wheeling toward the chain-link fence that met the sidewalk, like a paper airplane poorly thrown.

"We're all going to die," she remarked as she twirled toward us, her voice neither fearful nor facetious—unappealably stark. "We're all going to die."

Of course we knew, given her age, that she must have been repeating something she'd heard, at home, on the street—something in the air of the hour—but the way she delivered the announcement: whirling toward us out of nowhere, speaking at once to no one and everyone, had an uncanny, Cassandra quality.

My son glanced swiftly up at us with an apprehensive smile. I bit my lip, at a loss how to comment.

We all knew beyond doubt what the girl meant: We would all die in direct consequence of this new government. And I recall thinking, as I have thought so many times since, how astonishing it was that we were living in a technologically advanced, spectacularly wealthy, democratic country in which it was possible for an innocent soul to believe, in all seriousness and sanity, that the government was now out to murder her. Or, if one balks at the imputation of a plan to actively kill, then anyway to create the conditions that would make her death inevitable, collateral damage of some larger, rapacious power play. I thought of it in London when I heard terrified parents worrying about whether their children with diabetes would lose access to the insulin that kept them alive in the event of the no-deal Brexit being righteously threatened by successive prime ministers as a supposed goad to European negotiators, in the name of the will of The People. I thought of it when the U.S. administration began slashing clean water, clean air, safe food regulations, and school meals for poor students in the name of making the country work for real Americans.

How had it come about that the governments of two major centers of Western civilization had more or less declared open war on large parts of their own populations?

After leaving our son at the school entrance, we walked back down Willoughby Avenue, past the august façades of perfect mansions to the park, and began circling the buckling dark rivers of its asphalt paths.

"What's going to happen?"

"I can't stop thinking about that poor girl."

"What are kids going to be saying to each other in school? From now on—"

"How will the teachers respond?"

"I feel so sad."

Over and over, repetitions of the same questions, iterations of the same disbelief and disillusionment, threaded with faint reassurance. Vows of resistance mingled with abject fear for the young.

We walked down to the northern end of the park bordering Myrtle, glancing across to the dim brick huddles of the Walt Whitman housing projects, veering around toward the west side and its views of jabby glass condos soaring downtown, with their fitness centers and elevated party spaces, past the lonely, shady playground, up the rise bordered by the bleak hospital compound with its tower that would be sold for a hundred million dollars to become more luxury condominiums, and around to the park's southern edge, bordering pristine streets of enormous brownstones, and around again to Washington Park with its own giant homes, and on Saturdays the Farmer's Market: strollers, dogs, butchers, apples, toddlers, lumpen vegetables, lines for bread, eco-leaflets, friendly bump-ins, annoyed squeeze-bys, donuts, donuts, cider, cider donuts.

"If things ever got really dire, we could move."

"Where? How?"

"Somewhere in Europe, I guess."

"On what passport? With what money?"

"We could rent out the house for a year—at least to expose Rafael to some other culture—"

"And then you lose your job and our health insurance for good. Where in Europe?"

"What are we going to do?"

"What can we do? This is just the way it is now. Anyway, our house is falling apart, we can't rent it."

"We have to believe it can change—that this situation will change . . ."

A friend came running toward us, across the broad expanse of grass used as a soccer field at the base of the hill crowned by the monument. The mother of our child's best friend. She came toward us as though she'd just heard one of us had lost a person dear to us in an accident, bounding over the rutted grass beside her little brown and white dog. It seemed as if the whole scene were in slow motion, throwing her arms wide . . . hugging us, weeping.

"What's going to happen?" she said sniffing.

It wasn't a question any more than it had been when we said the same words, and we let her simply repeat them.

After we said goodbyes, we cut across the flat earth, up the slope to the plain granite column monument at the summit, the memorial

Walt Whitman had campaigned for to honor the Prison Ship Martyrs: men and boys who'd been seized by the British for disobeying the sovereign's decrees and stuck into the holds of old ships bobbing off Wallabout Bay. In one of the most brutal episodes of the conflict, without any overt strategic decision being made to torture the prisoners, essential resources were simply not supplied to them. Food and water were otherwise allocated. More and more people were thrust into the holds until there was no more living space. Hygiene was impossible. Disease ran rampant. Eventually, Whitman wrote, the British themselves grew ashamed, even shocked, at the proceedings of their officers, but meanwhile the ships had served their purpose.

More than 11,000 individuals perished in the hulks—many not even rebels, but people from all walks of life captured in random sweeps by the English after the Battle of Long Island, when soldiers began arresting anyone who declined to fight for the crown. Buried in shallow pits along the East River, their bones washed up for years along Brooklyn's shores. Youths playing on the banks would kick the skulls for fun, while wind blew the loose sand off bleached skeletons. Old atrocities coarsened the sensibilities of new generations.

Whitman felt it was vital that the dead be commemorated lest the path to our present-day liberties become obscured. These figures with their suffering and sacrifice were, he wrote, "the stepping stones to thee to-day and here, America." But he never envisioned the monument as a site of strict mourning, let alone jingoism. Rather, he conceived of the memorial conjoined with a refuge where the public could take nurture from the natural world; the two purposes were linked.

"The unerring instincts of the masses" had already fixated on the

grounds of the old fort as "a Place of the Ideal," Whitman reported—
because of its history, spaciousness, and the views it commanded. He
described being up on the site one Sunday just before dusk and finding a thousand people gathered, hundreds of children among them,
and being struck by the grace and amplitude of their leisure. The
young frolicked in the grass. Women and men promenaded to and
fro, while at their feet lay "a surprisingly splendid scene" embracing
six counties, along with "a sweep of noble river, with the metropolis
like a map beyond." Whitman had been moved by the "genializing
influence" of the physical place, which he said destroyed all the ob-
jectionable qualities often found in crowds, rendering the populace
mild and beautiful. The site demanded a park, he argued in his newspaper, along with a cenotaph honoring the victims of England's imperial cruelty, which the public, under the dignifying influence of
nature, would help consecrate.

Rebecca and I stopped by a fierce bronze eagle planted at one of
the quadrants of the hilltop platform, looking over the broad set of
stairs, across the treetops toward the gray wall of mist hiding Manhattan. Almost exactly eight years earlier, in mid-November 2008,
we'd been strolling at the same spot when we chanced on preparations for a ceremony to be held in honor of the reinstallment of these
sculptures (they'd been locked in storage for decades after repeated
vandalizations), along with the relighting of the lantern atop the
Doric column. We got to talking with one of the men organizing the
event. Rebecca told him that I was a descendant of General Putnam,
for whom the original fort had been named.

The man latched onto this as serendipitous and invited me to
take part in the program that evening. He asked me to make a short
speech. My participation would make a living connection to the

historical roots of the commemoration, he insisted. I felt misgivings. Of course I understood the superficial attraction of putting me on display. But what did I really have to contribute simply by virtue of a remote genetic connection to the man who'd been partly responsible for the star-shaped fortification with five cannons first built at this position—a fort which had to be abandoned when General George Washington was defeated in the Battle of Brooklyn? This Putnam himself, after the war, became involved with massive land acquisitions in Ohio and the Northwest intended to cater to the hunger for living space of the young men of New England, where generations of middle-class settlement had made affordable property scarce. After the purchases, Putnam then served as brigadier general in a successful, devastating campaign against the Shawnee, Lenape, and Seneca nations who were pushed off those huge tracts of territory by the settlers' approach. What could I say about him that would neither gloss over his colonialist depredations nor cheaply advertise my own evolved ethical character by way of pious, unenlightening indictments of the dead?

But we were still in the initial euphoria of Obama's election then, and I wanted to demonstrate civic spirit. So I consented, trusting that something worth communicating would come to me in the moment.

"That's wonderful. It'll be great," the man said. "Honoring the revolutionary past . . ."

Truthfully, even he seemed unsure what specifically I would bring to the occasion.

The night was autumnal and windy. When we climbed up the hill to the base of the pillar on top of the vault where bones and ashes of the martyrs had been deposited, the ceremony was already underway. Hundreds of people, luminous in the brilliant lights, were clustered around the platform and down the steps of the wide staircase. As different speeches rolled on about the terrible suffering of the colonial rebels and the long fundraising struggles to restore the monument, I kept waiting for inspiration to knock, but the door of my mind remained silent. I felt increasingly nervous. Then I heard my name being called.

I stumbled toward the speaker's spot, took the microphone from the hand of some beaming dignitary—and found myself utterly tongue-tied. I'd been paraded on stage as a kind of freak from a time machine, a Coney Island sideshow: The Past Incarnate. But I looked at all the people waiting for my speech, many of them student age, and longed to say something that would speak to the world opening before them, to what Henry James called "the hungry *futurity* of youth."

My hair whipping around my head in the gusts like torn sails, I raised my hand in an oratorical manner, trying once more to summon my thoughts, but suddenly the pause felt too long, and I began gushing inanities about the beauty of the occasion, the long history of historical occurrences at this location, and how wonderful it was that the eagles had been recovered, the light rekindled, and time and family—the endless struggle for freedom that we were all indebted to and somehow a part of... The wind surged. My eyes lifted to the tree branches writhing overhead and I felt momentarily mesmerized. Then I handed the mike back to the moderator.

I might not have descended so low as to say, "I'm sure my ancestor General Rufus Putnam would have been very moved by this gathering," but I had not risen to the occasion. And a terrible sense of incompleteness haunted me. I felt certain there was something I ought to have said, a gesture I might have made, but the message remained locked inside me.

Standing at the place now, the day after the election, the shame of that night burned in me again.

"I'm cold," Rebecca said. "Let's go home."

We wandered slowly back down the path. On Dekalb, a man in a suit barged by us, barreling toward the bridge to Manhattan, yakking excitedly into his cellphone.

That was the first time I found myself wondering how many people who'd voted Democrat woke up after the election and thought, *Well,* we *didn't elect him, and of course we'll vote that clown out of office next chance we get, but meanwhile, regulations and taxes are going to be slashed to the bone. The market's going to be on* fire . . . *Boys, roll up your sleeves and hold your noses!*

Over the ensuing days, we saw friends from time to time, and discussed meeting up at various rallies. We talked of "being there" for one another, whatever that meant in the context of our already unmanageably overstretched lives and our lack of clear presence on a day-to-day basis, even to ourselves. We spoke to our son about the history of protest in America, and the principle of political resistance. At one point I caught myself saying something to the effect that he should always remember how the true spirit of America was not represented by this man, but by the diversity and freedoms he despised—and felt dismayed by the ways what I'd said seemed merely to mirror in reverse the president-elect's own rhetoric about defending true American values on behalf of real Americans.

We went to work. We rode the trains, their shrieking, tortured, infrastructure acoustics like old amusement park rides. I pumped and jerked back and forth on elliptical machines, watching panels

of talking heads in studios at Rockefeller Center bat the headlines
about while getting mad and cracking jokes, waxing patriotic or
folksy-philosophical, rolling their eyes, growing nostalgic, quoting
history wistfully and prophetically, defiantly denouncing and sen-
tentiously aggrandizing, expressing disbelief, certainty, fear, disgust,
love, gratitude, humor, humor, and *horror*, until all their sloppy emotions and opinions sloshed together; sipping coffee from fat mugs
emblazoned with their network logos, grinning, sighing, revolving
to the topic of last weekend's big ball games, spinning in their chairs,
laughing uncontrollably, and getting silly just before it was time to
say "Okay, we're gonna take a short break," just like real people living in real, comforting normal-normal-normal Americas even if the
times were *craaazzy*—cutting away to commercials of happy-forever
moms in bright, clean kitchens and sleek execs emerging from silver
the-future-is-now cars.

We made meals, exchanging todays and tomorrows in broken
phrases. Pouring cups of tea and teaching our son Scrabble. The
black and gray kittens we'd gotten from a shelter the week before the
election rolled on the maroon carpet. Their obliviousness to the news
was therapeutic.

One afternoon, a friend of mine whose girlfriend had previously
been married to an investment banker called me to lament the election. He began groaning about what a slimeball Trump was, then
abruptly swerved and began speaking about a hedge fund guy he'd
come to know through his girlfriend's circle who, having formerly
been an active Clinton supporter, was now pocketing tens of millions
of dollars on different bets based on predictions of how Trump's presidency would "turbo-charge" the economy. My intimations the day
after the election, about Democrats deciding to make the ugly best

of their situation, seemed jeeringly validated. As he spoke about this man, the pitch of my friend's voice began rising manically. "Oh yeah, it's all working out for Steve and his *dudes*! They don't give a fuck what happens at this point! They've made their killing." The note of outrage and envy were equally hypertrophied. "Fucking frat-boy swine! They'll park the money in real estate and offshore accounts. Another car. Another fucking jet ski. Another 10,000-dollar-a-night whore. Another dumb-ass beach villa. Another private fucking plane. They've got no imagination. No sense of public responsibility. So they'll just keep buying more and more of the same shit until they burst. What do they care now if all the coming migrants get machine-gunned at the border, or if Trump declares martial law? They got in under the fucking Nazi radar!"

Finally I couldn't take any more of the diatribe. I cut him off as tactfully as I could and went outside. Feeling nauseated, I walked down the street to the park. Before the entrance, a woman was pivoting in place, speaking into her cellphone. "Yeah, well you know what I'm telling white people in my office? I'm saying, welcome to my world. Welcome to my fear! Welcome to the feeling Black people've been living with forever. You scared and sad? Oh *boo-hoo*!"

The static bourgeois melodrama of the immediate post-election period, with our sanctimonious, vacuous repulsion, plans for support groups, and a bottomless brunch of solidarity in brownstone Brooklyn, shattered. It was cold and mean out. The sky was blanked in pale haze. The feet of a jogger slapped the asphalt like pistol shots. A black SUV didn't bother swerving around a madly pedaling biker and missed him by a hair. He screamed curses from his entrails into the thick air.

I recalled a dinner a few nights earlier at which someone had started going on about how unspeakably alien the whole Trump phenomenon felt to him. "New York is just a different country," he said, shrugging. "I really feel it's true. The level of culture, the kinds of conversations you have here, the political engagement, the investment in the arts and the—you know, just the spirit I guess of social, intellectual . . . Well, you know what I mean."

"Actually," my friend Michael, a journalist, said with a smile, "I've been thinking about things from a different angle. If you take the three great debacles of recent American history: the Trade Tower attack and our response in 2001; the financial crisis in 2008; and Trump today, what they've got in common is that they're *all* totally New York phenomena."

"Media capital of the universe!" someone snickered.

"It's true," someone else said. "We're the heartland of darkness."

People chuckled, but the laughter rang hollow and quickly fell off.

I strode out again across the dirt and wan stubble of the soccer field, up the hill to the monument, returning to the place beneath the column above the steps that overlooked the shining buildings and gray elevated highways of Brooklyn toward the band of dull water, and onward to the cluttered glare of Lower Manhattan scrapers. Once more, I felt that November night in 2008 rising around me, the lights, the crowd, and the wind—the moment when the microphone was passed into my hands . . .

Of course what I ought to have spoken about that evening was the reason *why* Whitman began rhapsodizing in *The Brooklyn Daily Eagle* about the need for a memorial and park in Fort Greene. It was no spontaneous effusion at the sight of the public taking refreshment on the hilltop, but a response to escalating danger.

Whitman broached the subject in July 1846 as part of a screed prompted by an editorial in the New York *Tribune*, which was itself responding to a correspondent who'd written to oppose plans then being drawn up for the "*leveling* of Fort Greene." While the paper claimed to agree with this writer that the development was unfortunate, it added that objections were hopeless. "Trade and commerce are an irresistible power," the editors wrote. "The requirements of the rapidly flourishing city for 'more room' are constant and clamorous; and her citizens are justly proud of the rapid growth even while lamenting that in her progress a spot so haunted with lofty associations must be despoiled."

Whitman accused the *Tribune* itself of being the source of this letter, which provided an opportunity for its reporters to trumpet the glories of Manhattan's dynamism. He attacked the whole notion of the city's robust appetite for more space, especially insofar as this hunger was intended to legitimize encroachment on the room of others. "*Must* be despoiled," Whitman seethed. "What for, pray? Is the Dollar-god so ruthless that he grudges a few poor acres, (which the Spirit of the Beautiful, in fear as it were of his groveling fingers, has lifted high up above the level where he is accustomed to plod,) to the service of health, of refinement, of *religion?* Is nothing to be thought of on earth, but cash?" he fulminated. What injustice to "deliberately crush" the higher faculties we've been blessed with in the name of some pragmatically indispensable "desecration"!

I could have warned the present-day audience against capitulating to the notion that New York's business interests represented an irrepressible, indomitable force. *Don't believe the booming assertions of illimitable manifest destiny!* I might have cried, while citing the observation, sometimes ascribed to Frederic Jameson, that it's easier to picture the end of the world than the end of capitalism. That occluded vision signaled a surrender of the political, Jameson suggested—an idea further elaborated by Slavoj Žižek, and later synthesized in the work of the cultural theorist Mark Fisher, who, before the end of 2008, coined the term *capitalist realism* to describe what remains when beliefs have broken down "at the level of ritual or symbolic elaboration, and all that is left is the consumer-spectator, trudging through the ruins and the relics." (Or, we might add, the virtual jackals perpetually prowling the endless digital-image wasteland, chop-shopping and regurgitating their scavengings on new social media platforms in the form of flash shocks and flesh gags delivered one after the next in ceaseless, development-free series—a model of entertainment akin to the play of a gambler for whom, Walter Benjamin wrote, "the starting all over again is the regulative idea of the game.")

Fisher likened this "realism" to that of a depressive who's become persuaded that any positive alternative to their condition must constitute a perilous fantasy. He also pointed to Žižek's contention that cynical disavowal itself serves an ideological agenda, screening objective behaviors. "Even if we do not take things seriously, even if we keep an ironical distance, *we are still doing them*," Žižek wrote. For instance, we maintain that money is an empty cipher, yet act as if it has sacred value. The expression of disillusionment in capital is indeed integral to its operation, he argued—not so different, in truth, from Whitman in the nineteenth century, exposing the *Tribune's* rhetoric of lamentation over the proposed flattening of Fort Greene as part of a campaign to establish the inevitability of that obliteration of nature and history for the sake of more commercial activity.

The rededication ceremony at the monument was happening two months to the day after the failure of Lehman Brothers, when it was still plausible that everything could have played out differently had the president seized the plastic hour of the financial industry's meltdown to impose radical reforms—had he not chosen to rescue the banks, investment firms, and so on, effectively on their own terms.

That night I might have issued my own forecast about what continuing on this path would mean. The organizer of the event had solicited my participation in order to "honor the revolutionary past." I might have done so by driving home the imperative of revolution today. Only the words didn't come to me. And perhaps my silence at that moment was the true future forecast.

For one explanation of my floundering dumbness was that I myself was deep inside the system I was chomping to lambast. Indeed, part of the problem many of us faced was our swaddling in a vast cloak of complicity. Because, after all, how was one supposed to survive in the current economy? How did *I* make money? Filthily!

By the time I left Jerusalem at the end of the 1990s, I'd run out of cash and seen my personal debt ceiling collapse. For years I'd gotten by with piecework verbal peddling, teaching in different capacities and writing occasional pieces of cultural journalism. Only I hadn't really gotten by, since I kept having to borrow to survive, and so falling further behind. One of the understandings with my family about coming back to America was that I would henceforth give up the notion that the writing I cared about could support me economically, and would set about finding a "real job"—something I'd managed to avoid well into my thirties, even if I did continually labor at a motley array of not-real jobs.

Of course I dreaded the prospect, but I was also sick to death of scrounging and confronting the reality over and over that what I earned didn't quite add up to what I needed for rent, food, and so on. I'd had enough of beating my brains out trying to solve the puzzle of how to earn a living without compromising my values or exhausting my energies for writing creatively. I had young children. It was time to act like a grown-up, even though I'd never really bought the idea that maturity and regular, salaried employment were synonymous.

Nonetheless, I would get a full-time job and I'd write what I liked in the interstices, the way other artistic people did when they took their real-world responsibilities seriously. What exactly would I do? Well, it seemed clear to me I'd find work writing for somebody else. Some person or entity with a bank account. Working every day for a newspaper or magazine, presumably, or perhaps with a book publisher.

Several months after returning, having fruitlessly pursued countless leads in publishing and at not-for-profits looking for help writing promotional material, I was still unemployed. Without retracing the long, painful convolutions of my efforts to find work, I will say only that at the end of the fall I finally ended up being hired for $8.50 an hour by the customer service call center of Talk America: an infomercial marketer of products like Protein Power Package and of supplements for reversing the effects of male pattern baldness, of colon cleansers, brain builders, miracle diets, youth restorers, romance finders, money makers, and other all-around fate transformers. Talk America! And *tickety-tock*, America talked to me. I sat in Portland, Maine, at a tiny desk in a big fluorescent crossword puzzle of a room, taking call after call after call, the script for most of which went something like this:

"Hi, this is George at Talk America, how can I help you today?"

"You *fucking* liars! I got your Super Body Ultra Reboot machine and it's just a bunch of fucking broken plastic and springs with a bullshit video of some asshole lifting shit!"

"I'm very sorry if you're disappointed with the product, sir. It's been endorsed as you know by many of the world's top super body—"

"You get my money back overnight or you'll be sorry mother*fucker*—"

"We're happy to refund you your money, sir, if you're disappointed with our product, though we're very sorry to hear it. Are you sure you practiced the technique exactly as Buddy Beef Bronzer the Human MuscleDump demonstrates?"

(Inchoate, gore-spattered screaming.)

"Okay, well then, we can get the refund process started right away upon receipt of the merchandise, sir. It usually takes a few weeks until the next check printing, but—"

"YOU GET ME my FUCKING *money* tomorrow *morning*!"

"We're happy to provide you with a full refund just as soon as we receive back the super-builder product, at which point the refund can be processed—minus the $19.95 shipping and handling fee from our end . . ."

That was the point in the narrative at which I mentally winced and braced, the part that always spelled the start of real trouble. It was when the person whose body had not undergone an Olympian reinvigoration in a few weeks, whose brain had not yet hit trans-Einstein levels, who was still getting older, heavier, more drained, flaccid, broke, bald, clogged, and isolated, learned that the shipping and handling fees, on a box of junky bits one might feel annoyed by if it came as a bonus gift with a piece of gum from a vending machine, cost practically as much as the product itself that conversation broke down altogether.

"You know what I'm doing right now?"

"No, sir. Shall I indicate then that we should be expecting the return of your—"

"I'm loading my guns in the back of my truck. I'm going to start driving tonight. I'll be at your *fucking* offices in fourteen hours and I'll blow all y'all's fucking heads off."

"I'm sorry you're disappointed with the product, sir."

"Blow your *fucking* brains out! All over the walls! You cocksucking, motherfuh—"

Well, it made a change from teaching Keats and Shakespeare to gifted, eager young Russian immigrants at Hebrew University in Jerusalem.

I know the call sounds exaggerated, but I swear I received death threats in language almost identical to what I've just transcribed, and even short of people saying they would kill me, which did happen—twice—the rage and despair I listened to each day was monumental. I never questioned people's right to a refund. I never said much beyond vowing that I would do everything I could to expedite their refund, trying to calm them down, and then taking off my headset, leaving my desk, and begging my superiors to help the worst victims. Far more upsetting than the murderous dupes were the people who just broke down sobbing at the failure of their Talk America product, seen on TV, to have redeemed one single aspect of their tragic existence.

God, the endless lost tribes of consumers that the Talk America sales team managed to seduce. The *hope* they tapped into and turned into credit-card number read-alouds over the phone. The *faith* of those poor souls all over the country. On the rare occasions when someone sounded a little less desperate, I'd try to engage them in conversation, to gain some understanding of their larger experience. The experience, time and again, of failure, poverty, wrenching struggle, and betrayal, tacked onto the dream that a Talk America bauble would make their lives great again for the first time ever. Indeed, thinking back now on the hundreds of conversations I had at the center, how could I have been surprised for an instant by the possibility of Trump's election? He was like every Talk America product rolled up together in a single throbbing flesh totem. Trump was Talk America in commander-in-chief form.

But at last my Talk American education came to an end. In late winter, a friend in New York called to say that someone he knew who worked at a public relations firm in Midtown was looking for a writer and he'd given the guy my contact information. Shortly thereafter I found myself entering a black office building on the Avenue of the Americas that looked like a coffin of the gods slipped down from the clouds. I walked out of the elevator into a quiet reception room on the forty-second floor. I walked from office to office, greeting different executives whose long glass windows looked down over the dormant trees in Central Park, or across a panoply of skyscrapers resembling fossilized organ pipes.

Of course I took the job. Sixty thousand dollars a year and health insurance half paid by the company? I'd never made anything near that. I felt like a plutocrat.

I did manage to continually work on my own books while hiding in my cubicle in that office. I did try to subvert almost everything I wrote, living by the principle "bite the hand that feeds you," slipping quotes from Dostoevsky and Tarkovsky into a stump speech I wrote for the Duchess of York; weaving seditious political references through long, dry business documents. But notwithstanding the ways I tried to undermine what I was doing, I was still with the firm almost two decades later. ("Even if we do not take things seriously . . . *we are still doing them*.") What I'd thought would be a matter of a few years, long enough that I could crawl out of debt and find some more noble, decently paid work, turned into something closer to a life sentence. And each year the comfort of having my core expenses paid by the company became harder to dispense with, while those expenses slowly crept up. I was still working there, selling verbal snake oil to whoever would pay.

Sometimes I would try to console myself with the thought that most of the copy I wrote was for not-for-profits—hospitals, addiction-recovery centers, scientific research institutes, children's aid funds, and so on—but of course the truth was that this made the work more despicable. There was no reason to believe that a rehab facility that could afford to pay for a Midtown public relations program was any better than the facility that didn't have such a budget for self-promotion. It was a completely arbitrary elevation of nonprofit newsworthiness on the basis of money-raising prowess. As for the dozens of assignments I had with the philanthropic divisions of various large companies, I cannot think today of a single instance when the business agenda didn't ultimately poison and warp the project it supported. When it comes to corporate sponsors, there is no such thing as a benign public-private partnership; the public interest is always mutilated grotesquely to make it fit into the firm's bottom-line goals.

And anyway, it wasn't true. Most of what I was writing by 2016 consisted of new business proposals for potential real estate clients, explaining how the agency would place positive stories about their buildings in outlets monitored by potential buyers, investors, and brokers, along with larger "thought pieces" detailing the rejuvenating, dynamizing neighborhood impact these developments would have, aimed at local community boards and decision makers. It was pure chance that I never wrote anything for the Trump Organization itself. If I paid my debt for having so debased myself by losing a significant part of my time on earth to that labor, I yet excuse none of it. Not a day. Not a ghostwritten speech for the head of a single environmental initiative. Not a sentence. Not a word. Not a syllable. Why should my language have come from that woman or man's mouth at the rate of God-knows-what a minute? It was all lies and deceit. I allowed myself to become the voice of people I despised, or who had money enough not to have to speak for themselves. I sold the aspect of myself I cared for most deeply.

People talk frequently, often self-flagellatingly, about "bubbles" and "silos" in attempting to analyze why educated East Coast liberals had no idea what was coming in November 2016. *We were locked inside our precious little self-affirming feeds and mutually reinforcing insular exchanges*, runs the narrative. But I reject this diagnosis. Whether through conversation with friends who had loved ones in areas that did vote for Trump, or my own contacts with people in Fairfax, or my time at Talk America, or the grassroots reporting that did emerge from parts of the country left behind by the tides of globalization, I knew something about the resentment people felt elsewhere, and about the vulnerability to populist politics this sense of grievance engendered, even if I didn't register the level of vengeful elation-in-waiting.

Whenever one rides the subway, as I did every weekday for

almost two decades, one bursts the bubble of one's private existence and encounters a deeply heterogeneous array of humanity and socio-economic circumstances. A single walk down a New York City street can multiply perspectives and pop the self-validating narrative of anyone with their eyes open. People living in more narrowly patriotic communities where Fox News or the like is playing constantly in public spaces will be more susceptible to siloed viewpoints than someone navigating the urban commons. I was not in a bubble, but in a way my position was more culpable: With all my ideals, my sympathies, my higher literary, philosophical, and artistic fascinations, I'd found no means of supporting myself except as a parasite in the belly of the same system where the monster of the deal had incubated. The reason that I hadn't foreseen the results of the election wasn't that I was locked away, blinds drawn, with my cortado coffee and Roland Barthes; it was because I couldn't face the implications of my own participation in the system the president epitomized and sought to impose on creation. If there were bubbles involved, I was inside Trump's golden belch. And when I looked around there, like Dorothy waking from her dream of Oz, I recognized almost everyone I knew, hovering beside me.

6

· Zodiac Roulette ·

Month after month, Rebecca and I orbited the cenotaph in Fort Greene Park, clock-hands spinning on a dial without numbers, revolving faster and faster, trying to break through the nightmare. Up the proud little hill, around and around the familiar, comfortable blocks. Now and then, we fell quiet for a moment before a view of some faraway, flambé sunset against a skyline of scrapers, like a vitrine full of rocket ships, or as winter ended, an enchanting display of fresh life pushing up from the earth. Then we'd begin moving once more. Our voices would start ratcheting up anew, exchanging memories of earlier lives we'd lived in New York, together and apart, trying to grasp hold of our destiny—to determine where we were now, and what we might still conceive for the future.

Sometimes we'd walk further afield, through the spacious bourgeois silences of Clinton Hill, and east into Bed-Stuy, beyond the low brown cement Gospel House, on past little New Canaan Baptist Church, by Mount Zion Meeting House and the townhouse sheltering Mount Ararat Church; traversing the blocks alongside

Mount Pisgah, Mount Bethel, Shiloh, and Mount Hope, all the way to the tiny, multitone brick box featuring a long light-up cross with the words NEW JERUSALEM HOLY TEMPLE CHURCH OF CHRIST DISCIPLES OF CHRIST, INC. painted in white along its cloud-gray verandah. In daytime on weekends, the doorways gave bursts of glorious song; flowers bloomed in lacy nests on the hats of the women. God called to us from the depths of old Brooklyn. But it wasn't a God we could answer, or a Brooklyn we belonged to. All that had been excluded from our long lineage of freedom now stood between us and that, like an assembly of mourners blocking the entrance to a graveyard we'd turned up late to—after the body was lowered, after the eulogy was delivered, after the family had departed, *now* we wanted to pay our respects?

We walked on into the night, through jagged desolation. Gunning engines. Spatting strangers. Pit bulls straining to break chains. Sirens wailing everywhere. Doors swinging wide onto fluorescent liquor cages. Lights flickered and changed colors around the doors of corner delis with huge sandwich decals in the windows while cars roared by, audio systems raging, waving giant sonic flags over the ravaged darkness.

Some days we couldn't believe how fortunate we were, how much we still loved Fort Greene, how vibrant life felt. One afternoon, my sister and I sat in the window of a food court near the saurian rust squirm of the new stadium as a trio of young teenagers on the sidewalk propped a cellphone the other side of the glass from us, then stepped back a few paces and burst into individual dances, joyously springing, arms weaving, hands slapping, heads whirling. The happiness in their eyes brought tears to my own. *We can never leave this*, I thought. The next second, the kids snapped dead still and mirthless, retrieving their phone and moving on.

What was the "this" we could never leave? The delirious, spontaneous outburst had been a polished routine for the camera. "This" had left us, like the youths striding off to their next location shot, even as we kept blindly clinging to thin air.

We blinked and the streets of Bed-Stuy and Crown Heights were full of people with studied postures zipping by in short chinos and sockless loafers on electronic scooters, or careening down the sidewalk like extraterrestrial junkies, faces melted to their devices, thumbs flea-dancing the keys, furrowing solitary or wide-loading their way in oblivious squads to favorite all-you-can-drink brunch places, followed by the new, faster, CrossFit joggers, pounding everywhere in bolts of sweaty lightning. These sorts of changes had been happening for years—were we just seeing them differently in light of the election, or had they really gained traction to where they marked a paradigm shift?

Some days we walked west to the walls of the Navy Yard, alongside roads loosely paralleling the course of the river, down Flushing and Kent into the zones of the Satmars. Pale men, pushing up the bridges of their glasses and stroking their beards, tugging down the glistening brims on their black fedoras, darting around corners, into shuls and yeshivas. Jangly prayers battling for God's ear from behind barred windows. On Saturdays, mothers and fathers sauntered by in Sabbath finery, hands curling to the grip of old-fashioned baby carriages, preceded and trailed by scrambling, skipping, loping children beyond number. When I lived in New York in the 1980s I'd found a strange, poignant dignity in their bearing, those fantastically antiquated costumes, the insatiable passion for Torah. Now all I could think about was the stories of their rotten doings as landlords and the fact that this community had voted en masse for Trump. What a degradation of the Baal Shem Tov's original emancipatory vision!

We kept walking on through Bushwick into Greenpoint. The snazzy new apartment buildings with their own lush parks along the waterfront appeared holiday tropical: Rio de Janeiro on the East River. Picture-perfect people lolled in the grass, playing games with artisanal paddles and new types of electronics, wearing tight, flame-tint bathing suits on uniformly ripped bodies. Everything looked carefree. Perhaps all we needed was a little change of scenery. We could sell our place in Fort Greene and move half an hour away into one of the tiny, cute houses near these swank glass complexes, making a new home on one of the blocks with suggestive old seaport names. Think of all the money we'd save by splitting our house size in half and living somewhere with such lousy public transportation links! We'd bike everywhere and learn to kayak, and maybe finally to salsa. Some places had mini-beaches and marked-off areas where one could swim, and there were so many restaurants we'd never stop grazing. Every day after writing we'd take a walk along the river and we would sort of have escaped our current life without really having had to leave anything behind.

Burdened with less debt, I might even approach my bosses at the PR firm (or "shop" as the bosses now preferred to refer to the workplace, as though massaging people's images to make them appear less egregious resembled the labors of hale tradesmen in heavy canvas aprons), broaching the possibility of reducing my work schedule. I hadn't made any grand, principled decision to resign after the election, but I kept quietly dwindling the time I spent in the office. Coming in later and later, leaving earlier and earlier, until whole days would go by without my traveling into Midtown at all—and without anyone seeming to notice my absence. It was as if I'd quit without telling anyone I no longer worked there, a less dignified, not-so-mysterious Bartleby the Scrivener who preferred not to come in while still *sotto voce* pocketing the paychecks. I'd been there so long I'd become more or less invisible inside the bureaucratic labyrinth. How could you reprimand a nonentity for failing to show up?

Then we went to a broker and learned that all those sweet little houses on Java and India streets cost as much or more than our current home with its giant outstanding mortgage was worth. Then I tentatively raised the idea of paring back my schedule to my supervisor, who looked at me with a steady, clinically diagnostic gaze and said, simply, "That's not our culture."

"My blood pressure just keeps getting worse, even though I'm on medication and I think if I didn't have to commute so frequently or—"

Her eyes lowered. "I understand, but that's not our culture."

All I'd achieved by my request was to place myself back on the radar of management. "Our *culture!*" *You have no "culture,"* I wanted to scream. *You're a gluttonous corporate beast fighting fang, claws, and nasty bits in a jungle of howling, competing agency swine-fiends for more bloody chunks of soul-voiding business! You're the reason "culture" had to be created!*

But all the while, of course, I was inside the "You" I excoriated.

What would it have solved to simply switch neighborhoods, anyway, we asked ourselves. Had we lost our minds?

We just need to focus on our work, we told each other. *Bear down on the life we're already leading. Stop spending so much time floundering about in the sewer of the internet. Concentrate on family, friends, community—on nurturing political change, for God's sake.*

We just need to focus on the things that really matter. To figure out what those things are, more specifically. Compassion. Writing. Travel. The environment. Humanity.

Yes. We need to just concentrate . . .

"Should we think about moving upstate?" I asked one Saturday when the sun was dancing in the leaves of an English elm in the park, and I was remembering how much I loved visiting my grandparents at 12 Main Street in Cooperstown. Swimming in the freezing, dark jade lake below the country club. Walking through the soft, dreamy hills. Hanging over the garden wall alongside my three siblings, licking strawberry ice cream cones. Making out with the daughter of belly-laughing, alcoholic doctors in a toboggan sledding down a hill toward the snow-capped statue of James Fenimore Cooper.

"I don't want to move upstate," Rebecca said flatly.

"There's so much beautiful countryside."

"We'd have to drive everywhere and I don't drive and you don't like driving."

"Couldn't we live near a train station?"

"We'd end up commuting for hours every day and once we got home we'd still have to drive to get anywhere where we could really walk into nature—unless we were living too far away from everything else. I'd always be coming back in the middle of the night from some event or other for work. And so would you." When would we get to enjoy where we were or where we'd just been when we were always in transit between them? And what about global warming with all that driving, and farewell even the pretense to diversity, and even if they were only a couple of hours away how often would we really see any friends or family members once we settled in, and what exactly would we do there off by ourselves as we got older? How much nature did we want, anyway?

How lucky we were to be in brownstone Brooklyn, when all was said and done!

One night I visited Gabriella, the woman who'd helped raise our son with unfailing grace and lucidity. She'd grown up in Trinidad and had lived the past two decades in Bed-Stuy not far from the Nostrand Avenue subway. Turning onto her street from Putnam, everywhere I looked where once there'd been bodegas, a liquor store, a law office, and a barber shop, high-end boutiques and restaurants had sprung up like mushrooms in the night. The transformation is so trite by now—why even bother to notate it? But this had happened so dizzyingly fast! I'd been there shortly before the election and now it was practically unrecognizable. I felt like Rip Van Winkle if he'd gone to sleep for a few months instead of two decades and found he'd missed a commercial rather than a political revolution—or rather found that the form of the political had become private enterprise. Gabriella raised her eyebrows when I mentioned my amazement at all the new businesses.

"Oh yeah! It's completely changed since about a year! The police don't even bother coming here no more. They don't even bother." She laughed. I asked her what the transformation was like for her. "Well, it's got its good and bad. It's mixed, you know. The people that move in, everybody minds their own business."

"Mmm."

"They never look at you. Everyone's too busy. If they go in the laundromat, they turn their face away from you." She swung her head to the side, arching her brow haughtily. "They never smile. They never look at you, George." I shook my head. "They're just *too busy*." My head kept shaking. "They're all in their own world." She laughed again. "No, it's really true, I'm telling you! Everyone say so. If you go in the laundromat you can smile at the people there. But the new ones, *never . . .* You know, maybe they're Trump people, George!" She laughed, and I laughed with her.

But the worst of it was, I'm sure they weren't. None of them. Just as they weren't consciously avoiding her eyes; she was just completely invisible to them.

We hated New York. The self-involvement. The entitlement. We hated the changes. Those changes we were part of, and the changes that came after us, which we swore were even worse than the changes we'd brought with us. At least we talked to people and smiled at them. We looked people in the eye! Gabriella wasn't asking for anything from the newcomers! But just to acknowledge that we share a common space was too much for these people? Disgusting. Wretched city. Why were we there?

Where on earth should we be? And did that easy neighborliness really even slightly justify our existence?

Sometimes our conversation reverted to Trieste, which we'd visited several times, and where I'd savored the specters of the Austro-Hungarian Empire, along with the tickling aqua-glass embrace of the Adriatic. With its long blocks of elegant gray, yellow, and cinnabar Habsburg-era apartment buildings, in one of which elderly relatives of my father still lived, the bosky parks and languorous esplanades— that preserving absence of major tourist draws, along with the promise of quick train rides to the splendors of Venice—Trieste lingered in my imagination as a plausible elsewhere. Perhaps there we could learn how to think and see, to listen, and even to believe again. Plus, we'd learn Italian. All we wanted was a credible alternative, and Trieste seemed to have many of the really quite modest elements we were seeking: the sea, art, history, cafés, a relatively gentle way of life, breezy places to walk. Trains to everywhere in Europe. The ghosts of

James Joyce and Italo Svevo. Perfectly plausible ingredients to compose a life with—lacking only schools for our son, income-generating work for myself, health care, friends, a residential visa, a real reason to be there, or even a vague notion of what sort of existence we might actually create in that airy fantasy-land.

Well, perhaps Berlin would make the most sense then—we at least had friends in that city, and it was *so* progressive and rigorously cultured. We'd heard about any number of schools there with exceptional reputations. We liked the lakes and the trams, the bookstores and the art world. Only . . . Germany? *Germany*? Were the ghosts really just ghosts now? Plus, not to be trivial, but those long, bitter winters. And even if the ghosts were just ghosts, the idea of settling comfortably there still suggested a kind of unseemly pact with the phantoms who had nearly exterminated my own father. Why shouldn't a place that attempted to perpetrate a genocide still be haunted, even if the people living in Germany now bore no inherited responsibility? The ground itself stank with old dreams of world-annihilating super-humanity.

England? We couldn't think seriously of England after Brexit. With that country's implosion into regressive, racist jingoism we knew that transplanting ourselves to England would be a lateral move of the most flagrantly self-destructive kind.

A friend of ours who'd moved to Bangkok was the happiest of the ex-New Yorkers I knew. There was a certain attraction to the idea of moving somewhere in Asia, where a sense of the future seemed to be magnifying instead of contracting, albeit an entirely naïve, abstract one. How would we even begin to arrange such a total transference with a twelve-year-old child, when we ourselves lacked even a toehold in the culture?

Well, what about somewhere completely outside our frame of

reference, then? The nameless wilderness? The moon? The cosmos beyond our doomed solar system?

"Utopias are emplacements having no real place," Foucault wrote. "They are emplacements that maintain a general relation of direct or inverse analogy with the real space of society." The mirror is thus a utopia, he observed, for it is "a placeless place," in which one sees oneself where one is not, in an unreal space opening up behind the surface. I stared into the bathroom mirror, trying to make out the sanctuary in its depths. "I am over there where I am not," Foucault continued, seeing myself "where I am absent," while at the same time, "I discover myself absent at the place where I am, since I see myself over there." But what was I going to do in practice—crawl inside the looking-glass and live there with Alice?

Now and then I found my thoughts wandering to something Benjamin wrote on the subject of wishes. In folklore, he observed, "distance in space can take the place of distance in time; that is why the shooting star, which plunges into the infinite distance of space, has become the symbol of a fulfilled wish."

Perhaps the reason we couldn't fix on an alternative to Brooklyn was that we were really longing to move to a different moment in history. Meanwhile, away from our incessant, existential conversations about how we might reorient our lives, signs that the wind was in the sails of darkness kept multiplying, not only in the news but in the experiences of our own family.

My brother Jamie, who has become an ever more erudite, enlightening photographer of people and landscapes, lives in Bay Ridge and is married to a woman of Indian–Guyanese descent who designs toys and plays rock and roll. Her sister, who has worked in poorly compensated jobs at large, inconceivably rich auction houses, married a man from Morocco who died alone of a heart attack at home moments before she and their son walked in. The family's past encloses other traumatic tragedies. Yet my brother's nephew is a child of preternatural sweetness, gentle and thoughtful beyond words.

In early 2017, this boy was fourteen and in middle school. One sparkling winter day, I met Jamie in Fort Greene, and as we walked down Dekalb Avenue toward a chic Columbian restaurant, the diversity of its residents in the bright sunshine seemed a manifest refutation of what was happening in Washington. How resplendent and progressive our neighborhood was. What did *we* have to worry about? We were in Brooklyn.

That gush of feeling went into one file, while I listened to my brother's account of a trip down to D.C. he'd just made to visit our father in Fairfax. He described the funereal mood in the nation's capital, and some of the images he'd captured out the window of the train back to New York. He'd begun thinking of linking these photos together in a conceptual project, he added, and stopped to show me one photo he'd taken on the journey; but the first image that came up on his phone was a portrait of his nephew. I broke in to ask how he was doing, remarking how much my son missed him—it had been too long since they'd gotten together.

"Actually, he's not doing very well," Jamie said, with the slight, bashful smile he habitually adopts when he has grave news to report, as if he were somehow responsible for the injury, though he persistently sacrifices himself to sustain our whole family. I raised my face. "Yeah, he's being bullied, really badly, since the election. Kids are coming up to him saying now that Trump's been elected he's going to be sent back to his country—he and his mom are going to get deported."

"What!"

He shook his head. "They're mocking him, threatening him."

"My God."

"He won't let his mother speak to the school. He doesn't want to become known as a snitch. But it's getting worse . . . Honestly, it's tough for him."

This was Brooklyn. Bay Ridge, which had an increasingly obsolete reputation for being less diverse than most neighborhoods in the borough, yes, but anyway *Brooklyn*. All I could think, outside of my sorrow at what this boy was being subjected to, was that if this sort of harassment were happening to a student in the endemically heterogeneous New York City public school system, what was going on elsewhere in places where minorities actually stuck out?

That kind of testimony went in the other file. The file registering evidence that an irreclaimable rupture of America's promise had already occurred.

On another bright day, we went to a robust protest in Battery Park against the new government's ban on immigration from Muslim countries. Everyone was smiling and proudly, collectively insubordinate, and we joined in every chant and felt full of hope again. That went into the other folder. The we-shall-overcome-and-become-more-meaningfully-politically-engaged-than-ever dossier.

Everything that happened seemed to fall into one box or another; evidence of large consequence in the search for a solution to a problem we couldn't quite articulate, which yet consumed our consciousness.

But even on days when the system felt more resilient, I found myself succumbing to doubt as to whether the damage thus far inflicted, especially on young people, could be fully negated or even functionally integrated. Even assuming that my brother's nephew's maltreatment ended with the administration, for instance, how would he fit the remembrance of this period into his larger narrative of America, and of society as such? And what about the memories of the thousands of young children separated from their parents, among them children who'd been locked into cages? Could one just vote that experience away with a traditional change in presidencies? Whisk. Hooray. Gone. Try as I might, I could not visualize a normative end to this more or less democratically elected regime of bottomless greed yoked to pathological cruelty.

The next time I saw my brother's nephew he looked so worn and gaunt, so much older than his years, that my arms moved to embrace him before my eyes could betray my alarm.

All through this period, I kept thinking of Freud's 1929 essay, *Civilization and Its Discontents*, in which he contends that the fateful question before us is whether the cultural development of humanity can overcome the disturbance to communal life represented "by the human instinct of aggression and self-destruction." The duel between our love and death drives had reached a decisive phase, he wrote then.

Weren't we now similarly suspended between what Freud called the two "Heavenly Powers," Eros and Thanatos?

That summer of 1929, Freud rented a house in the idyllic Alpine countryside near Berchtesgaden, as he'd done many times in the past. Steep meadows dotted with tiny purple and yellow flowers, among slender grass spears and the gauzy, gray planets of dandelions gone to seed. Wooded hills bordering the property. Higher up, harsh-carved mountain faces, snow-speckled year-round. In one of these houses, three decades earlier, he'd written much of *The Interpretation of Dreams*. Perhaps, as he grew older, Freud felt a sentimental attachment to the region where he'd found the combination of pristine scenery and peace that enabled him to compose what he still viewed as his masterpiece. However, Berchtesgaden also illustrates the hazard of projecting any intrinsic link between a particular place and auspicious inspiration. Hitler chose the same location for his own retreat. He'd been coming to the region since 1923. In one nearby log cabin he'd written the second volume of *Mein Kampf,* and in 1928 he leased, for the first time, the chalet that he would eventually expand into a compound, the Eagle's Nest, which motivated other party officials to purchase property in the area and became the setting where Hitler staged the story of his own pastoral efflorescence for publicity purposes. By cultivating the image of his own domestic bliss there, he successfully recast himself in the popular press from a shrill, warmongering fanatic into a solid, home-oriented, nature-loving German burgher. The picturesque landscape around Berchtesgaden formed a backdrop both to the renewal of Nazi ideology and to some of Freud's greatest insights into dreams, the unconscious, and group psychology.

Freud wouldn't have known that Hitler had begun renting the rustic property in nearby Obsersalzberg. The leader's stature had shrunk dramatically since the night in 1923 when his militia seized control of Munich, occupying the government buildings and compelling the press at gunpoint to broadcast his revolution's victory. The putsch had been overturned almost at once. Hitler fled and was arrested. On his release at the end of 1924, *The New York Times* reported that the former "demi-god of the reactionary extremists" appeared "a much sadder and wiser man" than he'd been when he stood before a court the previous spring charged with conspiring to overthrow the government. His behavior while serving his sentence had persuaded the authorities that he and his political organization were "no longer to be feared," the paper assured readers. It was thought likely that he'd now retire to private life in his homeland of Austria. Although the initial sense that his imprisonment had "tamed" him (as the article phrased it) proved mistaken, even while the country's ongoing economic troubles burnished the allure of his nationalistic, xenophobic rhetoric, still, approaching the end of the decade, few saw him as a serious threat. One lesson that *can* be drawn from history is that it's folly to assume a poisonous movement with a charismatic head has been rendered harmless until that leader is, in fact, annihilated. Our cartoon devils and their little Rasputins will keep playing jack-in-the-box—popping back up into the public eye to wreak whatever mayhem they can at every opportunity until the lids on their containers are soldered shut. *For they have nothing else to do with themselves.*

Most of 1929 might anyway have seemed to present a lull in the political firestorms. There was a chance to breathe and reflect. Germany had just agreed to participate in a broad European conference aimed at bringing an end to the occupation of the Rhineland, while the National Socialists had been effectively wiped out in the Reichstag elections of the previous spring, garnering less than 3 percent of the vote. It was possible to believe that the political situation was at last stabilizing and the progressive sociocultural aspirations of the Weimar Republic were en route to being realized. Mies Van

der Rohe's Barcelona Pavilion, Germany's radical high-art contribution to the 1929 International Exposition in that city, fulfilled
the mandate assigned by its commissioner, Georg von Schnitzler,
to "give voice to the spirit of a new era." At the opening in May, he
announced, "We wished here to show what we can do, what we are,
how we feel today and see. We do not want anything, but clarity,
simplicity, honesty." As for Freud's hometown of Vienna, the biggest gripe one snarky reporter from *Vanity Fair* expressed in 1929 was
that the city had lost "all individuality" since the dazzling glory days
of its imperial past were replaced by dull democracy. "It has dress-
makers like Paris, nightclubs like Berlin, verdant suburbs like London, innumerable Jews like New York." Steeped now in "the eternal
European monotony of pleasures and appearances," an anonymous,
middle-class throng went "surging through its streets," while "dull
functionaries" packed the Emperor's old box at the opera.

Nonetheless, that holiday some compound of personal and historical misgivings set Freud's mind spinning on questions touching
the fundament of his life's work: Was civilization premised on renunciations so demanding that its eventual disintegration through
individual estrangement and madness was ensured? Perhaps he
himself achieved the equanimity necessary to persist only by way
of detachment, he mused, confessing to Lou Andreas-Salome that
his worst characteristics, "among them a certain indifference to the
world, probably had the same share in the final result as the good
ones—i.e., a defiant courage about truth."

In his younger years, Freud would sometimes spend hours in
the countryside guiding the children on mushroom-hunting expeditions, turning the outings into a game by acting as if the group
were stalking anxious prey. He told the young ones it was essential

to be quiet as they moved through the woods—"No chattering!" he warned—otherwise the mushrooms would hear them approach. The children must carry their collecting bags rolled up under their arms so that the mushrooms would not guess what they were up to. When Freud spotted an edible specimen, his daughter Anna recalled, he would drop his hat down quickly on top of it, as if it were a butterfly, to prevent the mushroom from escaping. She remembered also how he would instruct her to place fresh flowers daily at a shrine to the Virgin near the entrance of the woods in order to secure her aid in their quest.

When Freud was in nature with children, his rigid disavowal of religion and superstition relaxed, and the world became enchanted. Everything around their little forest band was mutable and potentially alive, he suggested, as he himself took on the role of animistic shaman.

But now he was in his early seventies and such excursions were beyond him, he told Andreas-Salome in a letter from the Berchtesgaden farmhouse at the end of July, announcing that he'd just finished the last sentence of a piece he'd begun on arriving there: an essay dealing with "civilization, sense of guilt, happiness, and similar exalted subjects." It struck him, he noted, as "quite superfluous," driven by no inner sense of necessity. "But what else can I do? One cannot smoke and play cards all day; I am no longer much good at walking, and most of what I read doesn't interest me anymore." In composing the work, he'd "discovered the most banal truths," he observed.

The text of *Civilization and Its Discontents* reiterates this self-deprecating line that he's merely trotting out tired, pedestrian insights. "In none of my previous writings have I had so strong a feeling as now that what I am describing is common knowledge and that I am using up paper and ink and, in due course, the compositor's and printer's work and material in order to expound things which are, in fact, self-evident," Freud writes at the opening of the essay's sixth section. His insistence on its redundancy is, indeed, so pronounced as to finally seem a kind of screen, perhaps intended to distract readers from fully registering the extremity of what in truth becomes an incendiary, quasi-nihilistic proposal that the entire project of civilization may not be worthwhile and—even should it have value—may be doomed by intractable elements of human nature. It's also possible that the veneer of ennui is defensive, hiding from Freud himself such discordant notes in the essay as its swings between hopelessness regarding humanity's future and the wildly ambitious suggestion that psychoanalysis itself might have a role to play in detoxifying the neuroses not only of individuals, but of "entire epochs of civilization."

Rereading Freud's essay in light of the ongoing struggles both sides of the Atlantic to define the character of national identity, it's striking to note how he introduces his entire discussion of civilization's prospects with a meditation on the etiology of human feelings of belonging. The question of what enables us to experience a sense of being at home *anywhere* rustles just beneath Freud's explicit argument, and his answer, once again, has as much to do with temporal orientation as with spatial qualities.

I thought back on a spring evening two years before the election when I was sitting with Jamie, his wife, Samoa, and my father at an outdoor café in Vienna near the steel and concrete box of Rachel Whitehead's Holocaust memorial at Judenplatz, the frozen library of unreadable books with spines all turned inward, titles unknown, commemorating the 65,000 Austrian Jews murdered, as the inscription declares, by "the National Socialist criminals." Earlier that day, we had gone with my father to the apartment building he had escaped from with his family in the middle of the night to avoid arrest and, we now know, almost certain deportation to Theresienstadt. He had wanted to return to the place where he'd spent the first part of his childhood. We'd gotten into the building and gone up to his floor, but as we came nearer to his actual doorway, he suddenly announced that he'd had enough and reversed course, moving back down the winding stone stairs so rapidly it was almost as if he were fleeing again. When we stood outside on the street once more, his face was hard—not frightened. Angry. Alone with a past I possessed only glimpses of, as if through tears in a shroud.

Now, several hours later, we were all unwinding together in the balmy June air. My father and I were saying something or other about Judaism and time, the survival and crystallization of a people through its cultural memory, in the context of the failing of American schools to teach history to the young. We were rehearsing, in other words, a somewhat pat valorization of the Jewish commitment to turning one's head resolutely back over time's shoulder toward the whirlwind. I will never forget the moment when Samoa, who is petite and often reticent, with a long fall of black hair, a shiny black gaze, and an irrepressible buoyancy, burst over our exchange to say she had no interest in looking backward, that she couldn't wax poetic about the devotion to remembrance, or all the profound, moving lessons of history. She wanted to look ahead, to the future—this forward spirit in fact was what she loved about America. The national disregard for history was precisely what conferred her own sense of belonging, she suggested. Because there was nothing for her when she looked behind her except painful thoughts of the suffering experienced and inflicted by her extended family back at her birthplace, along with memories of the acquiescence of the larger community in that unhappiness. History was what kept you from moving on to realize the promise of your own life, she declared.

Though she was speaking out of visceral experience, there are influential philosophical traditions that extol the liberation of forgetting, some of which aim to catalyze a new collective awareness. When John Cage was asked why he sought to infuse his music with elements of chance and spontaneity, he spoke of the importance of opening "our minds to possibilities other than the ones we remember"—possibilities beyond the compass of what we know as individuals. "Something has to be done to get us free of our memories and choices," he said.

In Samoa's telling, the ideal of devout historical consciousness lay nestled inside the compulsion to repeat, and repetition was equated with the fantasy of replication—whether in terms of one's own entrapment in sterile patterns of behavior, or the baneful nostalgia that found expression, for instance, in the slogan MAKE AMERICA GREAT AGAIN. In dreams of the serial production of some genetically whitewashed prior American identity, in other words. That past where a person like my brother's nephew could never truly belong to the United States by virtue of a simple racial calculation.

Much of my work has centered on stories that assume the urgent relevance of recovering lost or neglected history, but my family trauma lies further back in time than the torments of her immigrant story, and temporal distance from injustice supplies the credit line for theoretical expansiveness. She would not be who she was now, an ebullient person of manifold achievements, as at home as I was in that cosmopolitan Viennese café, had she not lived in conscious defiance of her past, history, and memory.

The ambiguities surrounding my own position—that the remembrance of what came before and the possibility of the future are fertilely conjunctive, like astrologically charged alignments of planetary bodies—were exposed by the phenomenon of the past now being erected as a "big, beautiful wall" against progress: that immaculate America at the origin of MAGA.

"Before I was shot, I always thought that I was more half-there than all there," Andy Warhol said. "I always suspected that I was watching TV instead of living life. People sometimes say the way things happen in movies is unreal, but actually it's the way things happen to you in life that's unreal," he wrote. "Right when I was being shot and ever since, I knew . . . The channels switch, but it's all television."

The statement anticipates the condition consummated in Trump's real America for real Americans in which the boundaries between actual trauma, amnesia, and mythologized memory are as fluid as the divisions between stations on a screen menu. It's not coincidental that throughout his career, Trump expressed a fascination with Warhol. Trump quoted Warhol's statement, "Making money is art, and working is art, and good business is the best art," three times in his book, *Think Like a Champion*, and once in the introduction to *Think Like a Billionaire*. More recently, he'd tweeted it repeatedly. After they met at a birthday party for his fixer-lawyer Roy Cohn, Trump asked Warhol over to Trump Tower to discuss a commission to make a portrait of the building. ("It was so strange, these people are so rich," Warhol wrote in his diary in April 1981. "And they don't have drinks, they all just have Tabs. He's a butch guy.")

Following the meeting, Warhol went off and created a series of eight multilayered silkscreens from a photograph of the tower, black, white, and gold—sprinkled with diamond dust. Consciously or no, Warhol's work had long explored Lacan's notion that "repetition is not reproduction"—that what repeats is something that occurs "as if by chance," instantiating the accidental and sometimes the shock of accident. As the art theorist Hal Foster observed of Warhol's serial imagery—especially the imagery of disaster—the form of representation it trades in works "to *screen* the real understood as traumatic. But this very need *points* to the real, and it is at this point that the real *ruptures* the screen of repetition," initiating a break not of the world, then, but of a subject, or rather a split between perception and awareness of a subject moved by an image. The repetitions in Warhol's painting thus simultaneously create a distance on the real and drive it into us, producing a powerful doubling effect. "I never fall apart," Warhol once said, "because I never fall together."

But when Warhol brought the striking images around to Trump and Ivana, the couple recoiled. The color scheme didn't coordinate with their plans for the lobby. More than that, the idea that the image *repeated* upset them; they couldn't see past the façade of sheer reduplication. "It was a mistake to do so many, I think it confused them," Warhol noted in his diary. Repetition seemed to reduce the value of the pictures, perhaps to dilute the monolithic potency of the tower itself.

Trump refused to go through with his purchase of the paintings, and Warhol hated him from then on. That infatuation with Warhol taken *literally*, without the doubling force of irony—without the layering of repetition of any kind—evokes earlier moments when the megalomaniacal intoxication with the idea of art collapsed into the real, such as Hitler's failure to gain admission to Vienna's main art school, followed by his decision, unconsciously or no, to reproduce Bosch's painting of *The Last Judgment* (which hung on exhibit in the school gallery) through the medium of his concentration camps. So Trump's hugely popular reality television show, which some see as the true explanation for his election, in which he enacts the role of omnipotent, infallible corporate executive, proved, retroactively, a preview to his appearance as America's all-mighty, corporeal executive-in-chief, thereby inverting Marx's famous dictum: History repeats itself, the first time as farce, the second time as tragedy.

But in truth this repetition is less successional than hollowly mimetic. After observing Hitler in the flesh, Carl Jung remarked that he seemed like "an automaton with a mask, like a robot or a mask of a robot." He never laughed. He only sulked. "He seemed as if he might be a double of a real person, and that Hitler the man might perhaps be hiding inside like an appendix, and deliberately so hiding in order not to disturb the mechanism." This reaction was not so surprising since what he really was, Jung opined, was the cavity into which the Germans had projected their own selves, "that is, the unconscious of seventy-eight million Germans." This was what made him so powerful. He was like a man "who listens intently to a stream of suggestions in a whispered voice from a mysterious source, and then *acts upon them.*"

In lieu of rescuing an actual past or envisioning a real future, the antenna-like demagogue amplifies and broadcasts the people's compendium of grievances as these fester in the perpetual present of an unattended unconscious.

Freud would not, anyway, have been overly concerned with the moral legitimacy of the plan to forge ahead without looking back, like Orpheus fulfilling the contract under which he might reincarnate Eurydice, but rather with its feasibility. No memory-trace, once formed, can perish, he argued, and in the right circumstances any remembrance might resurface intact. Drawing a comparison in *Civilization and Its Discontents* between the mind and the Eternal City, he asked readers to visualize all the epochs of Rome coexisting without any structure having fallen into ruins: the oldest layer, the complete *Roma quadrata*, a fenced settlement on the Palatine, thus sharing space with the grand House of Augustus, along with later palazzos and administrative structures—each building from Rome's long succession of imperial phases present in place simultaneously.

Attempting to act as though personal or national history can be summarily dismissed only leaves one more liable to being swallowed unawares by it; the Jewish commitment to memory reflects Jewish intimacy with the possibility of catastrophic regression, even from a pinnacle of cultural accomplishment. From the beginning, Judaism was always most concerned with ritualizing remembrance, thereby connecting individuals to the community of generations; ultimately enabling them to rekindle the experience of those who first received ethical consciousness at the Revelation on Sinai.

Near the opening of *Civilization and Its Discontents* Freud remarks that some time before, he'd sent a copy of his "small book that treats religion as an illusion" to an extraordinary individual whom he counted as a friend and who happened—despite people's tendency to falsely equate power, success, and wealth with merit—to have been recognized by the multitudes as a great figure. On having read the work, this man, the French humanist Romain Rolland (as Freud later disclosed) responded that while he agreed with Freud's judgment on religion's value, it was a pity he hadn't probed the *origin* of religious sentiments. It was something he himself had personal knowledge of: "a sensation of 'eternity,' a feeling as of something limitless, unbounded—as it were, 'oceanic.'" This mental experience of time and space blurring into a state of total belonging was a "subjective fact," not an article of dogma. It brought no assurance of personal immortality, Rolland added, but was yet the source of an energy that informed all the various churches and faith systems.

These views caused him great difficulty, Freud noted. Indeed, in a letter to Rolland written from Berchtesgaden while he was composing *Civilization and Its Discontents*, Freud remarked that Rolland's comments on the subject two years earlier had left him no peace. He couldn't discover any such "oceanic" feeling in himself, and investigating the feeling by conventional scientific means was impossible. Ultimately, he could see no pathway for exploring this impression of "an indissoluble bond, of being one with the external world as a whole," except psychoanalysis.

It's an unexpected place to begin a rumination on the problem he will summarize later in the essay with the question: "How has it happened that so many people have come to take up this strange attitude of hostility to civilization?" But in fact, as becomes clear, the great challenge he perceives for civilization revolves around the question of belonging—specifically whether a sufficient proportion of a given population can be made to feel that they are part of this endeavor for it to remain viable.

Freud presents a psycho-genetic diagramming of the oceanic sensation that ties it back to a newborn's experience. Infants at the breast do not initially differentiate between the ego and the external world, which is nurturing them, he asserts. They exist in a state of "limitless narcissism." Gradually the boundaries of the self begin to be demarcated in relation to the sources of feelings it wishes to prolong or, alternatively, to ward off. As the process continues, a tendency arises to distinguish from the ego everything that can cause pain, "to throw it outside and to create a pure pleasure-ego which is confronted by an alien and threatening 'outside.'" The adult's "ego-feeling" is thus but a "shrunken residue of a much more inclusive—indeed, an all-embracing emotion, which corresponded with a more intimate bond between the ego and the world about it." The persistence in the mind of this earlier sensation of "limitlessness" (like the lingering image of vanished architectural works in a temporally syncretic Rome) is the origin of the oceanic feeling Rolland alludes to, Freud contends. He denies, however, that this is the source of religion, which he attributes to exaggerated exaltation of the father and the fact that life is simply too hard for most people without spiritual palliatives. Slowly it emerges that this exposition of the feeling of oneness and its counterweight, the emerging sense of differentiation, relate, in Freud's scheme, to the evolving character of societies, not only the individual psyche. What Freud does *not* do is examine the question of why he himself has never experienced the "oceanic feeling," although in *The Interpretation of Dreams* he says that he was breastfed by his mother and so presumably would have gone through the same stages of ego differentiation he ascribes to the individual as such. Freud's failure to analyze his own lack of a boundless sense of connectedness bores down through the essay's eight sections, leaving a historical-biographical hole in which the political might gestate.

He turns next to the subject of religion and the solace it provides by injecting life with a higher meaning. If we take the religious lens away and look merely at people's expression of purpose through behaviors, it's apparent that their intention is just to pursue happiness and avoid unhappiness, Freud writes, the drawback to this scheme being the overwhelming evidence that "the intention that man should be 'happy' is not included in the plan of 'Creation.'" Human suffering can be traced to three main sources, he continues: our own bodies, the external world, and our relations with other human beings—in other words, pretty much everything. But it's the last of these causes that often brings the greatest psychological anguish, since it seems patently gratuitous.

Freud proceeds to itemize the ways people attempt to fulfill their appetite for perpetual happiness in a world where opportunities for pain always predominate: intoxicants, religion, yoga-style techniques, the arts, beauty in its various natural and manufactured forms, love, the sublimation of instincts, and finally the collaborative project of binding individuals together in civilizations, above all to neutralize the threat of other people by regulating the relationships of family, state, and society.

With this last entry, we reach the heart of Freud's theme, for in considering all the ways that civilization's benevolent mission to protect individuals and preserve the peace between groups has been unsuccessful, we learn that another element of "unconquerable nature," in fact "a piece of our own psychical constitution," has obstructed its realization. It seems that "what we call our civilization is largely responsible for our misery, and that we should be much happier if we gave it up and returned to primitive conditions."

Freud calls this notion "astonishing" since, however one defines civilization, it's plain that everything we most rely on to guard against suffering derives from this enterprise. Indeed, civilization represents the sum of our achievements. Along with creating laws, it helps us to cultivate the soil so that the earth yields its fruits and to craft the tools that defend us from nature's depredations. Learning to control fire and to build dwellings stand at the head of civilization's communal accomplishments in Freud's telling, but these basic developments are followed by a slew of others that enhance our individual bodily prowess. So, again, why *would* a large number of people become antagonistic to a project that, from a rational standpoint, improves their existence?

It's not a new problem, Freud acknowledges. The animus was evident already in Christianity's victory over the heathen religions, because that success was closely tied "to the low estimation put upon earthly life by the Christian doctrine." Another signal event in the history of this opposition occurred with the European discovery of faraway peoples who seemed to be living a more natural and desirable existence. "In consequence of insufficient observation and a mistaken view of their manners and customs, they appeared to Europeans to be leading a simple, happy life with few wants, a life such as was unattainable by their visitors with their superior civilization." Finally, the most recent event Freud identifies in this chain stems from the new understanding of the mechanism causing mental illness: the discovery "that a person becomes neurotic because he cannot tolerate the amount of frustration which society imposes in the service of its cultural ideals."

Beyond these specific historical developments, he points to another factor that has grown more acute with the advance of technology: disappointment. Humanity now exercises a degree of control over external reality that would have been inconceivable in the past, Freud writes. For all the access of pride that accompanies this dominance, he points out that it has not been accompanied by an increase in the quantity of pleasure people receive from life.

In the most lyrical passage of the essay, Freud rhetorically interrogates his own argument: "Is there, then, no positive gain in pleasure, no unequivocal increase in my feeling of happiness, if I can, as often as I please hear the voice of a child of mine who is living hundreds of miles away or if I can learn in the shortest possible time after a friend has reached his destination that he has come through his long and difficult voyage unharmed?" From the telephone and cable, Freud proceeds to catalogue a roster of improvements to the quality of life brought about by science, progressing finally to the extended span of years we can now expect to remain alive. "But here," he announces, "the voice of pessimistic criticism makes itself heard and warns us that most of these satisfactions follow the model of the 'cheap enjoyment' extolled in the anecdote—the enjoyment obtained by putting a bare leg from under the bedclothes on a cold winter night and drawing it in again. If there had been no railway to conquer distances, my child would never have left his native town and I should need no telephone to hear his voice." One by one, he goes through the benefits technology has introduced, demonstrating how they each respond to a corrosion of human intimacy brought about by the advance of civilization itself. "What good to us is a long life if it is difficult and barren of joys, and if it is so full of misery that we can only welcome death as a deliverer?" Each of us has become, as it were, "a prosthetic God," Freud notes, yet we do not feel happy in our godlike character. Though he does not say so explicitly, Freud suggests that a prosthetic God is fated to be forever haunted by the recrudescence of animal longings.

Perhaps the unanswered—often unarticulated—yearning for a previous state of unmediated, warm closeness, an echo of the primal bond to the universe, is why we keep demanding more and more from civilization, reaching far beyond the satisfaction of utilitarian needs. We also want green spaces for our towns, aesthetic beauty, cleanliness, and order, along with intellectual and scientific rewards. But the fulfillment of each wish invariably entails some new, proportionate sacrifice reflecting what Freud calls "the decisive step of civilization": The "replacement of the power of the individual by the power of a community." Hence though our desire for freedom may present itself as a noble revolt against unjust authority, it often springs merely from the psychic residue of an ancestral personality that culture has not managed to synthesize. All civilization in Freud's model is a zero-sum game for, in the last analysis, it is "built up upon a renunciation of instinct," which is precisely why, as civilization moves forward, the issue of belonging grows ever more troublesome. The oceanic sensation that Rolland alluded to derived from feelings of unconscious identification; however, the process of civilization that Freud subscribed to relied on people becoming more and more self-aware.

The damming of our drives imposed by civilization is most immediately perceptible in the erotic sphere since, for reasons bound up with social stability, the state only countenances the indulgence of sexual urges within narrow confines. (In Freud's time, inside wedlock for reproductive purposes, which seems quaint to us now, although it's worth bearing in mind that as new possibilities for chemically, virtually, and biotechnologically intensifying our sexual experience continue to inundate us, there will always be another level of erotic abandon to nervously prohibit or deliriously embrace. Sexual liberation remains chronically relative.) But it's also the case with respect to the other, more archaic, complementary drive, which Freud recognized the existence of almost ten years earlier in *Beyond the Pleasure Principle*: the instinct that encourages violence and all manner of aggressive action in pursuit of a return to, or the repetition of, an earlier state of things in which the organism was so primitive that it was essentially immune to disturbances from external stimuli. Oftentimes in contemporary life this latter drive, which Freud characterized as "the expression of the inertia inherent in organic life," did not manifest in straightforward fashion. A craving for maximal stimulation, for example, might conceal the desire for a flood of sensation that overwhelmed consciousness and brought the person to a Nirvana point beyond the reach of any further agitation. The organic instincts are fundamentally conservative, Freud argued. Just as "inanimate things existed before living ones," we are compelled to say *"the aim of all life is death."*

The elaborate biological myth Freud conjured to explain the logic behind the death instinct is less significant for *Civilization and Its Discontents* than the basic notion that a drive toward aggression and destruction lies at the foundation of our psychic architecture. Its gratification provides one of our most powerful experiences of happiness. This death instinct is engaged in a perpetual struggle with the erotic drive, which encompasses the kaleidoscopic varieties of love and seeks to bind us into ever greater unities. While civilization ministered to Eros, "the inclination to aggression is an original, self-subsisting disposition," which seeks to "dissolve these units and to bring them back to their primeval, inorganic state." In Goethe's *Faust*, "the Devil himself names as his adversary not what is holy and good, but Nature's power to create, to multiply life," Freud noted.

Humanity's collectivizing projects have thus prudently left room for the thrill of hate-flush destruction by excluding certain groups from the joyous new unions they promulgate, whether through what Freud dubbed "the narcissism of minor differences" (which, for example, drove bordering peoples to endlessly feud with one another), or, with respect to grander human endeavors, by such time-honored traditions as demonizing Jews. When the Apostle Paul enshrined the idea of universal love between people as the core value of the Christian community, "extreme intolerance on the part of Christendom toward those who remained outside it became the inevitable consequence." Recent history had proven no exception, Freud observed. It wasn't chance that "the dream of Germanic world-dominion called for anti-Semitism as its complement," and one could only wonder who the Russian communist regime would turn against once it had wiped out the bourgeoise. Those convinced that the elimination of private property and the equal distribution of wealth would remove the impulse to mistreat one's neighbor would do well to remember that aggressiveness had in fact ruled almost unchecked in primitive times when property and wealth hardly existed, Freud cautioned. But even recent, refined efforts at establishing a harmonious civilization enlisted a scapegoat to compensate for so much renunciation. The flaw in such schemes was that eventually all the scapegoats could be slaughtered, even as the pressure to continually replace them with new adversaries created a stress that might finally cause civilization to break down altogether.

Freud was positing a double or perhaps even a triple bind: Most of the large-scale social undertakings classified as civilizations throughout history acquired their internal cohesion not by transcending the death instinct but by channeling its expression toward an officially sanctioned enemy. In those rare instances where a more inclusive state of civilization prevailed, the ruling powers achieved this greater tolerance by harshly repressing the population's sexual and destructive drives, establishing the political equivalent of an unforgiving superego—with all the attendant morbid, guilt-inducing properties. If the development of civilization and of the individual were so closely paralleled, the possibility had to be considered, Freud wrote, that "under the influence of cultural urges, some civilizations, or some epochs of civilization—possibly the whole of mankind— have become 'neurotic.'"

Though he held open the prospect that a psychoanalytic examination of such neuroses might produce valid therapeutic recommendations, Freud allowed that this process would be fraught with unique challenges. For in considering individual neurosis, the point of departure must be the person's contrast with his or her larger society, but in a situation where the entire community is affected by the same disorder, no such standard could exist. How would one say what was normal if an entire civilization had become pathological?

The words ran along my spine like blades of frost down a windowpane. How many people that I knew were now speaking about the United States as if playing a match-up game between the society and a symptom checklist of madness?

Who could doubt that the administration had opened the

gates to a titanic wave of aggression? By setting off a domino-chain of exclusions, beginning with Americans versus non-Americans, then turning against vulnerable demographics within the country's borders—the undocumented, the poor, the sick, different minority groups—while the left, overwhelmed by the velocity and brazenness of the assault, began to fragment and go haywire—the president had incited something approaching a Hobbesian state of all-against-all, even as his own ardent supporters splashed and spouted in a jumbo hot-tub atmosphere of orgiastic togetherness. What if Freud's monumentally bleak diagnosis were correct and this was the moment when civilization's discontents triumphed?

Ever since the election, I had felt that we were witnessing the advent of apocalyptic capitalism. Trump was its ideal front man, but of course the system had been encroaching long before his ascendancy. Part of his attraction derived from his willingness to strip bare a truth people already intuited: The free market had merged with the death drive. Gutting environmental regulations in the name of business imperatives was its most blatant manifestation, but wherever one looked—the attempt to destroy the already crippled health-care system, the destruction of housing programs, food regulations, the national parks, public discourse, privacy, justice, beauty, compassion—the new America First regime promised an end to the renunciation of instinct in the name of "limitless narcissism." However, this stampede to brutality contrived to offer the worst of both worlds: People were running amok but in a majority of cases doing so online while hunched over at home eating junk food out of bags, so that they felt simultaneously liberated *and* paralyzed by stifled drives, provoking a state of brain pandemonium.

This too validated the model Freud proposed, for he'd argued in his essay that another challenge faced by civilization was that the happiness people desire is more intense than the serenity offered by a suite of pleasant days. It came rather from the abrupt satisfaction of wild needs which had been previously impeded, and was thus "from its nature only possible as an episodic phenomenon." Each fresh tweet or news flash provided an ideal neurotransmitter jolt, like watching the silver ball bounce between numbered pockets on a giant red and black wheel, waiting to discover whether what came up delivered a mini-hell or a micro-paradise, a gush of dopamine or a burst of stress hormones. I thought back on what my friend Adam had spoken of a year and a half earlier about a public that felt deprived of the unexpected, the undomesticated, the reckless, all-or-nothing, fantastical ecstasy. The president passed out dreams of cheap paradise and vengeance like chips at a casino to fevered fortune seekers.

Walter Benjamin described the way gambling made memory and history obsolete by invalidating the standards of experience. Inherent to the play was the principle that no game was dependent on its predecessor. The implications of this delegitimization of past knowledge for civic society could be significant, he observed. During the Second Empire, it became customary on the boulevards to attribute *everything* to chance. "This disposition is promoted by betting, which is a device for giving events the character of a shock, detaching them from the context of experience," Benjamin wrote. For the bourgeoisie even political events at last tended "to assume the form of occurrences at the gambling table."

Gambling and game-show politics represented the substitution of luck and diversion for democratic volition and learned expertise.

———

Day after day, instead of changing anything in my life, I sat before my screen, feeling like I was binge-watching the apocalypse. Or as if by staring hard enough at my newsfeeds I might torque them into displaying more favorable results, like some mentalist on 1970s television purporting to bend forks by force of telepathic concentration.

Meanwhile, voices across the spectrum of platforms kept asking, *Is this the end then? Last bets, please.* There was a certain titillating release in that prospect as well. Alongside pleasure, the most important element in gambling was peril, Benjamin wrote around 1929. The elation of winning, which produced a sense "of being rewarded by fate, of having seized control of destiny," was balanced by a "certain feeling of lightness, not to say relief," which the loser enjoyed by virtue of having avoided hubris. The best writing on gambling, anyway, focused on "acceleration, acceleration and danger," he declared.

Even so, the passive absorption of bad news, as if we were great sponges for darkness, was of course not the whole of everyday experience. Away from the jail guards of our monitors, we still worked, read, wrote, saw friends and family, went to parks, museums, cafés, and films. The conversation of ordinary being kept unfolding. Nearly every afternoon I saw my son arrive home from school amid his friends, brimming over with mirthful excitement about what the future would bring to them. Did I really think it was so simple as that the young were blind to reality?

The sense that there was something missing from Freud's account—a secret in the shadows of his own unexplained lack of oceanic feeling—continued to needle me with the possibility of an unexplored hope. Despite the seductive poignance of his conceit, was it *really* true that society's progress and our individual renunciations of instinct existed in a directly inverse relationship? There was an artificial either/or finality to the construct. I mistrusted the sense of mildly sybaritic absolution that came over me when I surrendered to the pitch of pessimism.

Something appeared scrambled in Freud's presentation of Eros as rooted in sexuality, which civilization sought to harness, and *the* primal instinct nurturing civilization's development. In our own reasonably sexually permissive society there were few signs of greater overall happiness. Whatever increase in sexual contentment had been achieved did not seem to have reduced the discontent with civilization as such. This suggested the potential for a third social impulse that didn't quite fit the agon Freud plotted—another way of thinking about love aligned with older, religiously inflected notions of *caritas*.

Why had Freud highlighted Rolland's celebrity stature in his essay unless on some level he were aware that Rolland might have experienced a sense of oneness with all creation because as an adult, unlike Freud, he'd been almost universally embraced by his fellow man? If all behavioral motivation "belonged" to Freudian theory, there was no role for contingent historical circumstance; his findings subordinated the world that had rejected him to his own temporally specific perspective. Might it be possible that the feeling of having an indissoluble bond with the universe manifested through a two-phase process? First experienced by almost everyone in infancy, it could then be reawakened among those fortunate enough to discover a sense of belonging within an adult collective. A particular group could obviously be more or less welcoming to the stranger in its midst. Thus the presence of the feeling Freud professed himself baffled by was not entirely germinal and random, but also determined by factors that a society could nurture or hinder through policies and education.

In denying the socially conditioned features of his own inability to feel a sense of belonging, Freud was repressing the political unconscious. This hadn't always been his practice. When younger, Freud himself invoked the realm of the dead against the social superstructure, to advance his own Eros-oriented revelation of the psyche's Stygian mysteries.

7

· Hunters in the Underworld ·

One delightfully, frighteningly warm March day in 2017, I took the youngest of my older children, Zach, to lunch at a chic new Italian place on Dekalb Avenue. We sat outside in the lazy sunshine, surrounded by tables full of beautiful, loud parties; loose jewelry and intricate tattoos swirled over the expensive small plates, tracing the conversations with blue, red, and green accent marks of faraway societies idealized for their anti-materialistic value systems.

Zach was in his mid-twenties then and living in Bed-Stuy, working as a paramedic for the city fire department. I could see his eyes shifting between the different groups, lids half-lowered. I saw flecks of their exchanges reflected in his pupils. I knew that look: not judgmental—he was only ever judgmental of himself—but inquiring, contemplating a way of life he could not enter into and trying to understand what held him back.

I've always thought of him as having the soul of an artist, which had nothing to do with the enchanting music he made in his free hours, but was rather a matter of his intense porosity to the larger environment—his poetic feel for the joys, pain, and sheer contradictions of being. I've always thought of him as blessed and cursed to persistently seek the scratch of the real, even when his own skin flays in consequence. Born in Jerusalem, he'd had that world taken away from him with our return to America while he was still a small child. As he grew older in New York, his sense of alienation magnified. The home I made for him in Brooklyn was never sufficiently warm or open to the world. He went to high school in Chelsea, at a public school that was largely a privileged monoculture. Nothing he learned there seemed important to him. He was always interested in the details and big questions of other lives, but none of his teachers spoke to that hunger. The social circles felt insipid. The ambitions of his classmates, alternately mundane or stratospheric, were in either case remote from his concerns. He only scraped through, but after he did so eventually began a course in emergency medical training and excelled at those studies. Now he worked the night shift in the depths of East New York, stepping into unspeakable scenes. People who'd been set on fire by their enemies or stabbed by psychopaths. Shot multiple times in cars, houses, and back lots. Youths hacked and smashed beyond recognition. The crimes and accidents you never read about because the victims live outside the ecology of the city's victorious self-image, and because the injured, more often than not, just barely survive, though God knows with what kind of compromised existence.

I thought as I looked at him of the people he'd helped save: the asthmatic children turning blue, serial summer-night overdoses, young men whose lungs had collapsed on the impact of a bullet or blade. Obese older diabetics having heart attacks. He was telling me now about intubating a conscious patient who'd suffered a seizure. His graceful fingers moved unconsciously through the procedure as he spoke, reminding me of the hours I'd watched them arching, sliding and overlapping; pausing, coming down and lifting across the keys of the piano he improvised on hauntingly—now they were performing another kind of counterpoint. Once in a while he spoke also about the people he'd seen pass away. The immigrant kid on the delivery motorbike run over by a truck his first day on the job. Sixteen years old, smeared into the pavement. The man shot in the neck, asking him, "Am I going to die? Am I going to die? Am I going to die?" Wide-eyed. Over and over. That question, his last words.

I looked at him, overcome with admiration and apprehension. For the physical damage he incurred carrying all those thrashing or heavy, inert bodies down long, treacherous stairways into ambulances. For the risks that might wait for him in the infectious turmoil of some larger disaster. For the psychic wound brought on by working in a world of such inexorable gravity, which divided him socially from his old school friends, who had jobs in sports marketing and PR, doing programming for financial firms and sales at high-end fashion boutiques.

On this day sitting at the restaurant, while the svelte long-haired waiters pirouetted between tables and those they served guffawed and clapped into the sunshine before slouching back to sip bright cocktails, flicking mildly impatient glances at their phones, like groovy pashas awaiting their elephants, I could see questions and bemusement through his eyes. The warm diamond air did not seem to touch him.

Finally, I broke in. "You don't look very taken with our companions." I smiled.

He gave a silent chuckle. "No—it's not that." He shrugged without meeting my eyes. "People are having a good time. That's good.

But what I was thinking was that tough as my work can be, I'm glad I have a job that brings things back to earth. It's the only way I can take being here."

"In the city?"

He nodded. "It's the only way the city makes sense to me." I could feel my brow furrowing. "I mean, it's when you see what lies underneath. People in all these life-and-death situations—when you see the reality, while all this"—his hand gestured vaguely over his head—"floats away somewhere above. Then you're like, Oh right, there's this whole other city most people here don't even know exists. It's full of vulnerable people who depend on public services. It can be dark and brutal, but it's actually *there*. All the money and attitude is just bobbing on top." He shrugged. "Anyway, it's the only way I can take being here." He laughed. But there was no mirth, only mourning.

I was both filled with pride at his devotion to this work, and heartbroken at the thought that New York felt so insubstantial to him apart from its underlying tide of lives in extremis. Like transit workers moving in the depths of the tunnels, he and his partners labored in the city's corporeal foundations, bodies in pain—struggling not to die, or fighting to be born; shuddering to be released, to be held, or simply to breathe.

What would his future bring?

I felt an abrupt impulse to wrench him away from all this—to hold him against me, to cover his being with mine until all threat had passed, but he'd left home years before, and the danger would never move all the way past him now. Wrench him away to what? What could my life offer him when it unfolded on the very surface he'd learned to see through—that provoked him to keep searching and searching for something more true?

I had thought when we sat down together to speak to him about a news story I'd seen just before leaving the house—headlines about some fresh move by the president against those least able to protect themselves. But the deeper inequalities—the breach he had thrown himself into—had of course long predated this administration. That older divide was there all the time, only it had been one I'd been able to turn my eyes from, when need be, more successfully.

I found myself thinking about the foundations of our own house on Cumberland, those formidable stone blocks that had supposedly been dug from the same quarry where the rock that built the Brooklyn Bridge had been excavated. It made a nice anecdote, anyway—the realtors had told us and we kept retailing it to friends with a slightly self-satisfied smile, as if we ourselves were somehow thereby dynastically related to that mighty, lyrical span. "Harp and altar, of the fury fused."

Yes, just look at that powerful stone, we might say, while subtly steering the onlooker to turn away from what we'd done with the space those blocks framed. The way we'd allowed our basement to become gorged with *dreck* we didn't need or know what to do with. All the extra belongings cramming our home's lower depths: a few dozen boxes of books we either had duplicates of or doubted we'd ever read again, bins of papers we knew we'd never page through, a not quite functional ping-pong table, a chandelier from my father's home in Vienna that had lost too many pieces to be put back together, a friend's abandoned jogging stroller, another friend's abandoned cross-country skis, somebody's half-on-loan drum set, a cracked red plastic sled, half-empty cans of paint, unused boards, extra chairs with different problems, a bed frame missing slats, containers full of warped LPs, garbage bags stuffed with old clothes slated for giveaway, bins jammed with cords and dysfunctional electronics, a rickety gray metal shelving unit scattered with stiff brushes, together with jars full of screws, nails, and odd tools, lamps with unsolved issues, stray bits of camping gear (though we never camped), deflated balls, a little old television—all steadily gathering Egyptian tomb layers of dust.

That was our underworld, what we lived on top of—perched above as if none of it existed. *La dee da, hum-dee-dee*, we're just sitting around up here on the throne of our light, airy living room. Pay no attention to that mass of dark, repressed objects lurking behind the curtain of the locked basement door.

Though in truth, increasingly, the basement had begun to flood, so that many of the things were also now regressing, going semi-amphibian, stained and furred with mildew, periodically water-logged. The floods were getting worse. The bilge, always dark, cold, and filthy, kept rising higher with each season's storm cycle. The last time we'd raced down the stairs with rolled-up trouser legs, gripping buckets, ready to start bailing, we found ourselves sloshing around up to our knees. It had been a frenzied battle against time to keep the whole room from submerging, the townhouse from capsizing, before the plumber arrived. I waited for the night when we'd wake up to discover we'd heard the inrush too late: The waters were already filtering up through the old dining-room floorboards, over the woven blossoms of the rose Persian carpet, rising higher and higher, seeping above the stamped-tin ceiling of that room onto the wide maple syrup–covered floorboards of the next level—surging up over the old upright piano, the pale gold and cream love seat passed down from my great-grandmother, the bookshelves and the painting by my friend Adam of a classical temple wrapped in rusty wires surrounded by a metal frame radiating red veins—turning the elegantly proportioned high-ceiling parlor into a pool—a giant bath, a *mikveh* for purifying the entire community of local property owners—*oh, that would need to be much bigger.* Rising and rising, now subsuming the lacy plaster moldings trailing the walls and ceilings, going up story after story to the floors that we worked and lived on, swelling and spreading until we found ourselves drifting away out the top-floor window on our mattress, floating off above the deluged brownstones of Fort Greene, clutching the sides of our soaking white raft like a dual-gendered Huckleberry Finn without Jim; sailing farther and farther downstream until the whole body of water suddenly turned subterranean, merging with the River Styx.

An almost naked man trudges up a rough stone slope, bent under a massive rock that he clutches to his crunched head and shoulders. Eerie fires burn in the background. Across the gutter from him sprawls an entirely nude male figure with chained arms and ankles whose guts are being pecked out by a giant black vulture: *Sisyphus* and *Tityus*, the two surviving paintings from Titian's *Four Great Sinners* series. Whatever wrong these men committed feels irrelevant; their suffering is transcendent.

I found myself spending a lot of time paging through art books in those days as the anger and money of the city bellowed louder. The images were train windows onto a fast-passing dreamland.

Conversation with Rebecca in that second year of the new regime turned ever more intently to the fate of our son Rafael. We could feel the atmosphere transforming around him, like a cocoon stealing the metamorphosis from the life forming within.

What kind of existence would enable him to flourish now?

Where would his imagination remain most individual and alive? What might we do to deliver him from the tormented patterns of being in which we felt ourselves increasingly locked here, like Titian's great sinners?

These pictures had been purchased by the discerning Habsburg patron Mary, queen of Hungary, for one of her hunting lodges in Flanders, where they were intended to be mounted in time to grace a fete in August 1549 honoring Prince Philip after his ceremonial advance through Northern Europe, on having been recognized by his father, Charles V, as the successor to the Spanish dominion. The enormous canvases depicting Sisyphus and Tityus, together with the lost portraits of Ixion and Tantalus, were fixed along one wall of the barrel-vaulted chamber, facing six huge tapestries of the deadly sins, with the seventh sin, Pride, the most serious, positioned above a dais where the queen herself sat enthroned near the emperor and the prince, watching the festivities. The atmosphere in the cavernous room, dominated by dramatic images of damned men undergoing an eternal repetition of the same tortures, conveyed to beholders the impression of being in the underworld where the Furies inflicted these punishments.

Scholars have puzzled over the question of why the grand hall of Queen Mary's château in Binche would have been turned into an immersive model of hell filled with grim imagery for a celebratory reception. One answer derives from the specific classical reference that inspired Titian's paintings: Juno's descent into the underworld, during which she made the extreme suffering wreaked on these sinners a reproach to the Furies for having allowed Athamas and Ino, a king and queen whom she considered yet more abhorrent, to continue enjoying the pleasures of their sumptuous palace. Wickedness appears on a spectrum in Juno's view—a point worth remembering at a moment when accusations of hypocrisy, along with the drawing of false equivalencies, are being deployed to muddy our perspective on all wrongdoing, nullifying the very possibility of judgment, except from a position of make-believe spotlessness.

In a number of Roman and Renaissance texts, the invocation of the Four Sinners prefigures the disclosure of yet more horrifying crimes. Mary of Hungary may have decorated the hall as a Juno-esque reminder to the Emperor that present-day heretics, such as the expounders of Protestantism then disrupting all Christendom, were getting off lightly relative to these antique wrongdoers. Then again, perhaps she just fancied the piquancy of watching decoratively costumed courtiers performing ultra-stylized dances amid the wild flames and cruelties of Tartarus.

Learned visitors to the château would anyway have felt themselves not only to be inside an evocation of the underworld, but also to be in the company of Juno's spirit. They may have recalled the earlier, paradigmatic account of Juno's invocation of hell from the *Aeneid*, where she summons the Fury of Discord to help her take revenge on those supporting her foes and humiliating her.

The epigraph to the first major work Freud composed at Berchtesgaden, *The Interpretation of Dreams*, is drawn from this latter scene in Virgil, a rebellious vow uttered by Juno herself: "If I cannot bend the powers above, I will rouse the underworld." With this quote Freud announces that he is launching out to explore the psychologically subterranean realm, because the potentates of consciousness have failed him in his quest for knowledge. However, the decision to begin his revolutionary study of dreams with Juno's promise to seek her avengers in Tartarus is thought to have a double significance:

Not only will Freud turn to the unconscious after having been un-able to solve the mysteries of neurosis by examining those parts of mental life we're aware of, he also channels Juno's voice to express his pledge to defy the socio-political circumstances that have hitherto obstructed his personal advance.

Juno is closely associated with Hannibal, Rome's nemesis—the Semitic hero who loomed large in Freud's youthful imagination. In *The Interpretation of Dreams*, Freud describes the moment from his childhood when his father reported that while he was out walking, a Christian had knocked his new fur hat off his head into the mud of the roadway, shouting, "Jew, get off the pavement!" The boy asked his father what he'd done in response and his father answered that he'd stepped into the road and retrieved his hat. Freud burned with shame at this admission, contrasting it with the stance of Hannibal's father, who forced his son to vow on the household altar that he'd take revenge on the Romans. Over time, Freud wrote, Hannibal came to represent for him "the tenacity of the Jews."

By the late 1890s when he began *The Interpretation*, after having been repeatedly denied the academic promotion he'd long merited, partly in consequence of anti-Semitism—and having encountered systematic resistance to the sexual aspects of his theories due to general bourgeois prejudices—Freud resolved to stir up the dream legions against his benighted adversaries.

But the underworld was fundamental to Freud's model of the mind's topography even beyond societal biases, since it gave a classical profile to the notion of a place where all the antinomies of individual experience were dissolved. Our unconscious wishes are characterized by their indestructability, he wrote in his dream book; "ever stirring, never dying," they exist in a Tartarian limbo from which they remain perpetually ready to emerge by allying themselves with a conscious desire, lending their momentous intensity to that weaker charge. Rather than being eliminated, these archaic yearnings only suffer a suspension of being, like "shades in the underworld of the Odyssey" awaiting the draught of blood that will allow them to "waken to new life." They are simultaneously dead and immortal.

Despite Freud's declarations of uncompromising allegiance to Enlightenment principles, speculations on the border zone between the unconscious and the occult realms of myth haunt his writing. Late in *The Interpretation*, he returns to Juno's oath while contrasting the psychological states of consciousness and sleep. "In waking life suppressed material in the mind is prevented from finding expression and is cut off from internal perception owing to the fact that the contradictions present in it are eliminated—one side being disposed of in favor of the other; but during the night . . . this suppressed material finds methods and means of forcing its way into consciousness. *Flectere si nequeo superos, Acheronta movebo.*'" The dream state allows for a heterogeneous vision, devoid of either/or choices.

Freud's mushroom-hunting expeditions were a frequent family diversion during this time, and mushrooms also figure in the work as a way into thinking about the limits of interpretation. It is customary, Freud writes near the end, for even the best-interpreted dreams to contain "a passage that has to be left in the dark." This is the point where a "knot of dream-thoughts shows itself . . . This is the dream's navel, and the place beneath which lies the Unknown." He then goes further, declaring that every dream-thought engaged with in the course of analysis will evade perfect closure, "spinning out on all sides into the web-like fabric of our thoughts. Out of a denser patch in this tissue the dream-wish then arises like a mushroom from its mycelium." The imminent natural world gave Freud his metaphysical image.

Elsewhere in his writing as well, Freud expressed belief in a spectrum of organic states that seems to resonate with his nonbinary views on psychological identity (his arguments, for instance, that bisexuality is universal, with each person manifesting desires on a gradient between the vanishing points of unalloyed hetero- and homosexuality). To one colleague, he wrote warning against the attempt "to disparage all the beautiful differences of nature in favor of tempting unity." In his view, it was just as arbitrary "to endow the whole of nature with a psyche as radically to deny that it has one at all. Let us grant to nature her infinite variety which rises from the inanimate to the organically animated, from the just physically alive to the spiritual." The unconscious, Freud wrote, might serve as a mediator "between the physical and mental, perhaps it is the 'missing link.'"

Such a lavishly polymorphous conception of the world and mind tempted some of Freud's advocates to feel they could project through his theories all manner of cosmic congruities.

When H.D. characterized Freud's idea of the psychic underworld as a confluence of past and future, as well as a counteragent to the divisive propensities of humanity at large, she was joining a line of heretical acolytes who expected the work of analysis to reach fruition in the supernatural realm. In words recalling Rolland's challenge to Freud's view of religion, H.D. likened the vast depths of human consciousness from which dreams arose to "a great stream or ocean underground." These depths of the psyche had remained unchanged since antiquity, H.D. wrote, and their overflow into the tiny domain of individual consciousness produced both flights of the imagination and madness. The oceanic estate was a universal property, she insisted, adding that while Freud didn't say so explicitly, "he had dared to imply that this consciousness proclaimed all men one; all nations and races met in the universal world of the dream." The secrets of the unconscious contained in these nocturnal visions "would forgo barriers of time and space, and man, understanding man, would save mankind," she prophesied.

When H.D. lay across the oriental-draped couch, her eyes turned repeatedly to the forest of symbolic figures on Freud's desk, the assembly that brought together Middle Bronze Age female statuettes from Syria, an Egyptian head of Osiris, a Greek Eros, a Chinese Buddha, and the Putnam Camp porcupine, among others. Inside his consulting room, it might have seemed perverse for Freud to deny her contention that he'd demonstrated how all time periods, nations, beliefs, and races converged in the dream world. As if what he really wanted from her was something else unspoken, somehow illicit.

She tells the story of a moment early in her analysis when, in the midst of speaking from the classic prostrate position, she swung around to face him, "stark upright," feet planted on the floor, provoking an outburst from Freud. He began beating his fist against the back of the old horse-hair couch, like "a child hammering a porridge-spoon on the table," saying that he'd listened to more secrets than any "popular Roman-Catholic father-confessor in his heyday." As if the mass of private knowledge he'd absorbed hitherto should have made the form of their exchange inviolable; by looking back at him, H.D. had shattered that mythological contract, no less than Orpheus had done on the path out of the underworld, though she found herself wondering also whether his temper were a strategy intended to shift the direction of her associations. Suddenly he broke out, "The trouble is—I am an old man—*you do not think it worth your while to love me.*"

She was left speechless. "The impact of his words was too dreadful—I simply felt nothing at all," she recalled. It was as though the Supreme Being had started beating the place where her body had been lying. "He must know everything or he didn't know anything . . . Did he think it was easy to leave friendly comfortable surroundings and come to a strange city, to beard him, himself, the dragon, in his very den?" He was too frightening, wise, remote, famous—too ancient. She slunk back into place, stretched out on the sofa, rearranging the rug that had slid to the floor.

Once more, it was as if her "thoughts were things, to be collected, collated, analyzed, shelved, or resolved." Her ideas were fragments, which he sometimes artfully pieced back together, "like the exquisite Greek tear-jars and iridescent glass bowls and vases that gleamed in the dusk" from the cabinets as she lay horizontal beneath his perch at the couch-end. As though the shards of her psyche were now becoming parts of his collection, while he presented her with his own cloistered vision of wholeness and immortality: The dead were alive insofar as they were present in memory or dreams, which he beckoned from her in that timeless chamber, coaxing those broken recollections to join the quiescent objects decorating his walls and furniture.

In that instant of Freud's eruption, with the fist pounding child-like at the point of her absence, she'd glimpsed the possibility that the whole psychoanalytic project was also Freud's private quest for boundless love and belonging—for the faith that his consulting room, cradling both Eros and the Sphinx, could return patient and analyst to a state of dyadic completion. She'd descried his dream of conjuring a dialogic womb—along with his bitter suspicion that if only he'd been a Christian confessor, she would not have torn herself from the spell. Why had Freud told her at the outset of analysis that she'd come to Vienna hoping to find her *mother*, when her mother was dead and the child in her that had called the woman "mamma" was dead also? H.D. wondered.

Of *course* his desktop exhibition was a maquette of that spatially and temporally unshackled realm where human yearnings for something more than mortality attain syncretic harmony, she concluded. "With precise Jewish instinct for the particular in the general, for the personal in the impersonal or universal, for the *material* in the abstract, he had dared to plunge into the unexplored depth," she wrote. "In the dream matter were Heaven and Hell"—a nonbinary proposition. Freud understood how to outmaneuver the mental censor she likened to Cerberus. She herself wanted the gates thrown wide. They ought to have been in total sympathy. And yet, though he didn't object outright to the extrapolations she made from his inferences, still, again, she intuited the insuperable division between them, that dispute "implicit in our very bones."

At its core hung Freud's refusal to concede that his theories offered any kind of astral chart to the future. He would only look back and further backward: the mind's archeologist, uncovering the secrets of all present-day behavior in the past. "I have not the courage to rise up before my fellow men as a prophet," he'd written at the close of *Civilization and Its Discontents*, "and I bow to their reproach that I can offer them no consolation; for at bottom that is what they are all demanding—the wildest revolutionaries no less passionately than the most virtuous believers." What solace could he tender when his work kept reiterating that all judgments of value derive from our wishes for happiness, and our happiness stems from the satisfaction of two primeval drives, Eros and Thanatos?

Again and again over the course of his career, like a perpetually recurring punishment for some original hubris, Freud found himself confronted with people's insistence that, even acknowledging life's miseries and the indefensibility of religion's fabulous antidotes, still in some muzzy aftermath we might glean the true oneness—just as hope was discovered fluttering at the bottom of Pandora's box after the last plague had flown off.

H.D. was typical in revering what she called, citing others, Freud's "courageous pessimism." She accepted his dictum that we're not "ready for discussion of the Absolute, Absolute Beauty, Absolute Goodness." But her affirmations seem predicated on the notion that a time will come when we *are* so prepared. Yes, Freud required that each individual do the laborious work of clearing away their own cluttered backlot of psychic rubbish, but once having done so, the stream of personal life would "run clear of obstruction into the great river of humanity, hence to the sea of super-human perfection, the 'Absolute' . . . There was another Jew who said, *the kingdom of heaven is within you*," she declared. "He said: *unless you become as little children you shall not enter the kingdom of heaven.*"

Her mention of the other Jew bears on Freud's recoil from the hope for eventual fulfillment, for he suspected that vague, shimmery eternity of soulful individuals who've evolved beyond formal religion of representing a false universal. Its lack of positive incarnation merely signifying, like the vacant stone at Golgotha three days after the Crucifixion, the promise that Christ has risen, His presence now invisibly filling creation. That vision of the future implied the sacrifice of his native identity. How many people in our own time have felt compelled to shy back from the promise of a global solution because they sensed how some core aspect of their private personality or history would be refused entry to the theoretically all-inclusive paradise?

The way these rationalists manqué approached Freud's ideas recalled adherents of Christian typology coming for the Hebrew Bible, imposing over its passages the interpretative matrix so beloved of American Puritans, which read all characters and events there as mere foreshadowings of the New Testament. So it was, Freud felt, that people sifted through psychoanalysis, searching for clues to some long-awaited, ethereal rapture, which was to be followed by total merging with the universe. (Although it was true also that his own *Interpretation* might be taken as an enquiry into the antitypes of Greek mythology.)

Jung had been the first notable exponent of the idea that analysis offered a prefatory guide to the practice of self-transcendence. He'd finally split with Freud on deciding, as he wrote in his memoir, that his real vocation was to investigate above sexuality's "personal significance and biological function, its spiritual aspects and its numinous meaning, and thus to explain what Freud was so fascinated by but was unable to grasp."

Always the notion that there had to be something beyond—surpassing, salvaging, completing, *denying* the real conditions of life in this world in the name of a supernal postscript. "The earth is a small planet, not suited to be a 'heaven,'" Freud retorted to one doctor who'd challenged him. "We human beings are rooted in our animal nature and could never become godlike." When feeling more benevolently toward humanity, he would attribute the importance of ridding ourselves of religion's illusions to the fact that if all the energies and resources aimed at the afterlife were redirected toward improving life here for the multitudes, we might actually get somewhere. "One should either fight ignorance and prejudice or attempt to increase man's control over nature, etc.," Freud told the doctor who suggested to him that if the general public only possessed more *knowledge* a miraculous transformation of life would ensue. Even so, he added, "it is equally probable that for the time being these men will offer us nothing but disappointment." In his letter to Lou Andreas-Salome announcing that he'd reached the end of *Civilization and Its Discontents*, he confessed that "in the depths of my heart I can't help being convinced that my dear fellow men, with a few exceptions, are worthless."

After Jung—indeed overlapping with him for a time—came my great-grandfather Putnam, fresh from late-night readings in Henri Bergson, Josiah Royce, the American Hegelians, his dear friend William James, and continually, like Scriptures, his guiding light, Emerson. Putnam, Freud wrote, "was not only the first American to interest himself in psycho-analysis, but soon became its most decided supporter and its most influential representative in America." In their very first conversations at his Adirondack camp in September 1909, Putnam also made clear to Freud that he would be among those advocating that the fundament of the psyche be searched for clues not only to how we'd become what we are today, but also to how we might facilitate our progress to a higher plane of being. In his inaugural letter across the Atlantic to Freud after their meeting, Putnam broached the idea that "psychoanalytic methods need to be supplemented by methods which seek to hold up before the patient some goal toward which he may strive."

Freud countered that while he knew analysts were unable to

adequately compensate patients for the loss of the fantasies that
came with their illness, the emptiness experienced in the absence of
neuroses was "not the fault of therapy but of social institutions." To
which Putnam responded that nonetheless, patients needed something more than for doctors to shine a light on the roots of their
symptoms. The study of human nature might be better begun at
the top than the bottom, he opined at one point. Analyzing a single
phase of a symphony, whether its first notes or culminating moment,
couldn't give a sense of its perfection. One could only do justice to a
work of art by learning to appreciate the entire composition, and so
it was with human beings, Putnam argued. If there were reasons why
people "should adopt higher views of their obligations [as based on
the belief that this is a morally conceived universe, and that 'free will'
has a real meaning], then these reasons ought to be made known to
them," he wrote.

"I feel no need for a higher moral synthesis in the same way that
I have no ear for music," Freud answered Putnam. "I am resigned to
the fact that I am a God forsaken 'incredulous Jew,' I am not proud
of it and I do not look down on others. I can only say with Faust,
'There have to be odd fellows like that, too.'" While he disavows
pride, there's a note of delectation in Freud's yielding to the Faustian
attitude.

But Putnam wouldn't relinquish his mentor's soul so easily. Indeed, throughout the seven active years of their friendship, he tries to
bring Freud around to his side, at times almost pleading with him to
take what he claims will be a tiny hop over the lintel of his own psychoanalytic constructions into the radiant universe of infinite connectedness. "The individual is not to be thought of as existing alone,
but should be considered as an integral part of the community in

which he lives, and eventually of what must remain for him an ideal or idealized community," Putnam wrote him in April 1914, three months before the start of the First World War. "The interests of the community are implied in every one's motives and emotions, and sublimation consists in making these implicit interests explicit—i.e., in thinking out one's social obligations consciously and in the largest sense. I feel sure that we should agree virtually as regards these propositions," he added, beseechingly.

How could such sentiments fail to appear almost grotesquely oblivious to Freud? Especially once war began—all the more so given his own unstable societal position as a Jew in a Catholic, pervasively anti-Semitic country? Shortly after the conflict broke out, Freud noted, "Well may the citizen of the civilized world . . . stand helpless in a world that has grown strange to him—his great fatherland disintegrated, its common estates laid waste, his fellow-citizens divided and debased!" The one positive insight to be reclaimed from the ruins was "the destruction of an illusion." How can we really condemn a nation for wrongdoing, when righteous behavior would place it at a disadvantage? Freud asked. Just so, it was no less unfavorable for the individual "to conform to the standards of morality and refrain from brutal and arbitrary conduct," he continued. Thus, it shouldn't really surprise us that the "relaxation of all the moral ties between the collective individuals of mankind" would have consequences for its separate persons also. "When the community no longer raises objections, there is an end, too, to the suppression of evil passions."

It was true, Freud acknowledged, that we'd hoped the abundance of common economic interests might serve as an "external compulsion toward morality," but it turns out "nations still obey their passions far more readily than their interests." The latter are merely "*rationalizations* for their passions." Nonetheless, he acknowledged, there remained an element of mystery as to "why the collective individuals should in fact despise, hate and detest one another—every nation against every other—and even in times of peace . . . It is just as though when it becomes a question of a number of people, not to say millions, all individual moral acquisitions are obliterated, and only the most primitive, the oldest, the crudest mental attitudes are left."

The one tangible consequence of Putnam's efforts to fuse his own neo-transcendentalist views with psychoanalytic theory was to help move Freud to probe the psychogenesis of religious impulses in *Totem and Taboo* and other works, which posit an equally fantastical, yet utterly dark counter-mythology: the origin story of a band of ancient sons who butcher their father to end that man's dictatorial control of females in the primal horde, then turn the dead patriarch into an omnipotent immortal in order to assuage their patricidal guilt.

Freud was right to detect something missionary in the older American's tone. Time and again Putnam reiterated his conviction that analysis must have an ultimate metaphysical objective, lest patients, having climbed free of their interior infernos, feel "as Dante would have felt if Virgil had deserted him somewhere on the slopes of the Mount of Purgatory." In his essays he went further, declaring that the chief service of the psychoanalytic explorations, made "under the impulse of Freud's genius, has been that of forcing us to recognize the repressed devils that lurk within us. It is obvious, however, that we should never have felt these tendencies as 'devils' and repressed them unless we had had a standard of good." This standard cannot be solely dictated by society, Putnam contended. Rather, we harbor "a dim recognition" that "belief in 'the good' is one of the most real of all our intentions." For "the mind contains a real, permanently abiding element which partakes of the nature of the real, permanently abiding energy of which the life of the universe itself is made." Here was where the psychoanalyst's role might expand: Doctors could show a patient how "to unravel the portion of his unconscious yearnings which point not alone toward his earthly genesis, but also toward his spiritual genesis." And this awareness would initially be expressed through civic engagement. Every person, no matter how ignorant, has "a broad sense of obligation, a sense of moral values independent of earthly success, as a sort of birthright," Putnam remarked. "To have failed to become developed in this direction is to have 'symptoms' that need attention." He was trying to enlarge the diagnosis of mental illness to include evidence of a stunted social conscience.

But the notion of analysts being licensed to make patients aware of higher responsibilities through the filter of whatever philosophical system tickled their pious fancy repelled Freud. The shared features of our ancient psychic life could not be consecrated as a beacon to some united, redemptive future, he insisted. Humanity's instinctual commonality was not positively actionable.

In the introduction to a collection of Putnam's addresses on psychoanalysis that Freud oversaw publication of after Putnam's death in 1918, he noted that when the distinguished American proposed a metaphysics of analysis, no one understood "which of the countless philosophical systems should be accepted" as the long-term goal of treatment, since "all seemed to rest on an equally insecure basis." The only thing one could do, Freud reiterated, was, by removing repressions and overcoming resistances, to make it *possible* "for people to be moral and to deal with their wishes philosophically," if they were so inclined. "The great ethical element in analytic work is truth and again truth and this should suffice for most people," he maintained, rejecting Putnam's hope that their worldviews might be reconciled in the theory of sublimation, which Freud had developed with reference to a few exalted geniuses like Leonardo da Vinci. Most patients would be incapable of conducting their primitive instincts toward a higher goal in this manner, Freud asserted, for they had "inferior endowments and disproportionately strong drives. They would like to be better than they can be, yet this convulsive desire benefits neither themselves nor society." Isn't it more humane, he asked, to work from the principle of telling people to simply "be as moral as you can honestly be and do not strive for an ethical perfection for which you are not destined"? Whoever is really capable of sublimation will end up on that lonely path anyway.

Freud's dismissal of the prospects for mounting a democratic program to nurture sublimation can be read as grossly condescending— or as critical of Putnam's arrogance in setting out to prescribe lofty ethics and life goals based on his own convictions, rather than trusting each individual to figure out for themselves the scale of their spiritual-intellectual ambitions.

All my life I'd felt torn between these disjunctive perspectives by the two lines of my familial inheritance: the pull between Putnam's idealistic faith in human nature, with its call to honor the collective by grabbing on with gusto to the long chain of interlocked responsibilities, extending from the self through society to infinitude—and the tidal tug of Freud's dark, worldly view, which despaired of humanity en masse and its respective experiments in civilization, locating whatever compensation might be had in the quest of select individuals to fathom the hard, deep truths of our mortal condition; labors that add, incrementally, to the intellectual progress of the public at large. Now, in this hour of political alarm, I felt the debates reigniting inside me.

I'd seen Putnam's position embodied in my mother's ethos of selfless service to family, friends, community, and the old Yankee values that seemed a part of her biology. What could be more nobly inspiring? After my mother died, my painter friend Adam's mother, Sara, who'd known her since childhood in the picture-book village of Cooperstown, told me, in her plain-spun New England contralto, "Marian was simply the most generous person I've ever met." The glow in my mother's gaze and voice communicated to those around her that the world doesn't have to look the way it does; if we all pitch in with all our hearts, everything might yet become grand.

I'd seen the other position, the enchantingly disenchanted Mittel-European, Jewish perspective in my father's mother's glistening, concealing, laughing, heartbroken, ardent, bitter, bountifully voracious eyes. What could be more poetically inspiring than the jagged multiplicity of Mutti's struggle with life? I can still hear her voice beguiling me to listen to another aria from *Rigoletto*, to absorb the passions in the texture of Van Gogh's paint, to give her a proper, warmly engulfing hug, not some stiff little Unitarian cheek-peck. Her flickering, harrowed look conveyed to us, *This*, my poor child, is what the world looks like. Thank God for love and art!

How deserted she seemed in that brick tower complex between ever-droning spools of roadway in Arlington where my father found an apartment for her after my grandfather died. I remember the dried-blood-shade sameness of the building's façade, covered-up smells in the lobby, plastic flowers the hue of cosmetics on a corpse, the fluorescent elevator like the inside of a too-warm refrigerator. She who loved beauty so fervently she made her long-buried European artistic heroes sing to life for me, even when I could not comprehend the terms of her rhapsody.

Why did she never find a good friend in America? Why did she never feel welcome? How could she complain about anything? The country had saved her and her loved ones. Why did the New World never cease being alien to her? What fault was it of America that this middle-aged woman, who spoke no English whatsoever when she arrived penniless, couldn't make a comfortable home in the country? None. None! But why could she never stop pining for something not there, while disdaining the hidebound rules she collided with everywhere—the suburban supermarkets that wouldn't let one sneak a grandchild a single tiny pink and brown candy from an enormous bin full of them, the lines she couldn't follow, the forms she couldn't complete without leaving gaps or a superabundance of commentary, all the zones of petty officialdom she kept heedlessly trespassing? Why is she always so damn *difficult*! my father would groan after hanging up the phone on her. And then he would scowl and stand at the counter, cutting hard, crumbly chunks of orange Cracker Barrel cheese, biting his tongue and breaking a saltine to wedge it on. When we visited her, my siblings and I felt we were stepping into another world that embarrassed, discomfited, and over-excited us with its emotional blazes, lush colors, and strange sounds—as though, in her presence, we entered a riotous jungle of culture with no compass.

And why was it *that* world which, as I grew older, I wanted to find again, rather than my mother's honest, clear New England commons?

And why now, having found what I've found, is that the world I struggle to transmit to my own children? *That* anachronistic vision of European-Mediterranean culture with its terrible foundations in empire, enslavement, slaughter, and exploitation? Yet surely those foundations were never uniform, any more than were the patterns that the culture manifested in its development through time.

My mind kept drifting back to Freud's effort to conjure for his readers an image of how the mind preserves *in situ* all phases of its evolution through a temporally composite vision of Rome. After devoting several pages to building this picture, he abruptly drops the whole experiment as an "unimaginable fantasy." Had he done so because its irreducible multiplicity undermined the strict clash between love and death drives he'd set out to chart? Not all of the buildings and phases defining Roman history were equally tainted by vicious greed for gold and power. Nor did many of the edifices represent a clear triumph for one or the other of Freud's antipodal instincts. Most represented complex amalgams of Eros and Thanatos. Though Freud pulled back from his diachronically synthesized model of the Eternal City on the grounds that we can't visualize such a montage, of course we frequently produce exactly such overlapping, mutant psychological scenes, coupling disparate epochs of our mental development. Furthermore, many individual buildings in Rome are themselves cultural chimeras, incorporating stones and architectural features from different structures and eras. Becoming aware of this layering is akin to gaining depth perception after confinement within a two-dimensional field. The new breadth transforms one's own place in the scene.

Freud's exercise finished with an effort to picture at the Piazza of the Pantheon not only that edifice bequeathed by Hadrian, but also the original building erected by Agrippa, along with the church of Santa Maria sopra Minerva and the ancient temple over which that was built. A person looking at the site might need only to "change the direction of his glance or his position in order to call up the one view or the other," he mused before abandoning the whole endeavor. But this mental switching of temporal slides is something most of us do naturally, for higher or lower purposes, voluntarily or compulsively, with whatever occupies our fields of vision: children, parents, lovers, landscapes, buildings—our own reflections.

Apropos Putnam and his assertion that our capacity to discern the devils hidden within us compels us to recognize a standard of good, can't we also, to an extent, learn to direct our attention to parts of the interior forum that flock with demons or catch the light? Or, even without imposing that moral glazing, just to pan our mind's eye toward *different* elements of the tableaux, which by virtue of contrast may reanimate our congealing perspectives? Nor is it only features reflecting the latter stages of our development that are invariably the most salient aspects of these hybrid spectacles. When Freud dismissed the doctor who'd challenged his notion of human limitations with the assertion that we're too anchored in our animal natures to become godlike, surely he was failing to fully reckon with the rows of diverse animal divinities studding his own desktop. Those who live in the orbit of animals often speak of their natures and drives as more variegated than the simple dichotomy Freud outlined.

Then again, was Putnam really suggesting anything other than that we focus more energy on our angels and happy sides? The House of Mirth is the House of Fools, says the author of Ecclesiastes, while the House of Mourning is the House of the Wise. For all the poignant self-sacrifice of Putnam's way, there was also something intellectually flimsy, indeed maddeningly Pollyannaish in his tone. "I believe that society really antedates the individual, in a logical sense, and that 'society,' in its turn, is the name for a conception which must be taken in an ideal sense," he reminded Freud in April 1915 while the Great War was raging. "And I regard this opinion not as an idle theory, of no practical bearing, but as extremely practical and I believe that the inferential recognition of it enters into all our thoughts and acts." When he'd written home to his wife in Boston from the Adirondacks during the psychoanalysts' September visit, he informed her, "Dr. Jung is the general favorite, big, nice and jolly . . . The other two are Jewish—one a Hungarian, the other an Austrian—but very intelligent, informal, appreciative. One of them very chatty, the other silent, but all certainly un-American." The two Jews, Ferenczi and Freud, don't get a name; they're sufficiently tagged by ethnicity. They were Jewish *but* very appreciative. The society that antedated their individuality diminished their humanity. No wonder Freud disassociated himself from its united ideal.

Yet all the same Putnam also continually, humbly, deferred to Freud, acknowledging that his entire view of human psychology had been illuminated, if sometimes distressingly, by what he'd learned from Freud, assuring him that any differences they might have would never be such as to prevent them "working side by side, although in most respects it will always be as teacher on your part and learner on mine." Whatever empyreal goals Putnam cherished in the depths of his heart, in treatment these beliefs found expression mostly through his commitment to enacting Freud's own stated position that psychoanalysis should be thought of as a phase of education. Could an educative process concern itself only with origins? Putnam wondered. It's a remarkable proof of the far-reaching significance of human freedom "that we can use it to destroy our freedom," Putnam wrote. This could be observed "in the subtle, instinctive keenness with which the young child, when not sufficiently impelled by his own natural resources and not sufficiently aided by education, instead of taking each stage in his development as a stepping stone to the next, grows old indeed in years, but clings nevertheless, in secret, and without fully realizing the fact, to childish forms of thought and emotion which should have been outgrown." The result, he observed, is an "autistic life," wherein emotions never serve as transitions to anything greater, but assume rather a fixed character "in and for themselves alone."

Questions of how a person could mature—what it means to be an adult in a constructive sense of the word—revolve ceaselessly under his musings. The task for the analyst as educator was not to dictate to patients any particular life goal but to encourage a kind of psychological plasticity. "Each individual must learn to see himself and the physician must learn to see him, as a collection of interwoven forces, all still living and still active," he maintained. Putnam was attempting to prescribe a commitment to the cultivation of dynamically pervious, open-ended identity. Rather than posing the problem of belonging strictly in terms of the individual's desire for acceptance in some larger group, Putnam reversed the challenge, suggesting that to decrease the incidence of narcissism in society it be "brought home" to people in childhood "that they belonged, not to themselves conceived of narrowly (that is, as separate individuals) but only to themselves conceived of broadly as representatives of a series of communities taken in the largest sense." In other words, we don't belong even to our own selves alone as isolate beings.

I thought, in this context, of his family correspondence, filled with observations on nature interspersed with endless meditations on the well-being of loved ones—rippling sleigh rides of recurrent names: Lizzie, Jack, Louisa, Tracy, Fannie, Molly, Marian, Marigold, Heliotrope, Snapdragon—mixed with references to myriad professional obligations among patients to whom he was forever struggling to bring some conclusive solace, notwithstanding the acknowledged limitations of medical science and his own capacities. Certain letters read like poems. "On the train" he jotted above one note to his wife near the time of Freud's visit to America. "Delightful an early morning ride is and it certainly *is* delightful," he began. "On the great sand-plain, at the foot of the moraine, I surprised an immense flock of blackbirds who had been hidden in a lovely field of blushing grey grain, and the effect as they rose, changing and brilliant in the sun, was great. I think I can appreciate both sides of the Louisa-problem better than some people from having noted countless times, how any masterful person—even Fred and often Charley—*whom I adore* affects me. It seems at first, in one's heart-sinking, as if it was necessary to react either by conscious subordination or insubordination. But . . . neither of these methods is the one to follow. It is a great satisfaction to learn on one's own, to admire the powers of others just as if they were one's own, and gradually to enlarge one's own field of accomplishment." The path to self-expansion lay through self-effacing empathy, he resolved.

Just to hear that sweet lyric of the everyday counterpointing his cumbersome aspirations to unveil a salvational vision of the cosmos changes the tenor of both. The individual is "a stupendous antagonism, a dragging together of the poles of the Universe," Emerson wrote. "He betrays his relation to what is below him,—thick-skulled, small-brained, fishy quadrumanous, quadruped, ill-disguised, hardly escaped into biped . . . But the lightning which explodes and fashions planets, maker of planets and suns is in him . . . here they are, side by side, god and devil, mind and matter, king and conspirator, belt and spasm, riding peacefully together in the eye and brain of every man."

Had Freud shut his lids too dogmatically against the heavenly drama in consequence of having been relegated by prejudice to society's lower depths? In our own time of crisis, mightn't Freud's relentlessly backward-focused gaze—wrapped in his collected objects and reminiscences—be construed as culpably stagnant? Was it really possible to argue that his own mythological constructions with regard to points like the origins of religion and the death drive were more rigorously genuine by virtue of being more disheartening? Not to mention which, though his invocations of truth and intellectual honesty were more stirring than Putnam's airy abstractions, we now know that Freud was actively falsifying parts of his patients' case histories throughout his formative period, making up the lives of the vulnerable, projecting onto them his own fantasies when doing so suited his evolving theoretical needs—something which would have been anathema to Putnam. Instead of twisting people's motivations into lurid cul-de-sacs of arrested sexual development, he was forever trying to persuade them to bring down the walls of their own narratives about themselves—to make them as capacious as the Adirondack night on a mountaintop where he could eagerly point out the galaxies with the scuffed tip of his old walking stick.

Was it better, à la Freud, to proclaim the need for honesty and more honesty while distorting people's most intimate fantasies and experiences, or like Putnam to keep asking patients to raise their eyes up and further upward, beyond what they could ever realistically hope to bring into focus? Was it actually true, as Freud claimed, that everyone capable of sublimating their lower instinctual energies into higher goals would do so on their own? Surely some people, given opportunity, might flourish beyond the harsh terms of their circumstances if only they were made aware of other paths, while in the absence of such exterior guidance they must founder.

But what a mistake it would be to attempt to erase Freud because of the numerous compromised passages in his story! When we've purged ourselves of all history's heroes for their gross human flaws, we'll find nothing left to nurture us but the smelly bones littering a reformed cannibal's banquet table. Putnam himself steadfastly reiterated until his very last paper, written the year of his death, that it was Freud's explorations of the unconscious that had opened our view of the mind's topography in ways that showed what a compendium of active, contradictory forces we all are, thereby making both real empathy and self-acceptance possible. Before Freud exposed the hidden feelings that provoke society's designation of a person as "mean," "cowardly," "perverse," and so on, how many people felt themselves "crushed and isolated under such epithets," Putnam wrote. Through psychoanalysis they had "learned to regain their own sense of companionship and self-respect"—refinding the spirited community of their individual selves.

As summer approached, I felt increasingly as if some urgent secret was concealed in the dialogue between these figures. Sometimes I felt the answer so close I had only to look up from my page above our brick-walled garden, past the upper stories of townhouses with their unraveled spiderweb fire escapes and chimney pipes, to glean the solution of what we should do now. I was aware also of the increasingly desperate edge to this search, separated by how few degrees from the decision to dart into one of those modest doorways in which even corporate Midtown still mysteriously abounded, overhung by a sign advertising the full panoply of psychic services: Tarot card readings, palmistry, astrological consultations. All the while I was poring over old papers, I was mentally crying, *Tell me my future!*

Finally, one evening, I did have the fortune cards laid for me, seated across a small table from a brilliantly made-up woman with merry, manic eyes whom I knew socially from her years as a torch singer, but who now, after storms blew adrift her own ship of fortune, had become a psychic to the lost stars of downtown. As she turned over rectangle after colorful rectangle, commenting all the while on the patterns emerging, it came back to me how when people enter into these occult exchanges, what they're often seeking is to *un*learn what they now believe fate holds for them—to discover there's another, very different chapter yet to live than those composing the story they've inhabited thus far. Not so much then to know what fate has in store as to reveal that their own burdened conception of tomorrow is full of hidden cracks in which all manner of scintillating twists lie quietly germinating.

I don't remember many cards she turned over for me, or what she chose to illuminate. I find myself thinking of Death and the Knight, but I see a reversed heart impaled by three swords, a circle floating in the sky with strange runes around its circumference, the Fool stepping toward a precipice in a soigné costume, balancing a long staff tied to a little pack of belongings over his right shoulder and pinching a flower in the fingers of his left hand. *He does not seem troubled by the fact that he cannot tell what lies ahead. New beginnings. Inexperience. Belief in the universe. Leap of faith.* What I recall her repeating, more and more vehemently, as she lay down each new image, was, "No—no, you do have a choice. You have a choice!" I found it hard to meet her shining gaze as she leaned over the table toward me. Hard to speak at all, so intense was her passion to make me see what she saw. The gold-dyed streaks in her waves of hair brought to mind bolts of lightning. Was this how Tyche once appeared to the Greeks?

My son Rafael came home from the park, boisterous and hilarious, with his jostling friends. Luminous technological devices pinwheeling between their hands; fragments of outer space that fragmented the here and now. Their ebullient irreverence in an uneasy compact with idolatrous subservience to the latest phones, apps, and platforms. These were their crystal balls. Yet instead of revealing what was to come, the magic props showed only the ever more inescapable totality of the present, with its endless succession of instantly replaceable superstars. We adults notoriously tried to limit access to these intoxicating objects, like working-class Victorian parents rationing doses of gin for their offspring before lurching around themselves to take a long swig from the bottle. And the young saw the grown-ups' hypocrisy, and felt their own addiction, and could find no exit from the morass of contradictions. They'd been placed in an impossible bind—but one that delivered frequent, tingly bursts of sensation.

The words began echoing inside me once more: *What would his future bring?* But that framing denied the role of our will. This child still lived at home with us; our choices became his own. The responsibility for what happened next to him was still in our hands.

What should we do, then?

8

· The Happiness of Pursuit ·

One

A muscular young man breaks into a party of mostly naked women bathing. He pushes away the ripply red curtain they've hung over a line to hide their ablutions, striding forward into the shallow trickle of water dividing him from their sanctuary: a glade overhung by lush trees and the ruins of some monumental edifice. The momentum of the youth's advance seems too strong to stop, even had he wanted to—and it's just possible that he *would* halt, were it all up to him. He seems utterly stunned by what he's exposed: a handful of glowing, gorgeous women, splayed, lounging, curling, bending. He's a hunter and he's dropped his big bow. His fingers spread wide in amazement. Some of the females are recoiling, concealing parts of their bodies with scraps of material. One hides behinds a tilting pillar with an antlered skull on top. The central figure, the most voluptuous of all, is seated on a block draped with a swath of plush maroon velvet. In her golden hair she wears a crescent ornament that rises like

horns from the strand of pearls threading her tresses. She rears back
from the intruder, legs split, lifting a piece of white fabric over her
upper half while fixing the dazed athlete with a stare of cool murder.
In the midst of so much bright flesh, it may take him a second to
register that she's linked to a second female who crouches just behind
her—a lithe Black woman in a loose, copper-striped robe that scoops
low down her back. This latter woman's right arm stretches over the
crowned woman's head, helping to hold up the material the white
woman is using to veil herself. The Black woman's left arm reaches
far down, fingers clasping the stone block the large woman is planted
on. The arc inscribed by both arms together forms a dark crescent at
the back of the figure on velvet. This anterior figure could be a min-
istering attendant, but it also looks as if she's presenting the white
lady—as if the Black woman were somehow behind the revealing of
the other one's nakedness.

Titian's *Diana and Actaeon* was the painting I kept turning back
to at this time. One of the pictures the artist created for Philip II
in the late 1550s and categorized as "Poesie," concerned prima facie
with the loves and betrayals of the gods, the scene seemed to throb
with issues of our own time: an intrusion of masculine power into a
scene of female vulnerability, violence counterpointed by the spec-
tator's foreknowledge that the balance is on the verge of shifting—
these women will have retribution. The skull on the pillar is a portent
of Actaeon's own death mask. *Now*, the women are being ogled and
psychologically brutalized, but at any second Diana is going to trans-
form Actaeon into a stag, which will lead his dogs to tear him limb
from limb, believing he's the prey they've been hunting for. Titian's
addition of the Black female to the myth made the painting yet
more hauntingly resonant, for the issue of race thus appears to hover

behind everything—framing the rupture of female purity, just as the issue of race haunts the scene of democracy's betrayal at the heart of present-day American politics.

Looked at through this second lens, it would be possible, indeed, to imagine that what the young man has actually revealed is the white woman's reliance on a Black woman's subordination to the process of shaping her own velvet lap of luxury. The disclosure of that dependency engenders her true nakedness. In which case, the young man's real crime is not the exposure of the women's nude bodies, but the tearing away of the curtain from a system of exploitation and subjugation that props up a white coterie's rituals of righteous self-purification.

Regardless, the image lent itself to being considered both as a scene of boundary-breaching masculine aggression, and as the drama of a person catching sight of a concealed structural truth about power, which they now must be punished for having uncovered.

Ovid himself thought of the story in this latter sense and felt its cruel tragedy to be a parable for his own banishment by Augustus in 8 A.D., an event set in motion partly in consequence of his having glimpsed something he shouldn't have behind the imperial curtain. In his account of Actaeon's story, Ovid describes the hunter "wandering with unsure footsteps" in pursuit of his quarry, then happening to burst into Diana's grove coincidentally, at the whim of fate. In his later work, *Tristia*, written from his Black Sea exile, he lamented, "Why did I see anything? Why did I make my eyes guilty? . . . Unwitting was Actaeon when he beheld Diana unclothed; none the less he became the prey of his own hounds. Clearly, among the gods, even ill fortune must be atoned for, nor is mischance an excuse when a deity is wronged."

How often since the election had it seemed that we'd stumbled into an obscene revelation about the truth of America, and that the price for this vision was a kind of psychological exile.

I remembered, some years earlier, going to see this painting with our son Rafael when it went on exhibit in London at the National Gallery, having been transported there from Edinburgh to celebrate the event of its purchase for the British nation from the Duke of Southerland when the period of the family's loan of the picture expired—a late-hour rescue after the threat of its being procured by a private collector became acute.

I imagined standing again before the large canvas now after the election, taking our son's hand once more and beginning to guide him through the maze of its references, the trails of glimmering suggestions that might help us reflect on our own quandary. "What comes to mind when you look at this scene?" I might ask him. "Why does the drama feel so momentous? What variations of exposure, searching, and vengeance are on display here?" I would say. All those stolen glimpses and accusing stares, the gawking, surveilling, and shaming—which of course we as spectators participate in.

I'd retell him the basic myth from Ovid in which Actaeon, grandson of Cadmus, founder of Thebes, wanders while hunting into the most secret grotto of Gargaphie, where the goddess Diana is bathing, humiliating and outraging her. "Red as the clouds which flush beneath the sun's rays were the cheeks of Diana as she stood there in view without her robes," Ovid writes. "Then she cast back her gaze; took up the water and flung it into the young man's face," speaking the words that foretold his doom as she did so: "Now you are free to tell how you saw me all unrobed—if you can tell."

At different points in our tour of the painting, I'd seek to somehow ask my son what he thought it signified for a scene of unforgivable transgression and impending bloodshed to be made sublimely beautiful. Could the chromatics of feeling articulate their own truth? Would that then still be tragedy? Was it possible there were forbidden scenes we ourselves might witness at the price of our ability to communicate what we saw? He'd been so well instructed in his little Brooklyn public school about the wretched effects of ethnic bias and social injustice in general—any inkling of the abuse of power by some privileged jerk struck him and his peers like a mallet to the kneecap that made the leg kick straight forward. Yet nothing they learned had any context, so once reflex slackened, all the discrimination they heard about swam together in a great murky palette of homologous, symptomatic iniquity, depleting their own ideational diversity, while the disease itself ran on unchecked beneath the surface.

I imagined now trying gently to draw out the thoughts conjured by the picture through a process on the border between poetry and analysis, leading him eventually to the question of how plunging into a work of such profundity might change our view of our own positions in the canvas of history and mythology.

Then I'd pull back the veil a little further and tell him that actually there was a whole other way of understanding this painting than those we'd explored thus far: a path into meaning that could be discerned solely through excavation of the choices Titian had made when staging the myth of Diana and Actaeon, especially the discrepancies between his vision and the story as recounted in the *Metamorphoses*. This alternative perspective didn't cancel the insights we'd been discussing until now, I'd stress, but gave them another layering, which could deepen certain tints and dimensions in our contemporary view, just as current events informing our own vantage point echo backward through time.

In introducing the idea that Titian's iconography reveals how he was actually drawing on multiple texts, classical and Renaissance, I would try to keep my son's gaze from drifting while talking a little about lineages of scholarship, which resemble older lines of theological disciplehood and illustrate how profane knowledge can sometimes acquire its own sacral quality through the process of transmission. For this work, it would be pertinent to learn the names of Erwin Panofsky and his pupil Marie Tanner, though it would be helpful also to know something about Aby Warburg, the art-theorist scion of a Jewish banking family based in Hamburg, who'd been Panofsky's own inspiration, and who before his death in 1929 had become recognized within the larger field of cultural history as a persuasive proponent of the principle *"Der liebe Gott stect im Detail"*—God dwells in the detail. The juxtaposition of his own diminutive physical stature and dark, melancholic eyes with his aura of personal magnitude might have struck intimates as illustrating the justice of this sentiment. All Warburg's searches through the minutiae of images and texts were aimed ultimately at celestial objectives: the delineation of what he called "a space for reflection" that would countervail our enslavement to the instincts that drive us to literalize our passions, turning terror and greed into blind physical action.

Some of Warburg's most important work involved tracing the genealogy of Renaissance figures and symbols back to their pre-Christian antecedents, a process that frequently demanded passages through the iconology of astrology, where he found a wealth of visual material for studying the principles of polarity and balance on which he felt the preservation of civilization depended. (Thus, for instance, the planet Mercury was neither good nor evil on its own but took the slant of its character at any given point in time from its shifting place in the zodiacal diagram of the heavens.)

The cosmically impelled motion of astrological figures through space resembled the inevitable periodic changes in place and context affecting individuals and nations, Warburg believed—a consideration that he hoped might temper the allure of ideological extremism. How could one project a fixed character onto anything when one observed the radical fluctuations of the heavens? As E. H. Gombrich, one of the scholars who grew up in his shadow, noted, Warburg was concerned with rescuing such conceits as the horoscope from their superstitious instrumentation as crude "hieroglyphs for prediction" and positioning them instead as psychological "aids to orientation" correlative with the arts of compromise that helped set in motion the greatest eras of civilization. In part, these diplomatic attitudes entailed simply refusing to lose sight of how there was always another angle of perspective to discover, so that neither the ideal nor the abysmal could be justly expunged from one's vision. Writing to a friend about the trouble he'd had with *L'innocente*, a modernist novel by Gabriele D'Annunzio, Warburg used words reminiscent of Putnam's to Freud: "I don't permit anyone to drag me through an *Inferno* whom I do not also believe capable of leading me across the *Purgatorio* to the *Paradiso* . . . I do not demand a *Paradiso* where everyone sings psalms in white robes and without genitals, and where the dear lambkins stroll about with the good yellow lions without fleshly desires—but I despise the man who loses sight of the ideal *homo victor.*"

In certain art works and linguistic conventions, Warburg believed, one could see embodied the benign interpenetration of competing systems of belief, such as Christianity and paganism, which suggested a way out of humanity's hopeless antagonisms, past and present. For the destructive irrationalism of a superstitious mentality was only the obverse face of the glossy, positivistic, contemporary mindset that claimed to render irrelevant all prior forms of being. The appropriate attitude before so-called primitive peoples and their ritualized approaches to humanity's abiding questions was intellectual humility, Warburg indicated, an example of which in his own character, adduced by Gombrich, were the words Warburg scrawled across the manuscript of a paper he'd composed on the serpent dances of the Pueblo peoples he'd once visited in New Mexico. "I do not want even the slightest trace of blasphemous science-mongering," Warburg wrote there. The anthropological interpretations he'd ventured were "intended as a help for those who come after me, in their attempt to achieve clarity and thus to overcome the tragic tension between instinctive magic and discursive logic. They are the confessions of an (incurable) schizoid, deposited in the archives of mental healers."

Though Warburg believed wholeheartedly in the ideal of progress, and the principle that civilization's survival relied on the methodical accretion of knowledge in all fields, including those concerned with the physical and material worlds, he was discomposed by the advent of the machine age, which he saw epitomized in the United States. Those who embraced the prospect of a mechanical deliverance from humanity's afflictions seemed especially prone to assume that the latest prosthetic enhancements of nature heralded a permanent transcendence of our unreasonable passions. Whereas in fact, he'd concluded by 1918, "Athens has constantly to be won back again from Alexandria."

Of equal importance, over-attachment to technologies appeared to him to corrode the mythopoetic forms of thought that spiritualized humanity's relation to the environment, and hence themselves represented features of progress. On his trip to the western United States, Warburg described capturing with his camera "the goldseeking intruder into the land of the Indians": Uncle Sam with a top hat above which stretched an electric wire that replaced the serpents of the Pueblo dances—themselves organic figurations of aerial lightning. The modern American had done away with pagan deities in the name of "infinite waves obeying the pressure of the human hand," but this did not mark an unqualified positive development. Instead

of worshipping the snake, "he kills and exterminates it." Men like
Edison, with their inventions promising "the instantaneous connection of electricity," threatened to "lead the globe back into chaos,"
Warburg contended. With their mechanical annihilation of distance, they destroyed what "science, emerging from myth, had pain-
fully conquered, the zone of contemplation that became the zone of
reasoning." The breathless speed of the telephone, the wireless, and
other forms of electrotechnical communication were promoting a
purely reactive society, in which reflection might eventually prove
impossible, opening the floodgates to new forms of barbarism. At
the end of his life, Warburg remarked that "the conscious creation
of distance between the self and the external world may be called the
fundamental act of civilization."

Panofsky, the German-Jewish art historian who'd taken Warburg
as his mentor and was seen by many as inheriting his intellectual
mantle, first came to America to teach at New York University from
his post at Hamburg in 1931, the year Freud changed the ending of
Civilization and Its Discontents by inserting a question after what had
been its last sentence. In 1929, the essay had closed on what was for
him an uncharacteristically sanguine note: The current atmosphere
of unrest resulted from people's knowledge that the forces of nature
had been mastered to such an extent that humanity would have no
trouble "exterminating one another to the last man," Freud wrote,
but we might anticipate that this awareness would act as a deterrent.
"Now it is to be expected that the other of the two 'Heavenly Powers,' eternal Eros, will make an effort to assert himself in the struggle
with his equally immortal adversary," he declared in the final line of
his original composition that summer in Berchtesgaden.

It seems an odd lapse from his habitual thought patterns for

Freud to have supposed that factual information about the risks of a given behavior would dissuade people from indulging in it. However, he'd been influenced in relaxing his pessimistic guard not only by the surmise that knowledge of their ability to eradicate the species would motivate his contemporaries to put aside their hostilities and forge new alliances, but also by the fact that, for the most part, the economic picture in the German-speaking world had improved over the past five years. With this relative prosperity, enthusiasm for National Socialism and other radical movements had subsided. So, despite his aversion to such prognostication, Freud felt moved to predict that "immortal Thanatos," which had held sway in world events since the start of the Great War, would now confront the erotic counter-force that just might prove a match for it.

Three months later the American stock market crashed, precipitating a financial crisis across Europe. This new tribulation, along with other developments, some foreseeable, others surprising, led to a remarkable surge in the Nazis' fortunes. In the election of September 1930, the party's share of power in the Reichstag rose from 12 to 107 seats. After years in which the tide had been turning mostly away from Hitler, now it rushed dramatically back again—another reminder that once such forces have been let so wantonly out of the bottle, their effects will play out for many years, notwithstanding interludes when the agents of darkness may appear comically enfeebled. In 1931, Freud felt compelled to reenter his essay and erase its hint of oracular confidence by tacking a question onto the end: "But who can foresee with what success and with what result?" The possibility of civilization's recovery was not altogether negated, but any hope of knowing beforehand what form this amelioration might take was gone.

When Panofsky went to New York that same year, he still

thought he'd be able to divide his time teaching between Europe and America. In 1933 he was dismissed from the faculty at Hamburg for the crime of his genetic origins and took up residence instead between New York University and Princeton, where he would impress peers with his relentless commitment to searching for meaning *everywhere* in approaching the interpretation of paintings, a quest that drove him to hunt especially, colleagues observed, in the most unexpected places—marginal visual features, hidden historical circumstances, riddles and disguised allusions—sites paralleling the shadow realms of psychology that Freud had devoted himself to on the premise that these held the key to the true self.

This shift of attention to the edges and underside was emblematic of a broader intellectual reorientation. After Warburg's death, his muse Gertrud Bing wrote of how he "hung on to the whole inchoate and untrammeled mess of everyday life, which other people try to dispose of—circulars, invitations, receipts, account books, requests for favors, complaints, all mixed up together." The wheat could not be separated from the chaff here, Bing said, for as she sifted through his estate, she discovered repeatedly how "the most trivial-seeming material gave rise to unexpected revelations about connected thoughts or concrete situations." Walter Benjamin, for his part, examining Baudelaire's creative method later in the 1930s, invoked the image of the ragpicker: "Everything that the big city has thrown away, everything it has lost, everything it has scorned, everything it has crushed underfoot he catalogues and collects. He collates the annals of intemperance, the capharnaum of waste . . . Ragpicker and poet: both are concerned with refuse."

These various thinkers, active in the morning period of our last century's cataclysms, each sensed that something crucial had been missed in society's optimistic, headlong rush into modernity—something that now needed to be urgently engaged with, which had been junked or ignored since it did not fit into the new order of utilitarian normalcy. A former student of Panofsky's remembered him reeling off a list of flamboyantly obscure textual references: "Who has read *Hisperica famina*?" "Do you understand the significance of Virgilius Maro Grammaticus?" When the class shook their heads, Panofsky admonished them: "You have yet to discover the value of useless knowledge."

This recalibration of significance did not imply nostalgically cringing away from novel forms of expression and changing lifestyles, but instead striving to graph their relationship to humanity's abiding concerns. So Warburg sought to understand how imagery in contemporary advertising both resurrected and vitiated figures from antiquity, such as an iconic female figure striding forward in rippling garments, whom he saw as the bringer of life and movement into otherwise staid tableaux: Judith carrying "with a gay step the head of the murdered commander," a seraph flying with good tidings to the placid Madonna—now visible in a nymph-ish "travelling-girl," luring the middle class off on prodigal vacations from a poster for the Hamburg-America Line. Benjamin liked to cite a Brechtian maxim: "Do not build on the good old days, but on the bad new ones."

Titian was Panofsky's ideal among the Old Masters. "No other great artist appropriated so much" or showed himself so "pliable while remaining so utterly himself," Panofsky wrote. Introducing the challenge of deciphering his art, Panofsky cited a legend from the life of Saint Augustine. One day while meditating on the Trinity, Augustine sought to clear his mind by taking a walk beside the sea. As he strolled along the shore, he came upon a young boy assiduously bailing out water from the waves with a scallop shell, then pouring the water down again on the sands. When Augustine questioned the child as to what he was doing, the boy answered that he was emptying the ocean. It struck the saint then that any human being seeking to penetrate the enigma of the Trinity was acting just as this boy was doing. So it was also for the historian attempting to interpret Titian's work, Panofsky asserted, which was why, instead of grabbing at the waves, he focused on collecting what the tide had left behind on the beach: "quaintly shaped pebbles, sea urchins, conches, and starfish."

I longed to find the words to tell my son why it seemed to me ever more the case that this kind of quest to discover new depths of significance in the overlooked details—the insistence on the presence of an inexhaustible multi-dimensionality to the productions of culture, psychology, and the natural world alike—itself constituted a form of political resistance. The perspective raised the possibility that the two ways of viewing the world I'd seen embodied in my mother and Mutti were not, after all, mutually exclusive. Perhaps it's true that the world we stare out at now is indeed the whole truth, but we don't absorb that world at a glance. If we look harder, more actively and receptively, we may watch the picture grow richly imbricated. This *is* the world, but it transforms under our concerted attention. Suppose that the domain of the city of Utopia "is not a 'something' that is 'outside' (i.e. beyond the world of sense), but is, as it says, 'no place,' which perhaps suggests no place *else,* but this place transfigured," Stanley Cavell wrote.

Yet so often the words I found to actually say to my son took the form of admonitions that sounded, even in my own ears, at once pallid and frantic. *We must not allow ourselves to be contained by our technologies. We must refuse to be summarized or shepherded by algorithms to advance someone else's commercial or political strategy!* "Until

I am dead, no one can ever be guaranteed to truly know me," declared the revolutionary director Pasolini. "For as long as we are alive, we lack meaning, and the language of our life . . . is untranslatable, a chaos of possibilities, an uninterrupted search for relations and meanings." It was this same spirit that inspired him to stridently identify with every type of "banned humanity"—with Blacks, Jews, Gypsies and the ragazzi of the streets against the claustrophobic consumer society he saw engulfing reality. You see, Rafael, the infinitude of the individual must be cherished or the collective will—your own nature I mean, the full— and then . . . ! I heard the words leave my lips and watched them shatter on the shoals of the virtual—felt him thinking, *but* this *is the world you've placed me in. What choice do I have but to make some kind of peace with its terms, pre-programmed and otherwise?*

I'd sat beside him recently while he played Spider-Man on a PlayStation at a friend's house, watching him fly from skyscraper to skyscraper on silken cords spun from his palms above the grid of a meticulously reconstituted Gotham. Every façade, every block, every neighborhood, evoked sites imprinted on my memory from countless hours spent plodding back and forth between them. Now he streaked and twirled like a twenty-first-century Ariel above the furiously jammed traffic and self-enclosed, trudging pedestrians— scaling buildings in seconds, leaping across wide avenues. All his feats achieved with a few rapid-fire marionette flicks of his fingers while carnage, smoke, and horror reigned on the streets. It all made sense. *It was all true.* This *was* the city today. Only the Spider-Men we looked up to were plutocrats who, instead of fighting crime, were the perpetrators, their gravity-free carte blanche the politically depleting fantasy of millions of exhausted workers who commuted daily over the tangled, prostrate bodies of those already defeated at some primary

level of competition. The longer I watched him play, the more I realized I was looking in a mirror of my own New York history. Hadn't
I struggled along every one of these glaring, blaring, blasted streets?
Dodging killer trucks and blithe sociopaths; supporting wasted, hurt,
and sick friends; trapped in crowds trying to escape the dark tunnel,
staggering under my own bags and illnesses; creeping over broken
glass between the murderers and martyrs? I remember that shattered
storefront. The shiny big box outlet mobbed by faceless shoppers
turning round and round in inexplicable circles. Those hard-jawed
black-suited businessmen with the big shiny watches—I'd stepped
into elevators with them, allowed myself to be backed into corners
while they folded beefy hands and locked briefcases over manically
ironed crotches. That shriveled cardboard-boxed couple with knees
up and backs against a wall, staring vacantly at passersby while stroking their sad hound—I'd pushed my loose bills into that very Big
Gulp cup. Those smoldering trashcans. That strutting sunglassed
supermodel tossing her glittery locks back while a photographer con-
torted all sides of her as though he were being electrocuted. The rat
with the long filthy tail making a dash for the sewer grate—I knew it!
The endless blinking, pounding limousine with limber girls and boys
waving their fists out the sunroof and shrieking. The gold chains in
the windows, the gold chains twinkling on the pumped chests of the
gym-droids, the gold chains strangling the ostrich necks of trustees
teetering out of gold taxis for the last Age of Midas Gala. The fire
bursting in glissando sequences along row after row of converted
warehouse windowpanes. I knew every stone in the game!

I opened my palms to the cracks of sky between scrapers, waiting
to see the plumes of silk spuming up from my flesh high into the dark
air, latching onto silhouetted water towers—releasing me at last, at

last, from the cruel New York asphalt, but the lines on my hands merely multiplied and crisscrossed, wrapping my own body in time. How many of these stones were stained with the blood of those I loved or whom I should never have allowed to remain strangers.

How could my son *not* want to spend his hours sailing in a terpsichorean sublime high above these endless, high-res incarnations of all the blurry urban realities I'd pulled myself through my whole adult life like a trampled snake who'd swallowed half the detritus of the twentieth century and now, stuffed and lost, was trying to slither off to some prelapsarian garden boasting lots of fresh fruit trees?

He was beaming, the white crescent controller waxing and sliding from view between his shifting hands, like moon phases in fast motion. Why would anyone ever want to leave this New York, not New York—the doppelgänger Big Apple of all access, and no insides? Caught in our endless interior showdowns, we'd ceded the real outdoors to the archons of a fantasy nightmare. Now the whole city lay snarled in the web of its own squandered superpowers.

How close the woebegone adults in Rafael's orbit were these days to simply crying, "Abandon all hope ye who enter here!" Wasn't that bound to provoke the craving for a converse invitation: "Welcome to the Party"—like the song by the young, gravel-voiced rapper Pop Smoke that blew up on YouTube before he got arrested for stealing the Rolls Royce Wraith that'd been lent him as a prop for his music video—before he got shot to death in another heinous gun crime? How could we salvage some vestige of the older categories of wisdom on which the transmission of civilization might still depend at a moment when it was clear the actions and failures to act of my generation might have ushered in the extinction of life on the planet?

———

I remembered being at a party in a tall, gray, unheated London house that had been broken up into a nocturnal labyrinth of flats inhabited mostly by older artists—a huge party with scores of voices echoing off the walls and high ceilings of its many rooms. Paintings, drawings, and sculptures smoldered and flared in the shadows, glimpsed in flashes between wan bodies in black clothes with opulent flourishes. This same party, I was told, had been happening in this house for decades. Exactly the same party, the same people, the same night, the same rain. *It's a Skeleton Ball*, someone said, grinning, *even if a number of us ghouls have gotten rather fat*. As the night wore on, the voices became hollower and hollower as they ricocheted off the stones until they sounded like clapping bones.

At some late hour I found myself in conversation with a petite male artist in his sixties with a knobbly flame-red, fine-featured face and brilliant blue eyes. We'd slipped into the subject of impending doom, talking over the latest headlines about the acceleration of climate change. After we'd exchanged some banal despondencies, he told me that in fact he did not feel altogether demoralized. He taught part of each year in Norway and the young people there *did* give some cause for hope, he said, adding that he wasn't talking about the eighteen- and nineteen-year-olds. No, he meant the thirteen- and fourteen-year-olds. The really young ones. "Because," he went on, and held up his right index finger, as if he were checking the wind direction, then extended his arm and panned it out in front of him in a wide arc. "They see in 365 degrees. They see what's *happening*. Where they live, they actually watch the ice caps melting. They see, and these kids—they're not going to relent." He paused a moment, then abruptly resumed in a steady, cool voice, his turquoise eyes boring into me. "You know, I have a whole theory about Moses and the Israelites—the whole wandering for forty years in the wilderness business. Egypt and Canaan, they're not so far apart, right? Forty years? *How* could they have taken so long? But you remember the story? How they'd barely crossed the Red Sea when the Israelites all began whining about how they wanted to go back to the fleshpots and be slaves under Pharaoh because the hardships of the journey were too exhausting. I think at that point Moses said to himself, 'Right, this lot—this generation—they're not able to get it. They're never going to be ready for freedom.' So what does he do?" My interlocutor stuck his index finger out again, this time pointing straight in front of him. "Moses says, 'Okay, my brethren, Canaan's over this way.'" Then the man swerved his finger around and aimed it another direction. "'Oh wait, I meant it's over here.'" Now the man swept his hand completely behind him. "'Sorry, over this way!' You see what I'm saying? . . . Moses *purposefully* kept the Israelites wandering around in circles for forty years so the older generation would all die off before they actually got there. So only the children would cross over to the Promised Land. Sometimes you need a fresh set of eyes."

If the events of recent years have demolished a certain picture of the world, the reverse move, trying simply to reassemble those pieces as they once were, goes nowhere. Perhaps we must give another hammer blow—this one against the particular fracture lines and disfigurations we've been left with by the solipsistic master vandal-predators. Perhaps we must sweep the last shards into a box that we can sift through in stray hours and look up from to the view that's opened in the space where they once hung. When the Twin Towers fell, the little balcony attached to my apartment on Lower Broadway looked down into a smoking void, but as the clouds from the chasm were torn away by the wind, I suddenly saw, through the space where those steely twin rectilinear phalli had thrust at the sky, glimpses of the mottled river flowing onward without emptying.

If the instantaneous triteness of our diagnoses of this crisis functions as a preemptive neutralization of critique, this does not detract from the sheen of green feathers on the wings of a parakeet that's landed atop one of the spindly, bare branches rising off the tree outside my window—daubing the billowing gray sky behind, like a jewel slipped by an unknown fugitive into a bundle of old sheets.

"We are all businessmen and women, whether you see it that way yet or not," Trump wrote in *Think Like a Champion*. "If you like art and can't make money at it, you eventually realize that everything is business, even your art." Wasn't this the reigning dogma of the hour? The notion that there's nothing behind the curtain but monetizable ciphers? Everything we see is just a palimpsest of perpetually scrolling price tags and global popularity rankings in the marketplace of ideas, products, resources, elections, faiths, realities. The perspective that would strip-mine our vision of all traces of an incalculable world structured like a language below the surface—in other words, the womb of the future.

Andre Breton, lecturing in 1935 on the Surrealist object, quoted Rimbaud's dictate: "I say that we must be *seers*, make ourselves seers." Dali, he said, had managed to attain this state through a process of "paranoiac-critical activity," which he'd been exploring together with Lacan since 1930. For Dali, the paranoiac mentality, unlike true psychosis, was "pseudo-hallucinatory" and enabled the person inhabiting its vivid contours to obtain "a double image"—the figuratively exact representation of two utterly distinct entities simultaneously at a single site. Dali was not using the notion of paranoia in a clinical sense, but rather concerning himself with the active systemization of confusion which would "discredit completely the world of reality." This was, Breton continued, a kindred process to the one Max Ernst had developed with his absurd juxtapositions of prosaic, ready-made realities, such as the umbrella and the sewing machine. These conjunctions, Ernst believed, permitted objects to escape their naïve purposes and pass "from absolute falseness to a new absolute that is both true and poetic: the umbrella and the sewing machine will make love."

Such experiments, paralleling Breton's own investigation of the "waking dream," could revolutionize our perspectives, he felt, in part because they disallowed the possibility of determining in advance what their outcome would be. To know where we were going was to know only the multiplication ad infinitum of narcissistic human folly. In a treatise entitled "A Short Prophetic Interlude," he announced that acrobats would soon arrive, "in tights spangled with an unknown color, the only color to date which absorbs both sunlight and moonlight at the same time. The color will be called freedom." For himself now, Breton wrote, he felt obliged "to take a public stand against every kind of conformism," including Surrealist conformism. The road for today was "obviously not the one with guard rails along its edge."

Contemplating the darkening political picture of Europe in the second half of the 1930s, Breton speculated on what might be entailed in deconstructing our unconscionably self-possessed positivism, which seemed to him a psychological engine behind both the capitalist and the fascist projects. His thoughts turned repeatedly to Freud, the seminal figure behind Surrealism's founding. Above all, Breton venerated Freud for having elevated dreams on a par with other psychic activities, rather than leaving them, like the night, "a mere parenthesis." He'd shown the necessity of reckoning with elements of the dream that sank back below consciousness once sunlight returned—everything that had been forgotten about one's activities from the previous day, "dark foliage, stupid branches. In 'reality,' likewise, I prefer to *fall*," Breton wrote, noting that he longed "to sleep, in order to surrender myself to the dreamers, the way I surrender myself to those who read me with eyes wide open." At this juncture, what he most wished to register was the "*hate of the marvelous* which rages in certain men."

Isn't it vital, we might ask ourselves now, to learn to fall before we find ourselves shoved yet deeper into the dirt? To see the roots and particles of earth, then revolve our faces back to the sky—to reach for the strained limbs of whatever nature is left us? And if we see a tall-hatted wolf playing piano in a cloud, why shouldn't we listen? Rather than debating whether the demagogic energies we see roiling about us do or do not constitute fascism, let's make ourselves into antitypes of Chamberlain emerging from his aeroplane on September 30, 1938, and announce, without palliatives, *This is "Fascism for Our Times." Now what shall we do about it?*

Notwithstanding their eventual alignment with the Communist movement, the Surrealists were among the first to recognize that conventional leftist ideology, with its strict focus on material equality and a just organization of the relations between labor, production, and ownership, was failing to reckon with fascism's appeal.

In 1933, Pierre Yoyotte, one of the early Black Surrealists, a mysterious figure with a tangential connection to a Dalinian faction of the movement in Paris, challenged the conventional view of Hitler and Mussolini's popularity. He argued that at a certain level of poverty, "one not easy to define," but in which people's basic physical needs were provided for, "the *misery of desire*" became more significant than economic hardship.

I salute that phrase. It crystallizes the challenge and possibility for progressive politics in our own time. No less urgent than the obligation to address society's calamitous economic disparities is the imperative of grappling with the misery of desire gnawing at today's "general public." It was Hitler and Mussolini's understanding of this principle that enabled them to orchestrate a potent counterrevolution against the working class's hunger for economic relief, Yoyotte stated, adding that "emotions survive on masks not realities." Thus the fascist leaders had developed a mesmerizing iconography of gestures, rituals, and symbolic objects that induced amnesia about the "money battles," while supplying mystical gratification. "Their infantile victories over the primary desires endow them ... with the appearance of a paradise."

Neither Hitler nor Mussolini had given much to their followers in terms of material satisfaction, Yoyotte continued, but this was exactly the point. "Capitalist inequality is in reality not the enemy of the hysterical exaltation of the hordes in black and brown shirts." Rather, theirs was an "essentially emotional and ideational revolution," he observed. "The great discovery and the essential originality of fascism is its utilization of the *irrational* as autonomous and important factors in the political domain."

Yoyotte charged the authors of communist propaganda with having disastrously neglected these truths. They had been "officially (and obtusely) suspicious of the discoveries of psychoanalysis that would have helped them fight knowledgeably against the irrational processes of family, religion, fatherland, etc." In contrast to their self-consciously righteous efforts, he lauded the young Dadaists and early Surrealists who, in the immediate aftermath of the First World War, had come together to begin systematizing what he called "the poetic tradition of revolt." Descendants of a few rebels from the previous century who'd "objected to the monstrous invasion of money," they dedicated themselves "to the defense of desire, to individual inspiration, to solutions that were diametrically opposed to the Mussolinian or racist militarization of their time."

Much of the poverty in the United States and Europe around 2016 manifested at the level Yoyotte identified as especially politically vulnerable—people fed enough to feel full, howsoever poorly (*fed up*); living with some kind of roof over their head, howsoever lowly; provided with endless cake on demand in the form of blood-and-sex-frosted entertainment, even if none of that online cake-content could actually be eaten. What dreams would be nourished in such circumstances? The most accessible consumables merely exacerbated the misery of desire that millions of individuals in these advanced, wealthy societies had been consigned to.

It wasn't that Yoyotte downplayed the urgency of economic revolution. To the contrary, he saw the development of a rational strategy for bringing economic justice to the people as essential, but felt it could only be delivered through a politics that responded to mass unhappiness with a poetically liberating vision. We would do well to ponder his judgment. *Our enlightenment project needs a romantic vehicle.* The left must conjure its own galvanic, metamorphic hope to compete with the ecstatic absolution from restraints of conscience proffered by the champions of "racist militarization."

To resist the bigoted, kleptocratic strongman insurgencies of this moment, we must study the material grammar of contemporary right-wing spectacle. We should learn the forms and etymologies of their bodily motions, facial expressions, sacred relics (MAGA hats, soldier statuettes, background family photos), postures at the podium, color choices in costuming (those fire-red ties), the formal backdrops to speeches, cosmetics, vocal cadences, graphics, event soundtracks—all the while thinking about how to design our own radical arsenal of choreographies and artifacts. The elements of pomp and revelry at an aspirational demagogue's rally have been shaped to manipulate no less carefully than were the props, music, and lighting accompanying a Hitler speech—even if the vocabulary targeting a present-day America First crowd is very different from that employed for a German audience in the 1930s. Stern, unanimous, martial discipline has been replaced by unbuttoned, rollicking, ritually mocking entertainment, but it too serves to reinforce a sense of simultaneously omnipotent and omni-threatened group identity. Re-invoking Lacan, the repetition of the past is not a reproduction. The left can't pretend to hold itself above the unconscious passions, nor is emotional denunciation or lamentation sufficient. There must be, as Putnam argued, some opalescent glimmer of the sublime to aspire to, for "The people who do not see visions will perish from the face of the earth."

In developing a lexicon to oppose that of contemporary

fascism—one that swerves the public gaze away from desolation, fury, and terror toward the prospect of desirable action—we should look everywhere, pursuing stories from history, art, headlines, conversation, and our everyday passage through the world for evidence of gestures that might nurture ideals of justice, compassion, and creative joy: The image of St. Francis stripping off his clothes in the main plaza of Assisi as he renounces his paternal inheritance; images throughout history of the armed maiden lifting on high the sword, lance, or torch of justice to inspire courageous solidarity among confused populations confronting a grave test. Abbie Hoffman and a band of free spirits hurling dollar bills from the visitor's gallery in the New York Stock Exchange onto the brokers below while yelling, "Take the money! Here's the real shit!", creating pandemonium— actually halting all trading (an action Hoffman himself called the "TV-age version of driving the money-changers from the Temple. The symbols, the spirit, and the lesson were identical"). The iconic pink hats of the 2017 Women's March. Buddhist monks immolating themselves during the Vietnam War. Willy Brandt dropping down onto his knees before the memorial to the Warsaw Ghetto uprising. The raised fists of two African American athletes at the 1968 Olympics, giving the Black Power salute during the playing of "The Star-Spangled Banner." Contemporary NFL players taking a knee during the playing of the national anthem to protest police brutality. Shock moves, such as that described in a legend from China's Yunnan province, which recounts how when a woman on either side of a tribal conflict raised her skirts and demanded an armistice, peace had to be declared. Or ACT UP's fitting of a giant condom over a reactionary senator's house to protect the community from his deadly politics. Projects of aesthetic resistance, such as the Soviet "paper architects" who made up blueprints for buildings they knew could never be built under the existing political system, but were meticulously envisioned nonetheless as gestures of pure, utopian protest.

Another Titian painting in London suggests the paradigm for an iconography of communicable liberation: *Bacchus and Ariadne* painted in the early 1520s, when the artist was a young man.

In this work, Ariadne twists toward the sea, gesturing with her spread hand toward the ship on which Theseus, the lover who has betrayed her, recedes toward the horizon. Bacchus, trying to break her backward stare—the nostalgic gaze we are all tempted at times to indulge in—leaps from the chariot. Holding her eyes with his, but revolving his torso in a sweeping contrapposto, he seeks to physically wrest her attention away from the vanished lover toward the wild, dancing abandon of his followers and ultimately the coronet of stars high above in the heavens that symbolizes the union of faithful love he now promises her—a constellation presaging her own apotheosis.

On the simplest level, it's an image of someone offering a new passion to a person who has lost an old love—striving to prefigure in his own body the act of ocular transference whereby she revolves her eyes away from the space of absence to the surrounding world and sky that may be hers for the beholding, through the poetry of Eros.

At a moment when every reasonable view of our situation feels devastatingly inadequate, and we feel condemned to tragedy, we must discover ways to cultivate a revolutionary imagination in ourselves and the young. How was that process undertaken in the past?

As Walter Benjamin surveyed the Surrealists' achievements in 1929, ten years after the birth of its outlook in Dadaism, he was untroubled by knowledge of the artists' eventual wrong turns and excesses. The form a movement evolves into does not invariably expose the corruption of its original conceit, any more than an idea that begins in depravity is invariably condemned to continue replicating its original errors as it refracts forward through time. Although by this point he felt that Surrealism had reached a pass when it must either collapse in a prosaic "struggle for power and domination, or decay . . . and be transformed," this did not decrease the significance of what it had been "when it broke over its founders as an inspiring dream wave." In those days, life had only seemed worthwhile "where the threshold between waking and sleeping was worn away in everyone as by the steps of multitudinous images flooding back and forth." It was in this period that Breton celebrated the story of Saint-Pol Roux retiring to bed around dawn after fixing a notice to his door: "Poet at work." A sign to which Breton appended the request, "Quietly, I want to pass where no one yet has passed, quietly!—After you, dearest language."

And what does it mean today that we fetishize the notion of a city that never sleeps? Is this to champion a city that never dreams? A city in which language never takes precedence?

Breton was the first to recognize the "revolutionary energies that appear in the 'outmoded,'" Benjamin reported. In the wake of the obliteration of civilization's self-image occasioned by the Great War and subsequent waves of economic havoc, he'd turned away from the vogue: giddy idols of novelty, new gospels concocted to glorify rapacious growth. Instead, he'd begun exploring early factory buildings, pioneering photographs, and objects that had "begun to be extinct"—grand pianos, out-of-date dresses, formerly fashionable restaurants. Such remnants were like embryos awaiting an attentional incubation through which the historical could be changed into the political, Benjamin commented. The Surrealists had understood how sites of destitution, social and architectural, "the poverty of interiors, enslaved and enslaving objects" might be "suddenly transformed into revolutionary nihilism."

These reflections were shadowed by Benjamin's own crypto-religious, revolutionary imagination. For, as he wrote elsewhere, there's a form of "worldly restitution" predicated on "the eternity of downfall, and the rhythm of this eternally transient worldly existence, transient in its totality, in its spatial but also its temporal totality." This "rhythm of Messianic nature, is happiness," he declared.

"For nature is Messianic by reason of its eternal and total passing away," while the effort to emulate its passing was the task of world politics. (Hence the invocation of nihilism.)

By bringing to light neglected aspects of prosaic realities, such as the vast atmospheric forces of "Godforsaken Sunday afternoons" in the poorer quarters of giant cities, Benjamin believed these might be brought to "the point of explosion"—the verge of what he called "profane illumination." Liquidating "the sclerotic liberal-moral-humanistic ideal," the Surrealists had declared that real freedom could only "be enjoyed unrestrictedly in its fullness without any kind of pragmatic calculation, as long as it lasts."

Such expressions of disdain for the dogmas of utility evoke valedictory remarks in defense of the artistic imagination made by Stefan Zweig as European civilization was breaking down around him. Though Zweig's writing aspired to psychological realism, he matched the Surrealists in his obsession with Freud's taxonomy of the passions. He too proclaimed the centrality of Freud's insights into humanity's interior struggles for the future of civilization as such.

In May 1940, two months before the fall of France, Zweig delivered a lecture in Paris, which he titled "The Vienna of Yesterday." The speech was laced with loving observations about the city's cosmopolitan, ethnically and religiously diverse identity. But its most original aspect is the case Zweig builds against the conventional measure of national vitality as revealed by economic activity in favor of one determined by cultivation of the muses. He presents the arts as a seedbed for ideas that might allow humanity to re-create civilization after a catastrophe—even though the various aesthetic pursuits had been practiced in the moment without concern for any potential real-world application.

Zweig's lecture reviewed Vienna's long history of devotion to the visual arts, music, and theater in particular. He described the almost fanatical dedication of Austrian performers and composers to their calling—as well as the passionate attention bestowed by Viennese audiences on these virtuoso exhibitions. Plays and concerts were only the professional manifestations of the city's larger engagement with the cause of beauty, he claimed, a love affair that would embrace any excuse for a pageant or celebration and drew 300,000 people out onto the Prater for a flower parade. "A wind of lightness blew down from the Danube and the Germans looked on us with a kind of mistrust, like children who did not take life seriously enough," Zweig wrote. "For them Vienna was the Falstaff of cities, wanton, wise cracking, jocular." How the Germans used to ridicule the Austrians for their frivolous pastimes! he exclaimed. For centuries they'd carped at the Viennese *jouissance*, which Zweig credited to the populace's live-and-let-live attitude. In the estimation of the Germans, on the other hand, the idea of *jouissance* was "always linked to effort, activity, success, to victory," Zweig asserted. Even the sage Goethe had promoted this attitude in a poem, which, since childhood, Zweig had felt to be "anti-natural": "You must reign and conquer / or be subservient and lose, suffer or triumph / be the anvil or the hammer," Goethe chanted. He himself, Zweig added, had always felt that "an excess of ambition in the soul of a man, as with a people, destroys precious values." He believed that a person or nation "should *neither* reign, *nor* conquer." Above all, it was essential to be free and leave others their freedom to enjoy life without being ashamed of taking pleasure in being.

Such attitudes led the Germans to disdain the Austrians as hapless idlers when it came to the practice of commerce and manufacturing, just as they were foolish incompetents on the battlefield. Lacking operative knowledge of any sort, the Viennese aesthetes would be consigned to history's dustbin, the Germans gloated.

And yet, Zweig declared, lo and behold, at the end of the First World War, when Vienna lay in ruins, with grass growing in its streets and its roads blocked the whole way from the fertile countryside to the capital—when the currency was losing value by the hour while trains languished without coal and the shops were empty of bread, fruit, and meat—that feckless immersion in the pursuit of aesthetic delight revealed another dimension, which the Viennese themselves had been unaware of until then. It was precisely all those countless hours spent practicing their arts and crafts, Zweig argued, which gave the city's residents the skills and creative spirit necessary to resurrect a metropolis that war and disease had nearly obliterated.

"The miracle happened," Zweig wrote. In three years, everything had been rebuilt. In five years, the city had constructed blocks of communal houses that became the model of socialist urban planning for the whole of Europe. Commerce resumed. Galleries and gardens were restored. Students from around the world converged on the university. "Vienna became more beautiful than ever before" and suddenly found itself at the forefront in a hundred vital areas—a beacon to the world, defending culture "against all forms of barbarism."

In Zweig's view, the art of the imagination, which the city had accorded primacy to, conveyed to the population a faith that the apocalyptic scenes before them in 1919 had no greater permanence than theatrical stage sets. The conviction that these sights could be transformed came in tandem with a vision for how the metamorphosis might be effected, one that went infinitely beyond what might be gleaned from any standard, practical instruction manual.

What should we do, we might ask ourselves today, if we wake to find the war has been lost—flames are rising everywhere, the wicked hold the thrones of power, the disease is still spreading, and all prospects for revolution, let alone reconstruction, flicker but faintly on the distant horizon?

At such moments, "individual resistance is the only key to the prison," the Surrealists declared in 1942, with the Nazi catastrophe raging virulently around them. Even before that crowning monstrosity, they'd begun enjoining people to draw courage from the "invincible force" of "human becoming," the ongoing transmission of humanity's vital messages and energies through time, which worked its own metamorphoses on the rank status quo. Those poetic works from the last century once seen as "the most hermetic or the most delirious are becoming clearer day by day," Breton wrote after Hitler's ascendancy, while work from the past that had prided itself on being immediately accessible had grown "dim." It was now strikingly apparent "that these difficult works have contradictorily begun to speak *for us*," Breton announced. In catastrophe, art that refused to pander revealed itself as a carrier of that fateful force of human becoming. Art, love, and dialogue remain aglow in the ruins, the semi-immaterial material from which to begin rebuilding our world.

It wasn't worth the trouble to speak out "so long as one knows nothing while pretending to know everything," Breton wrote the year the Final Solution was initiated. And it was still less worthwhile for people to oppose each other, "and still less worth the trouble to love without contradicting everything that is not love, and still less worth the trouble of dying." Only there was yet spring to anticipate. One could yet dream "of youth, of *trees in bloom*, all this being scandalously disparaged, disparaged that is by old men: I dream of the magnificent working of chance in the streets, even in New York," Breton wrote from exile there. He felt obliged now to side with the minority who were continually *"climbing higher"* through programs aimed at catalyzing the ever-greater emancipation of humanity. Twin errors of perspective he singled out as threats to that project were anthropomorphism and people's fancied centrality to the order of creation.

He recalled a day on which he'd found himself walking along an elevated gallery above a flowering patio in Pátzcuaro, Mexico, beside a person whose "fine nervous hand . . . had controlled some of the greatest events of our time." While the two paced, they were assailed by the cries of mocking birds that lined the space in twenty cages, and the prominent figure's hand relaxed by petting a dog that wandered between them. As he stroked the animal, his language became less and less precise, and he started gushing more and more fatuously about the dog—speaking of its "natural goodness" and "devotion." Breton objected to the projection of these qualities onto the dog whose true nature, he maintained, could not be apprehended, whereupon his companion became heated. It was as if this man who'd handled the levers of power could only calm himself by refashioning the world in his own image. This weakness was poignant, Breton allowed, yet he would not accept that the dog should be humanized. "I see nothing wrong with opening the windows on the broadest utopian landscape in order to make this animal world understandable," he declared. The "understandable" here connoted the conservation of the animal's unfathomable otherness, which appeared representative of a way of seeing the world that is definitively not our own.

Even when we find ourselves following the gaze of an animal, participating in its reconnaissance of a world with which we believe ourselves familiar, we know its interpretation does not match our own. The gap between translations is a space of liberation. Any voyage is now commendable, Breton continued, which like Gulliver's travels is made "in defiance of all conventional ways of thinking"— that compels us to reorder our understanding of reality's proportions, if not seeing the unseeable, yet not accepting our circumscribed viewpoints as the whole truth. In conclusion, he cited a thought of Putnam's dear friend William James: "Who knows whether, in nature, we do not occupy just as small a place alongside beings whose existence we do not suspect as our cats and dogs that live with us in our homes?"

Wherever we are—in a museum, on the street—we have an obligation to let our gaze linger, keep looking and looking until we begin to make out the disparate strata complicating the initial glimpse, restoring the strangeness, disordering apparent hierarchies, temporal and sociological. That task of returning our eyes, continuing to absorb more details, building up and layering our picture, then zooming back and returning from another perspective, is in fact the work of culture: a refusal of the transactional impoverishment, the enforced uniformity of ideas and ideals that forecloses hope for a discovery that might yet transport us beyond the binary chambers of a blood-stained rat maze or a gold mine of triumphant sensation. Suppose the process of recouping our individuality were less a matter of "working on ourselves" than of a more intense auditory and

optical engagement with the world outside us, fructifying our own
perceptual makeup. Hearing and sight being, not coincidentally, also
at the pinnacle of the hierarchy of senses in Titian's era, conceived
by humanist philosophers in the artist's circle as channels to divine
contemplation. They were, Marie Tanner wrote, "the gateways to
spiritual awakening."

Two

Tanner, one of Panofsky's American disciples, was still living as an independent scholar in New York City at the time of the imaginary museum visit with my son. In the mid-1970s she had completed an essay on Titian's *Diana and Actaeon*, which she dedicated to Panofsky, who was then dead, for whom it had been begun seven years earlier. The essay "stumbles through many areas that could have been clarified by his insights and knowledge," she wrote in a prefatory footnote, rather as if she herself were Actaeon pursuing the truth about the image of Actaeon through some uncanny grove of culture.

Tanner takes the presence of the Black woman in Titian's painting as a radical innovation, which holds a key to the interpretation of the larger work. The figure has no precedent in Ovid's telling of the myth nor, indeed, in any other classical version of Diana and Actaeon. She must be understood as something more than a servant to the goddess.

The woman's addition proves to be one of numerous changes to the traditional iconography distinguishing Titian's approach to the scene. In Ovid, at the moment of Actaeon's encounter with the bathers, Diana and Actaeon are physically close enough that Diana will be able to bend forward into the stream, bring up water in her hand, and toss the drops into Actaeon's face, which commences the process of his metamorphosis. Titian's version rejects the typical sixteenth-century rendering of the myth by eliminating altogether the flinging of water. In his painting the pair are too far apart for this gesture, and Diana is in fact leaning backward, not toward the rivulet. Moreover, the setting of their interaction is in marked contrast to the bosky grotto described by Ovid. What's notable here is the parabola of azure sky festooned with clouds, together with the weird mix of architectural fragments: a colossal Gothic vault backdropped by asymmetrical arches, a wide-mouthed classical font near Diana's feet that seems to be sinking into the streambank even as it gushes water from a grotesque head carved on its perimeter, the pillar leaning at an odd, unstable angle, and a large stone platform where Diana is perched, which might be the floor of some otherwise razed structure—everything bathed in a strange medley of shade and light.

Tanner notes that the earliest extant account of the house of Fortune, from the twelfth-century work *The Anticlaudian* by Alanus de Insulis describes a building suspended at a steep angle on a river bank, one section sinking toward the water, another rising up the slope; parts of it gleaming and part in shadow, certain aspects of it solid, others crumbling. "Here is Fortune's own mansion if ever yet the unstable abides, the wandering comes to rest, the mobile stays fixed. Its entire cessation from falling, the constancy of its motion, now tumbles, now stands in position, now sinks down and misfortune ascends; in its mode and plan it lacks reason."

Different elements of Titian's setting correspond directly with this description, and the goddess Diana, indeed, has a long history of identification with the figure of Fortune, partly linked to her possession of a two-sided nature, which in turn connotes her layered associations with the light and dark sides of Earth's lunar satellite. (Fortune's wheel, for instance, symbolizing her changeableness, is equated with the moon.) This connection also helps explain the tradition in antiquity, known to Renaissance artists and philosophers, of depicting Diana as dark-skinned. Fortune was sometimes thus represented as well—and also dualistically as half white and half black.

With Tanner's interpretive framework in mind, the Black

woman and the white woman in Titian can be understood not as mistress and servant, a pair embodying the dynamics of power and subjugation, but rather conjunctive aspects of a single character. The painting contains other attributes tied to Fate and Fortune as well, such as the skull, along with a mirror and crystal vase propped on the rim of the fountain.

It's clear, in other words, from multiple details that Actaeon is encountering Fortune in the person of the fleshy, cream-tone Diana, and that the figure behind her, Black Diana, is only nominally divided from her, due to the constricted sight-lines of our mortal vantage point. Race is invoked here as a reflection of the perceptual limitations consequent on our insufficiently developed understanding. Perhaps we're bound now to perceive the women as double, but we're called on also to keep striving to resolve these two characters.

Yet my son might say to all this, in effect, *So what? What does any of this change? Even in Ovid, from what you've told me, Actaeon was stumbling into his fate in the act of chancing upon Diana. Why does it matter that Titian chose to identify the goddess more closely with Fortune—and then to split Fortune's identity between two female figures?*

At this juncture I would need to introduce the idea that Titian's innovation lay first in highlighting Diana's affinities with Fortune, but then in recasting the implications of the individual's encounter with Fate to make that more fluid and volitional. As a point of entry, I might refer to our own sense of powerlessness over the past two years—and how this had left us feeling psychologically denuded and grasping for cover.

Since the election he'd heard the grown-ups in his world murmuring incessantly about how they felt themselves subject to a vindictive ill fortune. That sense might be suspended when we went out together lustily protesting, but such events left only the mildest afterglow. The marches and meetings were cathartic, but after the applause for ourselves at the close of one rally or another had ended, we returned to the ranks of more or less obedient citizenry, wondering whether anything at all had been accomplished. Soon, a sensation of paralysis would begin stealing back over us, like the psychological mist that arises while scrolling through headlines, thickening into emotional opacity whenever our aggressive will to defy the turn of events subsided ever so slightly. Part of us knew by this point that if we weren't actively attacking the ICE holding centers to liberate refugees, we weren't doing enough. If the physical separation of desperate, indigent mothers from their children followed by lethal neglect of the young as an exercise in flexing America First muscle didn't spark insurrection, what could? And the absurdity of that image of us as gray-haired guerrillas stumbling about in the southwestern desert compounded our feeling of abject helplessness. Didn't the mere fact of our ability to entertain such a fantasy show that things had already gone too far—in the political arena, in our minds, in both spheres consanguineously?

That sense of having become Fortune's victims, which we ourselves knew was not the whole, or even the real story—one which downplayed all sorts of complicities and opportunities—yet kept recrudescing. Each time we learned of another act by the administration targeting the edifices of civilization, or yet another mass shooting by a solitary man which changed nothing politically, we heard the crack of solid ground around us, as if the granite bedrock of New York were just a thin sheet of ice. We protested, we signed petitions, we supported local initiatives for reform of one policy or another—I talked at public forums about the historical warning signs of the hour—but nothing halted the feeling of lurching, by fits and starts, ever deeper into darkness.

Meanwhile, my job moved from the fifty-story black glass monolith on the Avenue of the Americas, where I had been since I got hired, into a new dogfood-shade, trash-toy blockcastle known as Worldwide Plaza, called this perhaps as an exercise in reverse psychology intended to obfuscate awareness of its utterly narcissistic provincialism—the shoddily triumphalist, suburban office-park construction, devoid of any trace of real functionality, let alone aesthetic merit. I found myself shifted from a cubicle with four walls, and a window looking out onto the stone faces of other Sixth Avenue skyscrapers, into a cubicle backing onto an elevator shaft that whined and wailed all day long like the soundtrack on a cheap carnival zombie ride, with a front partition made of glass looking over a busy corridor and the computers of other workers toggling between browser tabs filled with stolen shopping expeditions and social media updates. Instead of voices, there were just computer keys clicking, like tiny bags full of infant bones shaken by a mob of charlatan shamans. I felt naked and saw nakedness everywhere. *Am I really here?* I asked myself, looking down from the see-through wall at my strange, crooked fingers above the black panel of buttons, remembering out of nowhere my hands falling through redolent clumps of lavender as I walked at dusk between scarlet poppies in a ravine by an eleventh-century Georgian monastery in Jerusalem.

I came into the office even less than before. There was less and less work to do anyway, since in fact the agency no longer needed writers, given that the target audiences of their clients no longer read. Once in a while I generated some anodyne tweets for a developer or property management team, or drafted a new business proposal for a company looking for help navigating what my agency liked to call our "complex contemporary communications environment." Otherwise I read, wrote, and piled stacks of old books on my desk—higher and higher—trying in vain to hide my glass view behind the volumes that transported me from this corporate abattoir of individuality, until the office manager rapped on my pane and made me bring down the pillars of Benjamin, Bishop, Freud, Emerson, Mandelstam, Lawrence, Woolf, Proust, Yourcenar, Lampedusa, Brodsky, Sebald, Eliot, Arendt, Flaubert, Marx, Foucault, James, Dubois, Conrad, von Rezzori, Whitman, Kafka—down, down, down again into a ruined flatland of prismatic cover art. But a few days after they'd been disassembled, I'd slowly start building my beloved bound Babel back up again.

My superiors in the office gave me increasingly troubled, quizzical looks when we passed each other. Who could blame them? By every marker of normalcy defining the agency environment, I'd become an absolute lunatic. Though it's also true that when I think back on the snickering conversations I heard around the office at this period, while the administration was settling into its abominations as if into a La-Z-Boy recliner before a jumbo monitor ("I just can't *wait* to see Melania on *Saturday Night Live*!")—when I think back on the language being dictated to me for documents about the firm's capabilities ("We use the power of media to make ideas, organizations, and people matter. Every day we create, launch, and shape stories that connect our clients with the audiences they need to reach. Our core offering is sophisticated counsel that derives from a universal approach to all aspects of our clients' needs.")—I do think it would be possible to say that this culture itself was psychotic.

Don't look at me, I said in my head when my superiors glanced sideways at me as we edged by each other. *I have no idea what I'm still doing here.*

For the thousandth time, Rebeca and I reviewed the different choices we could identify from where we stood now, discovering once again that we lacked sufficient information to make *any* rationally good choice in response to what was happening, other than to continue on with our lives as they had been, which we indeed kept trying to do, even though the primary effect of the new reality on our day-to-day lives thus far had been to throw into garish relief the dissatisfactions we'd felt with our lives before. More and more we found ourselves thinking that we could vote him out of power, but we couldn't remove from consciousness what he'd revealed about ourselves. By which we meant—what, exactly? That we no longer knew who we were or what we were doing—that we had never really understood the narrative we yet continued to contribute to as we went about our regular business?

I took my son's hand again, feeling that irrepressible warmth of time-not-yet-lived-through, and turned back again to the painting, this time to the dreamlike friezes of philosophy that lay behind Titian's colors.

The fifth-century epic poet Nonnus retold the myth of Diana and Actaeon with Actaeon cast as a lovesick person who intentionally seeks out the goddess, in quest of the epiphany of her divine beauty. "I should never have desired the Archeress of the wilds," Actaeon's ghost tells his father in the poet's *Dionysiaca*, after he's been killed by his hounds. "I should never have seen the Olympian shape. If only I had loved a mortal girl."

Numerous clues indicate Titian's awareness of Nonnus's text, beginning with the fact that only in Nonnus does Diana make the gesture of veiling herself in response to Actaeon's invasion of the grove and rather than initiating his transformation with a direct action, she merely lowers her face. (Nonnus describes Diana maddening Actaeon's dogs with a nod.)

If Titian's Actaeon was influenced by readings of Nonnus, then he is not, as in Ovid, a helpless victim of fortune, but instead a hunter who's made the decision to actively pursue his fate out of love, albeit a Neoplatonic love representing the desire for more knowledge rather than a purely sensual Eros.

Suppose, by way of example, I might say to my son, that we were to decide *now*, even from our ineluctably obstructed viewpoint, to try to change our circumstances in the interest of exploring what other forms of life we might still discover and shape together. Even understanding that we might not be choosing a *better* life, yet being able to decide that we could position ourselves to see something more of the world, multiplying the horizon lines and focal points of our existence—as if we were electing to shift our eyes to some different section of Freud's psychologically representative Roman Forum. Should we exercise our will to enter on a course of action that would rupture our current existence, even not being able to plumb the consequences? Could the space of the unfathomed itself become the object of our hunt?

In the mid-1960s, director Ingmar Bergman sought to identify what remained after the forces of modernity had lain waste the cultural canon as that had been transmitted down through the ages. Excepting those artists who lived under authoritarian governments and could be punished for their dangerous creations, art now was basically "free, shameless, irresponsible"—animated by an intense, almost febrile motion, like "a snake's skin full of ants," Bergman declared. (He counted himself among these insects.) "The snake is long since dead, eaten, deprived of his poison, but the skin is full of meddlesome ants." Why keep making work in this situation, he wondered. People no longer needed theater because they existed "in the middle of a drama whose different phases incessantly produce local tragedies. They do not need music because every minute they are exposed to hurricanes of sound passing beyond endurance." Nor did they need poetry because the new understanding of their place in the universe confined them to poetically useless "problems of metabolic disturbance." People had made themselves "terribly and dizzyingly free," while religion and art were kept alive merely as "conventional politeness toward the past, as benign, democratic solicitude on behalf of nervous citizens enjoying more and more leisure time." With all these troubles, Bergman asked himself again and again, why continue? "The reason is *curiosity*," he decided. "A boundless, insatiable curiosity that is always new and that pushes me onward—a curiosity that never leaves me alone and that has completely replaced my craving for community . . . I note, I observe, I keep my eyes open; everything is unreal, fantastic, frightening, or ridiculous."

A new validation of open-ended curiosity was in the air when Titian painted his *Poesie*, marking a signal departure from earlier orthodox Church traditions, which were endemically suspicious of the inquisitive urge. (Thus Tasso, in his sixteenth-century *Jerusalem Liberated*, would comment approvingly on Odysseus sailing beyond the pillars that Hercules erected to mark the outer limit of the known world: "Odysseus paid little heed to the established signs, in his craving to see and to know.") The Renaissance marked the end of the valorization of contemplation from a position of repose, in favor of a more active conception of vision that would strive resolutely to go behind appearances. In fact, the modern age started not with the death of God, the philosopher Hans Blumenberg has commented, "but as the epoch of the hidden God, the *deus absconditus*—and a hidden God is *pragmatically* as good as dead." This conception helped precipitate a relentless, "restless taking stock of the world," which benefited both the arts and the sciences.

Pietro Bembo, a scholar and poet whom Titian painted and remained friends with until his death, wrote his own reflection on the drama of the myth of Diana and Actaeon that extended the line of Nonnus's interpretation. "Believing he was in love while he met his lady only in imagination he has become a solitary stag whom, like Actaeon, his hounded thoughts have pitifully torn," Bembo wrote.

In this model, Actaeon invades the sacred glade because he is following his own hunger to see something more than mortals are supposed to behold: namely, the sight of divine beauty, which is truth. The individual is complicit in Fortune's workings by virtue of *the will to discover*. There is hence justice to the operations of Fate. (A principle that can be traced back to Dante's idea of "blessed Fortune," which aligns Fortune with divine providence.)

Titian's visual constellations, influenced by these intricate literary precedents, may in turn have helped further loosen the fatalistic view of Fortune's powers in ways that would later find expression in yet more revolutionary approaches to the problem of determinism's relation to free will. In Titian's wake, the humanist Giordano Bruno proposed that each individual had an internal drive that goaded them to shape their own destiny: "the infinite universe and all its parts move in conformity to their own nature, which is the creation of the omnipotent First Cause, and thus are reconciled both Free Will and Fate," he wrote.

Retelling Actaeon's story as an allegory for the soul impelled by love in the hunt to contemplate the divine, Bruno gave imagistic narrative form to the idea that the divine could not be directly perceived by mortal creatures. The boundary of our capacity to do so is represented by the figure of Fortune, he proposed, just as, in Titian's painting, Diana blocks the hunter's advance. Actaeon's particular tragedy is that the object and impediment to his pursuit are consubstantial, Tanner noted, with the Black Diana, representing Nature as the multitudinous, infinitely detailed character through which divinity projects itself into this world.

In his *Heroic Frenzies*, Bruno describes a lover who begins to understand the measureless nature of the woman he adores in tandem with discovering the peril that results from becoming too intensely absorbed in reflection on the ideal. Speaking in the voice of Actaeon, Bruno exclaims, "I stretch my thoughts to the sublime prey [divine knowledge] and these springing back upon me bring me death by their cruel and hard gnawing." It's necessary for the soul to "proceed to traverse the forest of natural phenomena where so many objects are hidden under a shadow and cloak," he continues, "for in a thick dense and deserted solitude the truth . . . veils and buries herself."

At the moment of the encounter with truth in the form of Diana, Actaeon will have the revelation that he himself is related to the divine essence, incorporating a "two-fold substance" like the moon, light and dark, "the most brilliant and the most obscure, the beginning and the end, the greatest light and the most profound darkness, infinite potency and infinite act coincide." The climax of his chase thus marks the moment in which "the hunter becomes the hunted." Actaeon no longer sees hidden Diana "as through a glass or window, but having thrown down the earthly walls, he sees a complete view of the horizon," with the result that the dogs, "as thoughts bent upon divine things devour this Actaeon and make him dead to the vulgar, free him from the fleshly prison . . . And now he sees everything as one, not any longer through distinctions and numbers." This oneness is Diana, "which is intelligible nature."

Fortune thus reveals itself to be propitious by ensuring that no condition in the world of the living, with its circular architecture, will ever be static, Bruno wrote. "For fate does not wish that good follow good, or pain be the presage of pain; but making the wheel turn, it raises, then it hurls down, as in mutability, the day gives itself to night when the great cloak of nocturnal torches obscures the flaming chariot of the sun, so he who governs by eternal decree crushes the great and raises the humble," thereby sustaining the "infinite scheme."

We wanted to change our life, Rafael, instead of just being forced to submit to the ways the world was changing so alarmingly around us while we tried to stand tight and cling on. We wanted to show you another culture, even if it was only across one ocean from the one you already knew; perhaps that could become a skipping-stone to the larger beyond. "The art of losing isn't hard to master," Elizabeth Bishop wrote. We saw the inevitability of transformation through time, the evanescence of our position, and sought to seize hold of our fate, even as the world we'd known was falling through our fingers like water. "I lost my mother's watch. And look! My last, or / next-to-last, of three loved houses went . . . It's evident / the art of losing's not too hard to master / though it may look like (*Write* it!) like disaster."

The Actaeon conjured by Bruno is the hunter who inspired Lacan to describe Freud as "an Actaeon perpetually slipped by dogs that have been tracked down from the start, and which he strives to draw back into pursuit without being able to slacken the chase in which his passion for the goddess leads him on." Instead of being attacked by his dogs, he guides them back into the hunt, but there is no climactic vision to hope for. When Lacan's Freud-as-Actaeon reaches Diana's grotto, he discovers only the multilayered character of psychoanalytic truth, which "proves to be complex in essence, humble in its office and alien to reality," Lacan announced.

He would always return to this version of his great predecessor: the bearer of Actaeon's quest into modernity. "The truth, in this sense, is that which runs after truth," Lacan declared in one lecture, "and that is where I am running, where I am taking you, like Actaeon's hounds, after me."

What liberation may bloom through this notion that rather than capturing the truth, we are charged with its continual pursuit. The idea reverberates through the writings of the New England Transcendentalists as persistently as it sounds in the twentieth-century artists and intelligentsia confronting Europe's attempted suicide through war and fascism.

And so it is, I imagined saying aloud, in a once-upon-a-time voice, *that although we knew an hour would come when this regime would fall as the wheel of fortune continued its revolutions, in pursuit of our own destiny, the divine beauty of an unknown future—feeling that it was necessary for us to gain some distance on the world we'd become engulfed by, acknowledging the brief duration of this one life we've been given—we began plotting to change our position on the planet . . . Perhaps what I can't put into words to you, I may yet express through a gesture that reorients the view of our shared existence, toward the other side of creation.*

But I see that like Actaeon I've become so lost in reflections on the ideal that I've slipped past the hard facts that also drove our decision.

Before the end of the summer of 2017, I finally succeeded in getting myself fired. I was called into my immediate superior's office one day and told to shut the door behind me. She looked at me very directly from behind her clean table. I was impressed with the lucidity of her stare. She gave me an ultimatum that I would become a full-on team player, sitting at my desk during all working hours, attending all meetings irrespective of whether or not they bore on my own assignments, pitch in more proactively across all the agency practice groups—and so on and so on. If I did this, with the understanding that there would henceforth be continual performance monitoring under the eyes of a colleague who'd until now been my coequal, we would give it another try. She gave me two weeks to think about the offer. I took the two weeks, came back into her office, shut the door behind me, and then she looked at me very directly, watched my lips part, and said she was sorry I'd made that decision. Then she terminated me.

With the loss of employment, so went our health insurance. We discovered that we'd now begin paying almost four times as much as had been subtracted from my paychecks hitherto—of course minus the salary. There were other practical considerations as well, concerning our son's education, arguing for a move now if we were to make one at all.

We'd never spoken seriously about moving to London, but our son had dual UK citizenship, and there was the National Health

Service. After our endless *Sturm und Drang* about what would be the best place to move to, London was the place that proved immediately feasible. It was the act of departure I concentrated on at that point, not the port of arrival.

We wondered whether we could think about the new city as a perch—a lookout from which to explore more of the world—rather than an all-consuming home, the way New York had been. People said London was now the most diverse city in the world, we reminded each other. Friends in the city talked about the ease of traveling all over the continent from there—St. Pancras to Gare du Nord in two hours and nineteen minutes. We always enjoyed the days we spent in London en route to visit Rebecca's mother in the southwest by the sea, we told each other—not to mention the poignance of those visits themselves.

We took a few days away and flew to the city, exploring neighborhoods we'd never seen before. We loved the way London went on forever in all directions, its glamorous modernism juxtaposed with gray stone shadows casting backward into the deep night of European history. "Old cultures," said an English friend with a shrug, speaking of London and Rome simultaneously, and the cryptic layers of this phrase struck a chord that kept reverberating inside me, echoing the opening of *The Golden Bowl*: "The Prince had always liked his London, when it had come to him; he was one of the Modern Romans who find by the Thames a more convincing image of the truth of the ancient state than any they have left by the Tiber."

We closed our minds to what confused our fantasy. After saying we'd never move to England—Brexit had sealed that—we made a dozen excuses and completely unraveled and rewrote our take on the country. We walked and walked, from the splendid green spaces to the Jubilee promenade alongside the river, staring over the

brown-jade choppy scales of that grand, ancient serpent to the monumental salt-and-pepper balloon of St. Paul's, then wheeling around
and walking west to the opulently graffitied skate park near the Tate
Modern, where the boards of lanky, multiracial revenants of James
Dean slapped the concrete and abruptly went airborne. *We can do
this. We can change our life*, we said to each other. Or, to be more
precise, we could change in *this* way.

We rationalized our passions, the same way Freud wrote of
nation-states doing when making theoretically logical arguments for
war. Or perhaps we projected our passions back over our reasoned
submission to circumstances, for looked at another way, the entire
move was of course a practical consequence of forces over which we
had no control.

In the back of my mind, I sometimes already caught myself
dreaming of one day moving on from London to points farther east-
ward. Of returning to Jerusalem. Of going farther and farther, until
I vanished in the sunrise. "Housed everywhere but nowhere shut in,
this is the motto of the dreamer of dwellings," Bachelard wrote. The
image of "houses that integrate the wind, aspire to the lightness of
air, and bear on the tree of their impossible growth a nest all ready to
fly away, may perhaps be rejected by a positive, realistic mind." But "a
dreamer might say that the world is the nest of mankind."

As the idea gained traction, we grew anxious over the prospect of
telling our son. Suppose he cried betrayal—refused flat out to leave
his friends and the neighborhood he loved? Would we actually force
him to comply? Were we capable of such tyranny?

Yet when we finally raised the possibility of moving with
him (after convincing ourselves that it was feasible), as we tried to

communicate what perhaps we'd always been meaning to do—I mean what we'd always been meant to do—instead of darkening in dismay, his eyes lit with excitement. He smiled with a spirit of adventure that was beautiful to behold, inspiring us to spring forward. And when we told Rebecca's mother, widowed and alone in the house where Rebecca had grown up by the sea, she was overcome with joy. For thirty years, her daughter had lived thousands of miles away from her. The thought of her unexpected return at this late hour was a dream she hadn't dared to allow herself.

Putnam never tired of meditating on Emerson's "Fate," an essay that opens with an off-kilter, matter-of-fact immediacy: "It chanced during one winter a few years ago, that our cities were bent on discussing the theory of the Age," he writes there. "By an odd coincidence four or five noted men were each reading a discourse to the citizens of Boston or New York, on the Spirit of the Times. It so happened that the subject had the same prominence in some remarkable pamphlets and journals issued in London in the same season." Yet for himself, Emerson observed, "the question of the times resolved itself into a practical question of the conduct of life. How shall I live. We are incompetent to solve the times. Our geometry cannot span the huge orbits of the prevailing ideas, behold their return and reconcile their opposition. We can only obey our own polarity."

That final sentence continually recurs to me. For Emerson, it signified that the only "solution to the old knots of fate, freedom, and foreknowledge" is the adoption of a "double consciousness." Each individual, he wrote, is compelled to ride alternately on the horses of their private and public nature, "as the equestrians in the circus throw themselves nimbly from horse to horse, or plant one foot on the back of one and the other foot on the back of the other."

This festive, big-top figuration of individual responsibility to the universe betokens an acceptance of transience and the refusal of dejection. It serves for its advocates as a reminder that the world, *or I in that world*, may yet become such that we would desire it to be as it is. This argument, "if kept green," may make one's "grown-up acquaintances impatient," Cavell writes, for it presents "a continuous rebuke to the way we live, compared to which . . . a settled despair of the world, or cynicism, is luxurious." Indeed, that oscillating vantage point may overcome the segregation of Kant's two worlds "by diagnosing them, or resolving them, as perspectives"—another function of "polarity."

We knew what we were doing was wrong—leaving our family, abandoning the country where we had a rich, settled life and manifold responsibilities. We knew what we were doing was right—refusing to settle, to surrender the happiness of pursuit, showing our child another side of the world, making him aware that there were other ways of living, other voices, than those he knew from the life we'd made in New York. We knew what we were doing was *wrong*—running away from the battle, shattering a basic physical solidarity with our community at an hour when our country was in crisis. We *knew* what we were doing was right—that there was no battle we could meaningfully contribute to off the page at this juncture and that gaining distance might increase our perspective in ways that would deepen our response to what was happening, even while whatever was real in our solidarity would survive this displacement. We knew that moving to sorry, damp-souled England with its contracting horizons was an error. Why reduce our child's vistas that way—let alone our own? We knew the way America's proudly expansionist, the-limitless-horizon-is-ours mentality had taken a wrecking ball to cultures around the world. Why shouldn't we change our son's angle of vision while he was still pliable, if we had the capacity to do so? We knew that removing our child from his friends and extended family would constitute an irreconcilable fault line in his life. And we knew what it would mean to his grandmother in her last years to have the grandchild she loved with such vibrant grace nearby, and to have him forge new friendships with people from parts of the world of which he now knew nothing. We knew that the United States would always be our psychological homeland, and we knew that we were no longer at home there.

Perhaps somewhere beyond the great American city, through the mythic pillars of Hercules, lay the long-dreamed-of "complete view of the horizon," which was freedom. Perhaps we could begin life again. Or perhaps we'd merely die to our life in New York. We knew that we knew nothing, that we could only observe our polarities.

Many friends were shocked when we told them of our intentions. But a few remarked also, after a little time had passed, that the fact of our leaving the country, even if only partly as a reaction to what had happened politically, shook them in ways that had made them reflect on their own lives.

In the spring of 2018, a short while before our departure, a journalist friend organized a farewell dinner for me together with a cadre of half a dozen close male friends. We were to convene one early June night on the back patio of my house on Cumberland Street.

That afternoon I took a walk around Fort Greene Park, gazing up once more at Whitman's sober column memorializing the prison-ship dead, thinking about those poor countless souls smothering inside the holds, suffering disease and injury, praying and pleading for mercy—for release. How many times had I circled around that monument and snaked up and down the winding paths of the park? What would it mean to lose this axis to our lives?

On my way back up the street, I paused for a moment out front of Marianne Moore's old apartment building, that slightly wan Beaux Arts structure to which she'd moved in 1929, which had once displayed a plaque with a quotation from the poet. BROOKLYN HAS GIVEN ME PLEASURE, HAS HELPED EDUCATE ME, HAS AFFORDED ME, IN FACT, THE KIND OF TAME EXCITEMENT ON WHICH I THRIVE. I had felt exactly the same almost to the end of the seventeen years I'd been living in the neighborhood. I shared the boundless gratitude that pulsed beneath her words. Only something had happened, which meant these excitements no longer answered. The wheel of fortune had spun too fast and violently. The better half of our house lay in ruins.

When I tried to articulate what precisely had changed, the rush of images that suffused me always began with the ones that had haunted me since election night—the bright, flushed faces of the men and women in red MAKE AMERICA GREAT AGAIN hats rooster cheering as Trump walked into the private room at the Hilton, just across Fifty-Fourth Street from my old office building, to announce his big win.

Even if this president were only the composite ambassador of the country's worst features, in his capacity as the Frankenstein figurehead of apocalyptic capitalism, he'd yet succeeded in becoming the most powerful man in the world. If his presidency was just symbolically worse than others had been, *it yet was worse symbolically.*

Symbols matter all the more at moments when reality appears to be crumbling. They light the horizons beyond our defeat—either luridly or inspiritingly. Signifying nothing particular, communicating nothing explicit, symbols may yet "make transparent something beyond all expression" that conveys a "momentary totality," writes Gershom Scholem. They shape the aleph of a language that can bring forward the poetic tradition of revolt into our own time.

I saw again in my mind the president-elect moving onto the stage with his lips making their trademark *il Duce*, camera-gigolo pout of puissance. I saw him clapping for himself, then shaking his forever self-vindicating, victorious fist, the Entertainer-in-Chief taking the world's biggest spotlight. I thought of his impersonations of afflicted or distraught people, in which for a few seconds he seemed to become his victims at their most vulnerable, inciting roars of hilarity from the crowds at his rallies. "There's nothing funny about a clown at midnight," observed the early horror film star Lon Chaney.

What will we do the morning after? I wondered.

And I thought once more about Ezra Pound visiting Cumberland Street before heading off to Mussolini's Italy where, when war broke out, he would begin to fulsomely demonize the Jews on Radio Rome—another effort to literalize a nostalgic fantasy about resuscitating a mythical once pure, virile society in the grip of some foreign parasite.

Reflecting on Pound's incarceration after the war for spewing his propaganda, H.D. wrote, "The prison actually of the Self was dramatized or materialized for our generation by Ezra's incarceration." The prison for *everyone*—even those who shared none of Pound's rabid prejudices, she asserted. It's a dramatic appropriation—rather than stealing the light from those who create under the shadow of racial oppression, accepting one's share of the darkness blinding those who work the forges of hatred. Now that he'd been so reduced, H.D. found herself asking, "Who are these dummies, these ogres of a past age, these fearful effigies that wrecked our world, these devils, these dolls? Who are they? . . . Did they ever exist? Did Ezra ogre-ize himself by his association with Radio Rome?" Or had that ogre been Pound's true character the whole time?

After Elizabeth Bishop visited Pound in the psychiatric hospital, she composed an astonishing poem that both preserved the individuality of his disease and illustrated, through Pound's helpless mutability, the greater humanity channeled through his nature. For all his ideological intransigence, his voice was porous to the mercurial times and social context. In each verse, the adjective with which Bishop characterizes the man confined in the house of Bedlam shifts to highlight a different aspect of his persona. From "tragic" to "talkative" to "honored" to "old, brave," to "cranky" to "cruel" to "busy" to "tedious," to the final stanza where she juxtaposes a soldier home from the war with a boy patting the floor to gauge whether the Earth is round or flat, together with a Jew wearing a newspaper hat who dances cautiously down the ward, "walking the plank of a coffin board" alongside a lunatic sailor who shows a watch that tells the time "Of the wretched man / That lies in the house of Bedlam."

The question before us, H.D. recognized, finally had less to do with the origins of Pound's ogre-ization than with what we ourselves choose to make of the wreckage and dirges left behind by those who deny our commonality. His fate wasn't even sad, she decided, for even in his ogre-ized state, locked in the mental prison of his infernal views, he revealed "a reserve of dynamic or daemonic power from which we may all draw." The loam of his wretchedness proved transcendently fertile. "He lay on the floor of the Iron Cage and wrote the Pisan Cantos."

> What thou lovest well is thy true heritage . . .
> Pull down thy vanity, I say pull down.
> Learn of the green world what can be thy place
> In scaled invention or true artistry,
> Pull down thy vanity . . .
> How mean thy hates
> Fostered in falsity . . .
> But to have done instead of not doing
> this is not vanity, . . .
> To have gathered from the air a live tradition
> or from a fine old eye the unconquered flame
> This is not vanity.
> Here error is all in the not done,
> all in the diffidence that faltered . . .
>
> Nor can who has passed a month in the death cells
> Believe in capital punishment
> No man who has passed a month in the death cells
> Believes in cages for beasts.

The group of us at Cumberland Street had been sitting, chatting, and drinking wine for an hour or so that lovely spring night. Candle-light reflected off the ivy-covered brick walls framing the courtyard, flickering over the enigmatically smiling face of the Bacchus statue I'd purchased in pieces off a sidewalk in Soho from an eccentric antiquarian who'd since lost his lease, and across the tall, pale back of our solid, sold house with its long, gold-lit windows looking in on a life that no longer belonged to me, when suddenly my friend who organized the evening broke out in his clarion voice, "Okay, man, enough chit-chat. It's time. Explain yourself. Tell us why you're doing this. What the hell is this all about?"

My eyes fell. I was completely unprepared for the question. I could feel everyone staring, the pause striking all other conversation. My heart began pounding. Wind rustled the leaves overhead. I looked up at the sky, to the stars washed out by metropolitan incandescence.

At last the silence became too much and I began talking in a jumble of passion and platitude. Trying to put together my broken, reason-overwhelming reasoning. I spoke of my hatred of nationalism, my loathing for the capitalist—

"Yeah—okay." My friend broke in. "What the hell does that have to do with leaving New York?"

I babbled something about the corrosive hysteria that seemed to be pervading the atmosphere, which I felt myself increasingly consumed by. I said that I simply couldn't bear to live under the reign of this abomination. Everything I'd tried to do my whole life as a writer and individual had been directed against exactly what had now transpired. "*I have failed*," I said. "The same way the democratic institutions of the country failed. This isn't a test of anything. The test is over and we didn't pass—I didn't anyway. This existence is over. I can't continue to act otherwise. From where I am now, I have nothing more to say. Zweig writes near the end of feeling that he is living a posthumous existence. That's how I feel now here. I know everyone has a different response to what's happened—for myself, I have to try something else, even if I fail again—fail even more completely next time . . . I can't give up trying."

Histrionic though the speech surely was, it was also dead serious: The life I'd built here in Brooklyn over all these rich, complex years inside this beautiful house on the grounds of a lovely, vivacious neighborhood—the world it had been my fortune to inhabit for so long, with its friends, its thousands of books, and its beautiful fragments of old cultures—felt now like a space capsule cut off from the mothership, hurtling through the darkness in freefall.

After I'd said whatever I said, I remember the faces of my friends looking up at me still expectantly, waiting for something—something *more*, something less overwrought, more lucid, less sentimental. They sat before me in that peaceful Brooklyn garden, looking up at my face, then at last tilted their eyes down again to the table, like an indulgent but still damning version of the court in Kafka's *Trial*. They didn't want to judge me, but what choice did they have when I had judged myself and found myself wanting? What could they do but echo, *Mene, Mene, Tekel, Upharsin . . .* And yet this too I now see involves a degree of self-extenuation, for of course, in the midst of all my sadness and guilt, I was also ready to leave. Eagerly restless. I couldn't help, really, even being just a little euphoric with wonder before the mystery of what happened next. At that moment, under the weight of my friends' gazes, I felt like I couldn't wait to take off.

At a certain point my shoulders lifted, then fell, my mouth opened without any words leaving my lips, while my head began slowly shaking.

And still no one said much beyond a few sad, gently clinical murmurings of sympathy. Then those too fell away. Only the sound of chairs scraping uncomfortably on the slate tiles, of bottles clinking the rims of glass, broke the silence. But still I couldn't add anything just then to mitigate my own lack of a real answer to the riddle of my self-expulsion from Brooklyn.

It took quite some time before talk started picking back up again. At first when it did so the other voices around me were so low that mixed with the evening wind they sounded almost like murmuring waters, but eventually some laughter was sprinkled in as well, along with some sarcasm, a bit of empathy, a little burst of grief or jocularity about a news story, the latest development in someone's professional situation or love life. Then all at once the talk relaxed altogether in a gush, switching to a new addictive murder TV series, a ball game, summer plans in Italy, the new tapas place that had opened in Crown Heights. I felt more upset with each passing moment. I wasn't ready for this return to the everyday. I wanted to stay in the realm of the passions.

And just as I thought this, as if through some telepathic communication, the friend who'd initiated the interrogation broke in over the little dialogues into which the party had splintered.

"Hold on, though!" he said. "Hold on!—I've got one more question for you. We're not through here yet." He burst into a hard, staccato laugh. "You actually think you can get away?"

"No!" I shook my head. Shook it over and over, feeling now a strange, new force swelling inside me. "Of course not! Of course I won't get away! We wouldn't be leaving if we really thought we could *escape*! But I have to act as though I believe it were possible—to begin again *without* escaping. I have to make some gesture toward imagining a completely other life is still possible—and that this other life won't be just a repetition or betrayal of the life we lived here. I have to keep pursuing the dream."

I said all this. And then I broke off. For suddenly I saw the reason—the *real* reason for everything. The words rang out inside me, while I stared mutely around the table at my old faithful friends in that strange Brooklyn symposium.

"Don't you see—there is nothing more American I could possibly do than to leave America right now in this way."

———

And so, like my ancestor Mary Chilton in reverse, one midsummer day we sprang from the New World onto a vessel aimed the other direction—in a completely spontaneous, utterly predestined motion, we took flight without knowing where we might finally land.

We plunged into the unknown. We leapt, and discovered we'd flung ourselves into the dark, tangled branches of our own nature—I mean soared into the majestic green trees of the Heath—I mean flown into all-embracing Nature as such.

The sky behind the tree outside my window in London now switches from thunder gray to nacreous. Birds appear and disappear in the shining leaves like an unending magic show. Suddenly fanning their wings, alighting on a slender perch, then vanishing again. A flutter, a flash, a balancing act, a vertiginous inversion. One can never tell in advance what will emerge next. This possibility of surprise, a living cabinet of curiosities—a dance in which hope and despair coexist.

FINIS

· Acknowledgments ·

I am enormously grateful to my UK agent, Sarah Chalfant, whose generous support and perceptive suggestions were essential to the writing of this book. When Rebecca Nagel, my American agent, became involved in the project, she too provided substantial assistance, for which I'm very thankful. I am honored and grateful that Jack Shoemaker chose to publish the book. He along with the whole team at Counterpoint and Catapult have been responsive and helpfully thoughtful throughout the publication process. I'm especially thankful to Laura Berry, Yukiko Tominaga, Katherine Kiger, Dustin Kurtz, Lexi Earle, and Nicole Caputo.

This book is hugely indebted to the conversations and insights of friends. The kind early read and incisive editorial suggestions of James Lasdun made an inestimable contribution to the book. My talks with Adam Cvijanovic always provide vital inspiration to my writing, and were especially important to shaping a number of arguments in this book. I'm grateful for both specific insights and the friendship of Michael Greenberg, Alexandra de Sousa, Jonathan Nossiter, Natalie de Souza, Deborah Eisenberg, Wallace Shawn, Sina Najafi, Nina Katchadourian, Sandy Tait, Hal Foster, Spencer Finch, Jeff Dolven, Eyal Weizman, Ines Weizman, Paul Holdengraber,

Barbara Holdengraber, Nancy Fishman, Barbara Richards, Danielle McConnell, Christopher McConnell, Carne Ross, Karmen Ross, Jane Myat, Simon Lewis, Alba Arikha, Tom Smail, Frederick Kaufman, Alan Berliner, Shari Spiegel, and Anne LaFond.

This story is a family adventure of sorts. The vision of America that my parents, Marian and Martin Prochnik devoted themselves to articulating and enacting remains an inspiration to me—as does the deep generosity of their love. Barbara Mead has provided an unfailingly kind and benevolent model of the traditionally stoical English character. I've dedicated the book to my siblings, Elisabeth, Jamie, and Ethan. I feel inexpressibly fortunate for their understanding and love. Their supportive intellectual curiosity is always sustaining, and their understanding of the unusual genetic-historical confluence we emerged from has enlarged my own in ways that were critical for the development of this book's themes. Samoa Jodha also helped substantially to expand my thinking about the role of memory in preserving individual and cultural ideals. This project is deeply informed by the disparate perspectives of my children, Yona, Tzvi, Zach, and Rafael. I have been continually grateful and impressed to see the ways that their ebullient spirits allow them to keep dreaming with open eyes—their own dreams have helped to catalyze my hope that positive change is still possible. For Rebecca, my love and thankfulness are immeasurable. Without her conversation home would be unimaginable.

GEORGE PROCHNIK was awarded a Guggenheim Fellowship in general nonfiction in 2021. He is the author of five books of nonfiction including *Stranger in a Strange Land*, which was a *New York Times* editors' choice and was short-listed for the 2018 Wingate Literary Prize in the United Kingdom. His previous book, *The Impossible Exile*, was shortlisted for the 2016 Wingate Literary Prize and won the National Jewish Book Award for Biography, Autobiography, and Memoir. Prochnik is also the author of *In Pursuit of Silence*, *Putnam Camp*, and *Heinrich Heine*. He has written for *The New Yorker*, *The New York Times*, *Bookforum*, and *Los Angeles Review of Books*, and is editor at large for *Cabinet* magazine. Born in Grand Junction, Colorado, Prochnik currently lives in London with his wife and their son.